How to Beat Better Tennis Players

How to

BEAT BETTER TENNIS PLAYERS

by LORING FISKE

Illustrated by B. J. Wilson

Doubleday & Company, Inc.
Garden City, New York.

Library of Congress Card Catalog Number 74–97660

Copyright © 1970 by **Loring Fiske**

Contents

CONTENTS

Introduction

To look at a group of tennis players, you would think they were normal, peace-loving citizens. They speak in modulated voices, they never throw things at each other, and they are usually dressed in spotless white. They seem the very model of well-bred, cultured people. They play according to rules demanding chivalry, honesty, and sportsmanship.

Yet tennis players are the most competitive cutthroats roaming loose in civilization. Although they mask their intense urge to win under a chivalric code, they play tennis for one reason: to beat the hell out of an opponent.

Some players claim they play for exercise. Hah! Try doing push-ups and skipping rope and you'll get ten times as much in half the time.

Some claim they play for business reasons. This may be true when playing with clients, but once they face a nonbusiness opponent, they turn on the pressure to whip him.

Tennis players are mostly lean, hard-driving, aggressive, intense creatures of whom Julius Caesar spoke: "Yon Cassius has a lean and hungry look . . . such men are dangerous."

Tennis players hunger for competition, not easy victories. They scorn the sportsman who hauls in dozens of fish or shoots down helpless animals with no effort. They want to test their strokes against a suitable opponent and maul him until he cries "Enough!"

The caste system was not invented by the Russians or the

East Indians. It was invented by tennis players trying to avoid "dubs" (meaning anybody they can beat 6–2, 6–2) and who complain bitterly because "slightly better" players (meaning anybody who beats them 6–2, 6–2) won't play with them.

Once you realize that winning (legally, of course) is the main purpose of a tennis match, you'll win far more often because you'll concentrate much better. If an opponent starts giving you a line about playing only for the fun of it, suggest you alternate serving for five minutes and do not keep score. Will he agree? Not on your life.

Against such an opponent, you should check the height of the net, call the score after every point, and never give him any free extra serves. This fellow is trying to disarm you into giving him all the close but out calls and bears as much sympathy for you as a barracuda.

What is the best kind of tennis game to play? You see dozens of players using different strokes and methods, and yet each seems to succeed to some extent. Every player better than you tells you his private system, and if you listen to enough of them, you'll become completely confused.

Actually, before you even lift a racket, you are already largely committed to play within a definite range because of your physique and temperament.

You may yearn to blast a serve and rush the net like Gonzales, but if you are short and heavy, forget it. You can't reach up to serve as hard as a tall man, and if you crowd the net, a smart player will lob you to death. However, if you stay back near the service line, you can't volley forcefully.

Even if you're tall and rangy, it still depends on your possessing the net rusher's temperament, which is that of a Mississippi River boat gambler. You must enjoy the risk of winning or losing a point quickly; you must seek to earn points rather than outsteady your opponents.

Suppose you're the opposite type: the retriever. You don't hit hard and you can't volley too well, so you avoid the net. Does this limit your improving your game? No, you just have to learn more about the percentages on shots, how to size up your opponent's weaknesses, and work on your own shortcomings from the backcourt.

Can a retriever beat a hard hitter? Well, way back when Ellsworth Vines was the hardest hitter in tennis, he met Bitsy Grant in the Nationals. Bitsy couldn't break a pane of glass with his forehand and was the shortest man ever to win the National Claycourt. He proceeded to whittle Elly down and out of the tournament.

Then there is the composite or college professor type. He figures out what his opponents dislike and gives it to them double strength. He hits hard at times, defensively if need be, storms the net occasionally, and uses his head every minute.

Bobby Riggs, one of the greatest players pound for pound, squeezed more operating efficiency out of his strokes than most taller, heavier, and harder-hitting opponents. He served more aces on his second serve by outguessing foes than any cannonball server.

Many players try to emulate the current champion. If he rushes the net, they rush up even though they're slow. If he hits short, punchy drives, they try to copy his style. But in the long run, you can improve most by playing according to your own temperament and capabilities.

If you like to slug, go ahead, but once in a while try hitting easier and disconcert your opponent. If you hate to take chances, stay back and outsteady your opponent. If you enjoy undermining your opponent's game rather than blasting him off the court, disregard your slugger friend's advice and patiently whittle him down.

However, regardless of your temperament and physique, you can improve your game without going through rigorous training or practice. You can win more often by making use of the principles set forth without changing your strokes at all.

Naturally, to become a champion you would have to learn effective strokes, practice endlessly, focus your energies to only one goal, possess an athletic body, and be born with lightning reflexes. For that you don't need this book. You need courses in etiquette, dancing, financial counseling in haggling for higher expenses, speechmaking for personal appearances in being honored for your achievements, along with a good tailor in order to befit you for your lofty career.

But if you simply want to improve your game and become more sought after as a tennis partner, this book will help you. It is based on many, many years of playing, coaching, and watching champions, tournament players, and beginners. On the success patterns they have developed and the percentage plays they use.

As a player, you will improve if you emulate the champions in some ways and forget them in others, if you try to play like a tournament player some times but only like yourself at other times, and if you keep going over the principles set forth in this book until you know them as well as a gambler does the odds at poker.

Even if you make use of only a few of the ideas, you will add new dimensions to your game and increase your enjoyment. For tennis is a complex game for complex people who disdain simple sports like bowling, which rely mainly on a strong back and the plodding patience of a mule train. Victory goes not merely to the strong in tennis nor to the swift of foot nor to the cunning, for a player armed with persistence and knowledge may defeat any of them.

Here then are some general principles to lift your game and increase your victory percentage:

1. *Keep trying.* You may not swing your racket like a champion, but you can play like one in another way: Keep trying.

A champion tries hard under all conditions of weather, court surface and lighting, personal difficulties, and against all types of hostile crowds, officials, and opponents. In becoming a champion, Jack Kramer schooled himself so well in overcoming difficulties that one felt that if he took on the devil himself, Jack would be no worse than even money in betting.

When your opponent hammers back your best shots and piles up a lead, you may feel you have no more chance than in arguing a traffic cop out of a ticket. But every tournament sees matches in which one side scores an impressive lead and then fails to hold it. If this happens to experienced tournament players, it can happen in your match.

Your opponent may be a front runner who swings with confidence when ahead and tightens up under pressure. You may take longer to warm up or to figure out his game. Or he may tire or become upset over missing an easy shot. Any of a hundred different incidents may change the entire course of a match. So despite the score, keep trying.

Of course, you won't pull out all your matches this way, but you will form the victory habit. The habit of trying constantly throughout a match and thus putting more pressure on your opponent. This is the habit of champions who never quit and thus snatch victory from seemingly certain defeat.

Don Budge was lagging 1–4 in the fifth set to Baron Gottfried Von

Cramm in a Davis Cup Interzone Final in 1937 and seemed certain to lose. But his long-standing habit of always trying despite the score enabled him to reverse matters and triumph.

2. *Think deep.* International Business Machines posts signs: THINK. Tennis players, especially weekend players, should mentally post signs: THINK DEEP.

How high should you hit the ball over the net when your opponent is on the baseline? Most players will surprisingly say, "Just skim it over the net." They have seen the pros return balls low over the net, but they forget that the pros rush the net constantly; thus the proper answer to a volleyer is to keep the ball low. But most weekend opponents do not rush the net, and thus you should give yourself more margin for safety by hitting the ball high over the net when he is on the baseline—at least a racket length.

You will not only increase your chances of returning the ball safely but most of all, by hitting higher over the net, you will be sending the ball deeper—within two feet of the baseline. Watch the drives of average players and notice that they land at about the service line—just perfect for an opponent to step in and crack.

Naturally, if you want to make an angled return, you will keep the ball lower over the net. But assuming you and your opponent are both on the baseline, it is far better to drive the ball out than into the net. Once the ball goes over the net, the wind may slow it down, your opponent may play it by mistake (and his remorse may disturb him for the next few points), or the ball might hit him.

Keeping the ball deep raises the percentages in your favor. It is then harder for your opponent to surprise you, because it takes longer for the ball to return to you, it is harder for him to storm the net, and it is harder for him to make a sharp angle.

If you are forced back of your own baseline and your opponent remains on his baseline, you should aim the ball two or more racket lengths over the net. The ball has farther to go, and you should allow for the added distance by lifting the ball higher.

So think deep, hit deep, and keep your opponent backcourt. He will then be likely to return short and give you a chance to move in for the kill.

3. *Take the offensive.* The odds favor the aggressor who forces his opponent to defend himself. A favorite phrase is "jerking your opponent around the court," which means making him play *your* way rather than his. If you keep him scrambling and running, he

can't get set to cut loose with his own winning shots. So put the pressure on your opponent and never let up.

4. *Get your first serve in 70 percent of the time.* Most players crack their first serves with all their might and vaguely hope they go in. It doesn't matter if they get 10 or 40 percent of their first serves inside, for they still crack the ball with all their might. Then they serve a weak second serve, which their opponents knock off for points.

Actually, you should first concentrate on getting 70 percent of your first serves inside, regardless of speed. Then, still maintaining that 70 percent average, you should work on gradually increasing the speed.

You may read the full detailed explanation for this Golden Rule of 70 Percent in the chapter on the serve. But meanwhile, lower your speed to get 70 percent of your first serves inside. You'll win a lot more points that way.

5. *Watch the ball.* This sounds so simple that it seems a waste of time even to mention it. However, many players miss absurdly easy shots because they look away before hitting the ball. If, when you are chasing a ball, you want to glance across the net to locate your opponent, fine. But as you close in, you should focus on the ball, *especially the last two feet of its path.* Not only will you hit the ball better, but this will force you to concentrate harder.

Many tournament players with slumping games find that if they simply watch the ball more intently, their games will improve. You can lift your game the same way by watching the ball until you see it hit the racket.

6. *Upgrade your physical condition the easy way: Walk more.* Since tennis is two-thirds running, you can improve your court covering by getting into better physical shape.

The chapter covering training and conditioning presents many exercises, but you can start now on the easiest method: Walk farther than usual. Take the long way around to go places on foot. Park a block or two farther from the store. Walk downstairs instead of waiting for the elevator. Walk around the block before going to bed. Walk more and longer, and you will gradually build up your endurance the easy way. You will find that you reach more balls on the court and thus increase your chances of winning more points. So start walking!

The Backhand

Mention backhand to the average weekend player, and he will scowl and mutter that it's the toughest shot to make. And for most of them it is.

Yet hundreds of tournament players possess sounder backhands than forehands. Typical is Pancho Gonzales, who was famed for his terrifying serve and booming smashes but who hit his backhand with far better control than his forehand. He could drop the ball with feather softness at a net rusher's feet or lob with the same motion way over the net man's head.

Actually, it is easier to get your weight into your backhand, easier to make an angle, and easier to c-a-r-r-y the ball on your racket by following through.

When you run wide for a forehand to try to hit crosscourt, you find that your body gets in the way and you have to make a deliberate effort to turn your shoulders. But in swinging on your backhand, you can follow through easily, because there is nothing in your way.

Improving a weak backhand will not only enable you to return more balls and win more points but will also cut down the extra running you do to cover it up by taking balls on the forehand. Cutting out this extra running will provide more reserve strength for you to win those crucial third-set battles.

You can improve your backhand in many ways:

1. *Hit the ball at least a racket length over the net when*

1

your opponent is on the opposite baseline. Most players hit too short, and if you overcorrect, you will find you are hitting a few too long, but many more will be landing a couple of feet inside the baseline.

2. *Hit twice as many balls on your backhand than usual.* Don't change anything else, but merely hit twice as many.

You hit your forehand better than your backhand, because you probably hit at least five or ten times as many forehands as backhands. So naturally, your forehand gets better. So if you don't feel like doing anything else on the backhand, just go out and hit twice as many balls on that side. You can't help moving better, judging the balls better, and hitting better.

Lots of good players have developed pretty fair backhands by practicing endlessly, even though their form would give the shivers to a tennis coach.

Johnny Hennessey became Wimbledon doubles finalist and ranked No. 4 nationally while flicking his backhand as though brushing at annoying mosquitoes. Yet he could angle the ball wide, hit deep or barely over the net, or lob tantalizingly beyond an opponent's outstretched racket.

He developed this backhand by rigorous practice. Will you develop a similar backhand if you practice constantly? Not unless you possess his great sense of timing and great talent in when to mix up his shots. But no matter how you swing at a backhand, if you hit twice as many, you'll improve.

There is only one slight fault about practicing any old way. If you use awkward form or a 1910 swing, you will find yourself on a plateau, and not even a superjet will lift you higher.

So let's consider the main causes for players' not hitting their backhands one-fourth as well as they should.

3. *Start moving sooner and preparing sooner.* Players who start right off for a ball on their forehand will dawdle when a ball goes to their backhand. Then they fall backward as the ball seems to leap at them.

Ken Rosewall's magnificent backhand has been likened to Zeus' lightning bolt, to Merlin's magic wand, and to a bag of tricks bequeathed by Houdini. He never seems to hurry when facing booming serves, and yet his backhand retaliates with fearful effect. He partly attributes his great talent to preparing sooner than on his

FIGURE 1

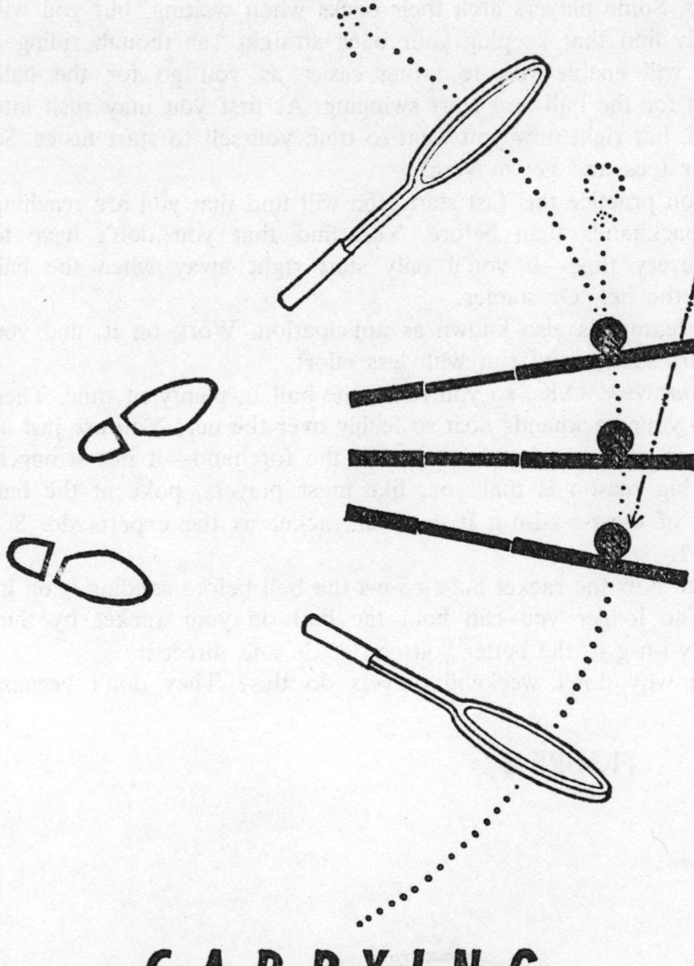

C-A-R-R-Y-I-N-G
THE BALL ON THE RACKET

forehand. Certainly he prepares sooner on his backhand than others do on theirs.

The instant the ball crosses the net, you know whether it's going to your backhand or not. Get started sooner by waiting with your weight on the balls of your feet, your knees slightly bent, and leaning forward. Some players arch their backs when waiting, but you will probably find that keeping your back straight (as though riding a horse) will enable you to swing easier as you go for the ball.

Head for the ball and start swinging. At first you may rush into the ball, but right now you want to train yourself to start faster. So on your toes and get moving!

As you practice this fast start, you will find that you are reaching more backhands than before. You find that you don't have to sprint every time—if you'll only start right away when the ball crosses the net. Or sooner.

This feature is also known as anticipation. Work on it, and you will start sooner and run with less effort.

4. *Footwork.* O.K., so you reach the ball in plenty of time. Then why do your backhands float so feebly over the net? You are just as strong on your backhand side as on the forehand—if not stronger.

The big reason is that you, like most players, poke at the ball instead of c-a-r-r-y-i-n-g it on your racket as the experts do. See Figure 1.

Notice how the racket c-a-r-r-i-e-s the ball before sending it on its way. The longer you can hold the ball on your racket by thus c-a-r-r-y-i-n-g it, the better you can guide and direct it.

Then why don't weekend players do this? They don't because

FIGURE 2

they cramp their feet into awkward positions. They keep their feet too close together (only six inches apart), fall over backward because they started their swings too late, or stick the right foot way out by itself and parallel to the net as in Figure 2.

Your feet should be placed about twelve to eighteen inches apart, with the right foot slightly ahead and diagonal, as in Figure 3.

FIGURE 3

Try placing your feet that far apart, and you will find that you can transfer your weight easily from back to front foot.

Why does your right foot extend diagonally instead of parallel to the net? Because then you can hit your backhands crosscourt. With your foot parallel to the net, you will tend to hit down the line to your opponent's forehand.

Everything favors your hitting crosscourt to your opponent's backhand: It is usually his weaker side. The net is lower through the middle. You can hit harder and with more safety. You can force your opponent more out of court than you can with a down-the-line shot.

Meanwhile, back to your footwork on the backhand: As you hit into the ball, transfer your weight from the back to the front foot so it rests flat on the ground. The heel of your back foot should then come off the ground, while the ball of the foot remains in contact with the ground. If your back foot comes up entirely into the air, you will make a great pose for the Ice Follies, but you won't follow through to c-a-r-r-y the ball on your racket.

Practice shifting your weight from back to front by stepping toward an imaginary net and transfer your weight. The more you practice this, the more of a habit you develop so that when you swing on your backhand you will put your weight into it.

Why emphasize footwork ahead of the grip or the swing? Because if you watch a dozen top-flight players, you will see one using the Eastern grip, another the Continental, one taking a high loop on his backswing, while a fourth takes his racket straight back. But they will all perform alike in stepping into the ball.

You could have the best grip and swing, but if you didn't move into the ball as you hit it, your backhand wouldn't rate with a boy who used the Western grip and swung his racket like a fly swatter—but who stepped into the ball.

Here's how to practice moving up to the ball:

Facing sideways to the net, slide your right foot about a foot forward so that your feet are now about a racket's length apart. Then drag your back foot up to within fifteen inches of the front foot.

You want to keep your feet apart at all times so that at any instant you can hit into the ball.

Figure 4 shows how you can practice shuffling into the ball.

FIGURE 4 ══════ NET ══════

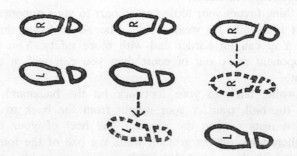

You can practice going backward the same way for high balls on your backhand.

The more you practice this, the sooner it becomes a habit. Practice a little every day whenever you can—on the court, in the back yard or patio, or when hitting balls against a wall.

5. *Hit the ball waist high.* You'd be surprised how many players run backward to take the ball on a lower bounce below the waist line. This is all right if you play a slugger and want to play four feet back of the baseline to give yourself more time to get set.

But if you run back for balls of ordinary speed, you run unnecessarily and force yourself to play a much harder shot. For the lower you have to hit a ball below your waist line, the harder it is to keep it in court. And the farther you run back from the net, the harder to surprise your opponent, for you give him more time to prepare for your shot.

Most of all, running backward will find you falling away from the ball at the instant when you should be stepping into it.

Some players assert they have more time if they run back, but actually if they just stood there and started swinging sooner, they would have even more time. Usually these players prefer lower bouncing balls because they tilt their rackets back (or "open the face") too much so that when they hit a ball waist high it sails out. The remedy is to keep the face of the racket straighter or more perpendicular to the ground ("closing the face") so that the racket meets the ball more solidly.

Stand before a mirror and swing, and see if you are tilting the face of the racket way back. If you are, that's probably why you run back toward the fence.

Practice swinging your racket with the face straighter, and stand your ground on the court to hit the ball around waist level. Start your rallies by hitting your backhand to accustom yourself to taking the ball higher. You'll find you save a lot of energy, can make better angles off the backhand side, and put more pressure on your opponent.

6. *Take more backswing.* Most players take a healthy swing on their forehands but poke or push at their backhands as though trying to tag the ball. If you are muscular and can hit powerfully like Lew Hoad and possess his lightning reflexes, you can get away with a short backswing. But even he becomes erratic at times compared with the computer-like steadiness of Rosewall. So in order to put your weight into the ball, you should take a good backswing. Rosewall makes a loop on his backhand by bringing his racket back head high and then pulling it down in time to swing in line with

his waist. This loop backhand covers more distance and requires more time.

Try a few swings before a mirror to see how big a loop you are taking, and how far back. If you do not take the racket back to your left shoulder, you are robbing yourself of power. One advantage is that it gives a feeling of rhythm. A disadvantage is that of not taking it back far enough and flipping the racket over the ball in the follow-through. Rosewall takes a high backswing and opens the face of the racket way back, but in hitting the ball he straightens the face so that it is almost perpendicular to the ground. Most of all, he c-a-r-r-i-e-s the ball on his racket by hitting through on the same plane so that the racket holds the ball longer.

Another school of thought considers a loop backhand as requiring too much time. It favors the Don Budge backhand swing: taking the racket back around the waist line to your other hip and dropping a little under the ball so as to lift under it. This swing is the simplest, and if you are rushed, you don't take as much backswing and can still make a fair shot.

Of course, the outstanding feature of the Budge backhand was that he took balls shoulder high and moved into them as they came off the ground on the rising bounce. This technique requires great natural talent and endless practicing and is not recommended when learning a steady backhand.

If you are used to taking a loop on your backhand and don't want to spend hours changing to taking it straight back, just try to modify the loop. Cut down taking it so high.

Remember: *The follow-through is more important than the backswing.* You can flail the air over your head with your backswing, but if you will bring the racket down in time to meet the ball and follow through to c-a-r-r-y the ball on your racket, fine.

To summarize: The simplest swing is to take the racket back around your waist line, keeping the elbow, a little bent, away from the body, with the face of the racket tilted back only slightly. Your wrist should go back in line with your left hip as you bend your knees and lift a little under the ball as your weight goes forward. You should drop your right shoulder as you hit into the ball.

As you hit, you should pivot your shoulders so that your chest faces the net and your racket keeps going to point to your opponent's backhand corner at about eye level. Your elbow should be a little bent and your arm should straighten out but not be stiff as a broom as you finish. Keep your racket perpendicular to the ground at the end of the stroke.

Feel that your racket is c-a-r-r-y-i-n-g the ball, and make yourself follow through in line with the flight of the ball.

Everyone tends to lift his racket higher on the backswing than necessary. To correct this, use your left hand to hold the throat of the racket to guide it back on the swing, and then let go.

7. *Keep away from the ball.* The average player lets the ball get too close to him on his backhand and thus has to cramp his swing. Keep your elbow a little away from your body, and reach out for the ball.

A good way to keep away from the ball is to think of hitting the outside seam that is farthest away from you. See Figure 5.

FIGURE 5 ===========NET===========

Also, by hitting the ball on the outside seam, you will be aiming more to your opponent's backhand, where you should hit most of your balls.

8. *Grip.* If you use either the Continental or Eastern grip, you are using the most popular grips. Two other grips are completely out of favor today, because they impose handicaps on players. One is the Western grip, in which your hand is placed as though picking up a racket that is lying flat on the ground. You swing at the ball with an upward brushing motion, which makes the ball bounce higher than with other grips but which robs the ball of speed. It is a bad grip to use

on low, bouncing balls and is practically unknown among tournament players today.

An offshoot of the Western grip is placing the thumb against the handle so that it extends much more to the racket head than the fingers. The result is that the player tends to push at the ball rather than to stroke or c-a-r-r-y it.

If you use either of these two grips, make sure you follow through to c-a-r-r-y the ball longer on your racket. You can try to modify the grip by sliding your hand toward the Eastern grip gradually over a period of time. Then, after a few weeks, you will find yourself using a more popular grip and controlling the ball better.

The Continental grip on the backhand is the same as on the forehand. You place a racket on edge, and then shake hands with it. Some players prefer using the same grip for both, because they claim they don't have time to change from the Eastern backhand grip to the Eastern forehand grip or vice versa. If you watch nine-year-old players change from one grip to the other easily, you might disagree with that view.

Actually, it is a matter of habit. If you practice hitting balls on the backhand holding any type of grip, you will find that after a while your hand has learned the grip and will automatically assume it. The physical education majors call this "the kinesthetic touch."

The Continental grip requires a strong wrist and is adapted more to low bouncing balls as a player tends to tilt the face of his racket back more or "more open" than with an Eastern grip. If you play an opponent with a Continental grip, give him high bouncing balls and he will chop rather than hit them.

The Eastern grip is the most popular, because it's easier to hit the ball with power and control. Standing the racket on edge, you put your hand on the top plane and spread your fingers apart more than in the forehand grip. Your thumb can be wrapped around the handle or diagonally along the handle, but make sure that your fingers reach farther toward the racket head than the thumb.

This backhand grip will also enable you to volley more forcefully than with the Continental grip. So if you are just starting out, you may find the Eastern grip more helpful all around.

If your racket turns in your hand on hitting a ball, don't blame it on the grip. Unless you have a very weak grasp, this happens because you have mis-hit the ball, either on the wood or off center.

You mis-hit either because you have misjudged the bounce of the ball, haven't moved quickly enough to take a good swing, or because you took your eyes off the ball.

If you have used a backhand grip for many years and cannot spend hours practicing every week, then keep it. Work instead on improving your footwork and swing, which are far more important than the grip.

9. *Practice.* The easiest way to develop a backhand is to throw balls up yourself to hit them. You don't have to think about running or judging the bounce, because the ball is right there. Here are some practice suggestions:

A. Stand about two feet back of the baseline over by your backhand corner. Throw the ball at eye level to bounce on the baseline waist high, and step forward to hit it across court to your imaginary opponent's backhand corner.

Try a couple of practice swings, and watch your backswing to make sure you are swinging the right way.

The idea is to develop your backhand swing into a habit. The more you repeat it, the sooner it becomes a habit—that's why you don't have to think about tying your shoe laces. You've done it so often it's automatic. But the first time a child tries it, he finds it very difficult.

You should stand way over to one side to practice hitting to the other corner. This shot is the most important, because you are hitting through the center, where the net is lowest. You can thus hit harder and keep it in because you have more area for safety. And you are usually playing to his weaker side.

Watch where your drives land. If you keep hitting down the line to the other's forehand, you are hitting the ball too far back, in line with your belt buckle or your back foot. You want to hit the ball in line with your right foot or a little ahead of it. Either throw the ball farther ahead or do not charge into it so much.

B. Another way of practicing your backhand is to hit a ball on an elastic cord. Tom Stow, a well-known California coach, has developed a device he calls "Stroke Developer." An elastic cord goes through a tennis ball and is suspended from a yardarm attached to a pole or fence. The other end of the cord is anchored to a hobble of heavy wood.

By hitting a ball on a cord that gives way with the stroke, the

11

player can practice hitting backhands, forehands, and serves without going on a court. You can practice moving into your backhand and taking swings without having to judge the bounce of the ball.

You can buy this device from Mr. Stow, or you can make one yourself. You can buy the heavy elastic "shock cord" from an outlet store, and by piercing the ball with an icepick, you can draw the cord through the ball. Then attach a piece of small pipe about three feet long to a board that can be fastened to a pole or fence, and dangle the cord from the pipe. Any heavy slab of wood or brick can serve as a hobble for the other end of the cord.

C. Find a player to hit to your backhand with medium-paced balls. Rally and do not play games, because you want to concentrate on how you are hitting your backhand. Or let him practice his serves, and you take as many balls on your backhand as possible.

D. If you can't find anybody to rally with, get a game with a decidedly weaker player. Use your backhand as much as you can. If you play a stronger player, you will feel compelled to keep the score fairly even and will favor your forehand as usual. But against a weaker opponent, you can practice your backhand much more and still keep ahead.

The important feature is to groove your backhand by repetition so that your swing and footwork become automatic.

Bill Tilden furnishes a fine example of determined practice. He lost to Billy Johnston in the 1919 Forest Hills final when handicapped by an erratic backhand. That winter he worked on the stroke with Arnold Jones, and by spring he had developed a backhand that could score outright winners consistently. Armed with this new weapon, Tilden reigned for years as Imperial High Potentate of tennis.

E. Practicing against a wall or backboard presents advantages and disadvantages. It makes you move your feet, watch the ball, strengthens the wrist, and can provide strenuous exercise. In addition, it affords a distinct psychological pleasure in hitting a ball smack in the middle of the racket with all your might. Psychiatrist pupils of mine have suggested it is even more valuable for releasing frustrations, if only temporarily, and in letting off steam.

However, although many coaches extol backboard practice, many more see little point in it. Perry T. Jones, former Davis Cup captain and long the leading figure in Southern California tennis circles, votes against it. He thinks it causes a player to shorten his backswing and his follow-through and that the bounce of the ball varies completely from actual tennis play.

Certainly nothing beats rallying on a tennis court, for you sharpen your eyes and feet to move and to swing at balls with varying bounces, speeds, and lengths. In hitting against a wall you never know what depth you are getting on your drives. Yet depth is a very important feature of tennis. The pros hit deep drives compared to the shallow drives of average players. If you hit a hard ball short, it merely sets it up for your opponent to crack it back even harder—and deeper.

Thus if you can't find anyone with whom to practice on a court, you will at least get some practice from hitting against a wall. But this practice should serve only as a minor substitute for real practice on a court.

10. *Develop your backhand chop.* The most dependable weapon in your arsenal should be your backhand chop. It is far easier to control than a forehand drive, although it lacks the speed and power of a drive.

When you hit a backhand drive, you take a bigger backswing, *lift* under the ball, and follow through farther. When you chop, you take a shorter backswing and chop down on the ball, with a shorter follow-through.

When you drive backhand, the ball on bouncing spins in the direction of the back fence and tends to rise, as shown in Figure 6.

FIGURE 6

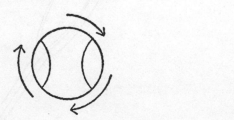

This topspin also makes the ball keep going faster toward the fence.

However, when you chop your backhand, the ball on bouncing tends to spin back to you and to bounce lower, as shown in Figure 7.

FIGURE 7

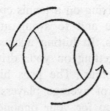

NET

This backspin makes the ball sit up and wait or skid.

Then why do players use the chop instead of the drive? Because you can return thunderbolt drives and serves much easier and guide the ball with greater accuracy. Because you take a shorter backswing, you have more time to prepare for a fast serve. The backspin also tends to pull the ball down into the court and keeps it from sailing out.

Best of all, you can chop a serve down at a net rusher's feet and cause him more trouble than a hard-hit backhand drive that goes high over the net.

How to make the backhand chop: You bevel or tilt the face of the racket back so it is "open," as in Figure 8.

FIGURE 8

14

Holding the same grip as for the drive, you chop down on the ball to put slice or underspin on it. The more you chop downward, the more backspin you put on the ball and the more it slows down on hitting the ground.

Remember: Take a shorter backswing and a shorter follow-through than with the drive. But as in the drive, move your weight into the ball so you will c-a-r-r-y the ball on your racket. Also, keep your elbow from touching your body, so you can swing more freely. Bend your knees as you hit into the ball, and put your weight down on your front foot so that it rests flat on the ground.

If your chops go way out, either follow through more or "close" the face of your racket more by tilting it more toward the perpendicular.

If your chops go into the net, do not chop downward so much or try opening the face of the racket more.

As on the forehand, do not chop low balls with as much force as a ball around your waist line.

High-bouncing balls: Most weekend players would rather face cannonball serves than high-bouncing balls on the backhand. The instant they spot a high-bouncing ball, they either scurry around to take it on the forehand or take off like a flight of ducks for the back fence. They want to take the ball no higher than waist high and sometimes race back far enough to take it knee high. Are all these trips toward the back fence necessary?

No.

Can you hit a ball around your shoulder as well as around your waist line?

Only Don Budge could slam into them for placements. But the rest of us can learn to handle them that high with skill. Actually, it is easier to return high-bouncing balls than a fast ball around your waist line. A high-bouncing ball travels much slower than a ball with a lower trajectory. That gives you more time to prepare for it.

It gives you time to run back. Lots of players make the mistake of running back while the ball bounces and are pulling away from the net as they hit the ball. You should either start faster or stop sooner in time to get your weight going toward the net.

A tennis axiom holds that generally speaking, the farther you stand from the net, the harder it is to win a point. So why handicap yourself in running ten feet back of the baseline for a ball you could handle at the baseline?

O.K., so you stop running way back and thus give yourself time to get set for the ball. Then since the ball must travel a long way—sometimes eighty feet—you play it *two* rackets high instead of the usual *one* racket high over the net. At least two, and possibly three.

Why that high?

Because for your opponent to loft a high ball to you, he must be standing way back on his own baseline. Unless he is a confirmed net rusher, he is not charging into the net but is waiting back at his own baseline.

If you return the high-bouncing ball only one racket high over the net, it will most likely land right on the service line—just right for your opponent to pounce on it. So think deep. Return the ball way back to his baseline.

If your opponent rushes the net, don't try to pass him. The odds favor him more than a thoroughbred racing a poodle. Lob the ball high over his head. He'll have to turn around and run back, and he won't like that because he'll have to run too far. He'll then quit rushing the net from back of his own baseline.

Assuming he is staying back, when you return the ball deep to his backhand, you put pressure on him. If he hits short, you can come up and drive the ball to start him running. If he returns deep, be patient and return deep to his backhand. He may keep running back to take the ball low. This is fine for you, because he will then be working harder than you, and eventually it will tire him sooner and cause more errors on his part.

If your opponent rushes in but stops at the service line, try chopping the ball down at his feet. Then if he rushes all the way into the net the next time, lob over his head. By mixing up your shots according to his position in the court, you make it harder for him.

Most of your high backhands should go back to his backhand side, because the odds favor that return. However, if he hits a short return and then remains in his backhand corner, chop down the line to his forehand. This is a harder shot to make, but it will pull your opponent away from covering up his backhand.

Problem: Your opponent is running around his backhand and

hitting a high loop shot to your backhand. Should you try to return to his forehand to pull him from his backhand corner?

Answer: Once in a great while you should chop deep to his forehand from back of your own baseline, but usually you should hit back high and deep to his backhand corner. For if your chop to his forehand falls short, he can come in and whip the ball at an angle to your forehand for a winner.

If you are unintentionally hitting your backhand to your opponent's forehand, you are hitting too late—the usual fault of weekend players. If you find your backhand going too far across court outside, you are hitting too soon. You should then either wait a little longer for the ball or move up for it.

Practice: 1. Now is the time to look up old Joe Slowpoke, who pushes back all his shots. The fellow whom everybody avoids when they want "a fast game." He lifts the ball high and slow, so they come down like feathers—and with about as much pace.

Against him, you'll get plenty of practice running back and stopping in time to step into the ball. Because the ball floats over so slowly, you'll have plenty of time to think *how* to chop, and how high to direct your returns.

2. Throw balls up high and a little behind you. Then glide back in reverse of Figure 4, page 6. By practicing this, you accustom yourself to moving back and to putting your weight into the ball instead of flicking it back with your wrist.

3. Find an erratic, hard-hitting junior, Slug Happy, who loves to crack every ball. When he bats balls at your backhand, you will have to start your swing sooner, and this will speed up your stroke. When you play the average player, you'll find you have lots more time in comparison.

The Serve

Want to know an easy way to improve your serve?

You needn't take pills or special exercises or lift weights.

Cut down the speed of your serve until you get seven out of ten first serves in.

You may protest that you won't be hitting your serve as hard as you can. So? You don't hit your forehand with all your might every time, do you?

A common delusion persists that a player must wallop his first serve with all his might. So he winds up and lets go. About two out of ten times the ball goes into the court. The other eight times it sails into the fence or thuds into the net.

His opponent grins in anticipation and moves in to knock off the weak second serve. The server feels the mounting pressure, so he tries to serve a hard second ball and instead serves a double fault.

The server alternates between serving "sitting duck" easy second serves or double faults and complains later that his serve was "off" that day. What he means is that the pressure of his opponent threatening to murder his weak second serve eight out of ten times made him tighten up.

Your main purpose in serving is not to ace your opponent. You should instead strive to put the receiver on the defensive by forcing him into weak returns or errors. Push him back to the baseline when returning your serve, because this cuts down his angles and gives you time to prepare for his return. Because usually the farther the player is from the net, the harder it is for him to win a point, you increase his chance of making an error. Remember: Eight out of ten points are won on errors.

Actually, the fearful part of facing the top pros is not only that they serve cannonballs but that they average three out of four first good serves. In the 1960 Masters at the Los Angeles Tennis Club, Hoad averaged 76 percent and the winner, Rosewall, 78 percent of first serves going in. Think how much easier it would be to break their serves if they got only 20 percent of their first serves in!

You may assert that you possess only two speeds on your serve: Very hard and very easy. So how can you learn a third speed of medium pace?

Consider how you run for a ball. When you first started playing, you raced madly for every ball. But you soon learned that you could saunter for slow balls, increase your speed to reach ordinary balls, and race for hard-hit shots to the corners. Thus you have learned to vary your speed of foot.

You can learn to vary your serves the same way. Most players in trying to ease up on their serves stop the racket at the moment of impact, and the ball then sails through the air with the greatest of ease—way outside or into the net.

The best way to control your serve is to make your racket follow through as you do when serving hard. The racket will then c-a-r-r-y the ball longer and guide it better. This applies whether you cooked up a homemade serve yourself or possess an orthodox serve like the pros.

If you have the time, the balls, and the court, take a basket out and try serving by yourself. Keep track of how many balls you get in out of ten. Your low percentage may amaze you. So cut down your speed—perhaps too much at first—and get your seven out of ten.

O.K. Now try serving a little harder. At first you will be like a man learning to drive a car—you'll drive too fast at times and then slow down too much. But after a while, you'll accustom yourself to a medium pace while serving seven out of ten inside.

Also, as you serve medium pace, you'll find that you're more relaxed than when trying to put over a cannonball. Getting most of your first serves in also saves you a lot of energy that you can use for running for balls that now elude you.

This doesn't mean that you should serve at medium pace all the time. When you practice, occasionally fire some sizzlers to build up your muscles and increase your speed. In a match, unleash an intended cannonball once in a while. Tilden, Budge, and Kramer all used to cut loose like that when needing points. But mainly, keep to that seven-out-of-ten average. When you better that percentage, serve harder.

If you can't practice your serves by yourself, take on weaker players. You can then feel free to experiment, because you can always put on the pressure to beat them. Try serving with medium pace to see how many first serves you get in.

Lift of the ball. For most players the next easiest way to improve your serve is to lift the ball higher on the toss. Most of us do not throw the ball high enough to reach way up for it. We then adjust our swings to hit a ball that is lifted too low or to one side and thus cramp our serves.

The higher a player can hit his serve, the greater his chances of serving harder and getting it in. Most powerful servers stand over six feet—Ellsworth Vines, Don Budge, Jack Kramer, Pancho Gonzales, and Arthur Ashe. They could reach up and crack the ball hard because of this advantage in height.

Another advantage to reaching up is that you will be more likely to straighten out any kinks or sidearm motions in your serve. If you lift the ball low, you can't help putting too much sidespin on it, which reduces the speed.

Many players pop the ball up to serve like a toaster popping up a slice of bread. You should cradle the ball in your hand, lift your arm upward, and release the ball only when your hand goes above your head. Then you are lifting the ball only a foot or two from your hand compared to popping it up from your waistline.

You should lift the ball a trifle higher than you can reach. If you lift it too high, you will have to check the smooth motion of your serve and thus lose your momentum.

Bad weather conditions. What if it is windy or if the sun glares right into your eyes as you serve?

If it is windy, you might well lift the ball lower and shorten your swing to make sure of keeping your serve in court. Certainly on a very windy day, make sure of getting your first serve in—even a slow serve may bother your opponent because of the wind's tricks.

Against the wind, hit harder. With the wind, serve easier, but be sure to follow through and put more spin on the ball.

If the sun blinds you, try tossing the ball higher, lower, or to one side, as well as changing your stance slightly to avoid staring right into the sun.

Consider the bad conditions as a challenge to conquer, for if your opponent is inclined to self-pity under them, you will hold an edge. A favorite psychological trick of some players is to try to make their opponents feel it is a bad day for tennis and not worth contesting for points. Thus a player of equal merit will quit trying and so lose a match he could have won.

Mechanics. Is your serve one of your best shots? If it is and you serve with an unorthodox swing, you might better retain the swing than try to make a drastic change. Unless, of course, you are a junior who has lots of time to practice and wants to improve beyond his present plateau.

Assuming that you want to serve like the pros, you should stand close to the center service mark, with the left foot diagonal to the baseline, your left shoulder pointing at your opponent, and your right foot parallel to the net.

For the slice service, you should lift the ball about a foot ahead and diagonally to your right, as though you were the Statue of Liberty holding aloft a torch—in this case, a racket.

Point your racket at your opponent, and take it back close to your side, as though it were a pendulum, while you lift the ball up. Your weight goes back to your right foot. Bring your racket up in back of you, and then drop the head so that it almost scratches your back. You then reach up, snap your wrist, and hit the ball as your weight goes forward.

To direct the ball, snap your wrist as though throwing your racket, and your racket follows through on your left side. Most players unintentionally serve mostly to their opponent's forehand, because they snap their wrists in that direction. To overcome serving to your opponent's strong point, practice mostly at snapping your wrist as though throwing your racket at your opponent's backhand.

Flat serve. To serve a flat or cannonball serve, you throw the ball in front of you and hit the ball with the face of the racket open so that the ball carries no spin. That is, you hit the ball from behind and slightly above. The pros and ranking players use it from time to time.

Here I must part company with the tactics of the pros. They practice for endless hours and can tell where and how they are serving. The weekend player just doesn't have the time, and often he doesn't even know that he is not lifting the ball where he intends. So why try to use a different type of serve that may throw your regular serve off?

If you hit hard and put a little spin on the ball, you will control it much better than the player who blasts flat serves and rarely gets them in. You can afford to put a little spin on the ball for the sake of a little less speed on your serve. Also, it is easy to get mixed up on where to lift the ball if you keep changing from a flat first serve to a spin second serve or an American twist (to be discussed later).

There are more variations on the serve than any other stroke in tennis, so that no absolute rule may be laid down. Rod Laver practically never hits a flat serve, for he just tosses the ball up in the same place and swings harder. Pancho Gonzales and Dennis Ralston take a short backswing instead of the full pendulum backswing, and other players do not "scratch their backs" as they drop the head of the racket. Yet they all serve well.

Ralston lifts the ball in a very complicated manner compared to Jack Kramer's simple toss. This could cause his greater number of double faults, because the more complicated you make a stroke, the more features that can go wrong.

However, all great servers lift the ball high and pour their bodies into the stroke so that they move into the ball with all the power of their shoulders. And they all snap their wrists at the moment of impact.

The American twist. Lift the ball so it would drop on top of your head or a little behind, bring your racket back, and after "scratching your back" move your racket from left to right so that it finishes on your right side. The top- and sidespin make the ball hop high to your opponent's backhand.

You should use this serve to rush the net, because the ball bounces higher and slower than with the slice serve; this serve also gives you more time to reach the volleying position. The high bounce should make it harder for your opponent to score winners, because it forces him to stand back farther and cuts down his angles.

This serve is not intended to win points outright, although it may cause your opponent to become overanxious at seeing you rush in and thus hurry his shot. You may use this as a second serve even if you stay back, because it affords a change of pace from your usual lower-bouncing, faster first serve. In fact, many players find it harder to return slow, high-bouncing balls than faster first serves.

The American twist does make greater demands on the back and stomach muscles than other serves, so when first learning it, take it easy and don't overpractice it—especially if you feel twinges in your back or stomach muscles the next day.

A good way to build up those muscles is to do back-bending and twisting exercises. If you're normal, you won't go through a long, tedious session, so try to do just a few exercises every day. You will limber up those muscles and be able to increase the number of American twist serves each time you play.

This serve exacts a heavier toll on women than men, it seems, perhaps because we men are supposed to be more muscular. A great player like Darlene Hard could serve the American twist all afternoon and rush the net because of her superb condition. But the average woman player who plays for fun would do better to limit this serve for doubles mainly, and then only if she rushes the net on her serve.

In any event, all servers should warm up with other serves first before using the American twist in a match.

Placing your serve. Most weekend players consider speed the most important feature of a good serve. Actually, the main difference between the pros and the average tournament player is not the great difference in speed as it is in placement. Sit as a linesman in a pro match and then at the usual amateur match, and you'll be amazed at how few really close calls you get in the latter. In one game with the pros, however, you may call five really close ones to the line.

Stan Smith, the 1968 National Open Doubles champion, told me Pancho Gonzales' serve bothered him more because of its accurate placement than its speed. Pancho accepted a bet recently that he couldn't knock over a can of balls set in the backhand corner of the ad court in ten attempts. Pancho warmed up and then knocked the can over on his third serve. Try it yourself some time to see how long it takes you to hit the can.

The fact is that if it weren't a license to steal, you could bet the average tournament player he couldn't knock it over in thirty attempts.

Naturally, it's more fun to crack a serve really hard past your opponent than to whip one over that he fails to return. But you should ask yourself whether you want to enjoy serving a rare ace or beat your opponent. When you learn to place your serves, you can always add the speed later.

Lots of players find it helpful to glance at their opponent's court, mentally aim at a spot, and then serve. This helps them unknowingly to swing the racket head in that direction. The trouble is that your opponent may soon learn what to expect.

The pros never tip off where they're aiming. As a linesman in dozens of matches calling serves on the center service line, I've tried to figure out ahead of time where Rosewall, Gonzales, Hoad, or Laver were going to crack the ball. You simply can't tell until they hit the ball.

You can do the same. Simply snap your wrist in the direction you want the ball to go, and the racket head goes that way.

Practice against a weaker player by concentrating on placing the ball to the corners. The more you practice, the sooner it becomes a habit and improves your serve.

Where to serve? Usually you should serve mostly to your opponent's backhand and occasionally to his forehand "to keep him honest" and to prevent him from edging way over to cover up his weaker backhand.

However, some players like Rosewall prefer receiving the ball on their backhand. Your opponent thus may have a steady backhand but a hard-hitting, erratic forehand. Then you could win more points by serving to his forehand.

If you don't know which side your opponent prefers, serve right at him. He will then move to take it on his favored side.

Beverly Baker Fleitz, the beautiful hard hitter, used to change her racket from one hand to the other so she was always hitting forehands. But when a ball came right at her, she would move to take it on her right hand. Players knowing this would serve most balls to her left-hand side.

Pancho Segura once told me that he tried to serve close to a tall player like Gonzales, who preferred running wide to hit a sweeping drive. Tall men like to use their leverage and find close balls uncomfortable.

However; against a smaller, agile player like Rosewall, Pancho served wide, because the former can't reach as well nor get the leverage.

A good way to tell which ball a player prefers is to fire a few wide serves to a small man to see how he handles them; and serve a few balls right at a tall man to watch if he can scramble backward to take a good swing.

Everything else being equal, it is far better to force a player out of court to make him run to the other side and thus wear him down.

Avoid serving all the time to an opponent's weakness. You give him so much practice that it will improve as the match goes on. Also, he can get set if the ball always lands in the same area.

Warm up. Most players try a couple of practice serves and then start serving. They don't want to keep their opponent waiting, they feel, while they try a dozen serves. Yet the server can't possibly serve well when cold—any more than a major league baseball pitcher could pitch well if he tried only a couple of warm up pitches first.

One good way to warm up is to try an easy serve when starting a rally instead of as usual with a forehand drive. By serving easily, you give your opponent a chance to practice his drives, but most of all, you are warming up your overhand motion.

You may also ask your opponent if he wants to try a few serves. Then he won't feel you are delaying the game when you try a few yourself. Also, if he has to go way over to pick up a ball, serve a couple into the fence.

The pros try at least thirty to forty serves before starting, and these are players who have perfected their games. If anyone could go without a warm up, the pros could, but they realize the value of limbering up their serves as well as their drives and volleys.

Second serve. The second serve is the poor relative in frayed cuffs of tennis. Most players try to avoid using the stroke and consider that the sooner they get it over with, the better—probably because so many players merely tap their second serve so that it floats over the net, where an opponent can destroy it with his forehand.

Yet Bobby Riggs once aced Pancho Gonzales twice in a row—on his second serves to the forehand.

You may not ace your opponents, but you can develop a stronger, more reliable second serve.

For most players, merely follow through more. Instead of stopping your swing halfway, make yourself follow through more and thus c-a-r-r-y the ball longer on your racket. The longer you c-a-r-r-y the ball on your racket, the better you control it.

You may use the American twist for your second serve if you know it, or work to develop it. But if you don't know it, lift the ball so that it will fall on top of your head. Then swing your racket to brush upward and over the ball and thus add spin to the ball. This will also make the ball bounce higher and force your opponent to stay back more. You then finish with your racket on your left side.

Many teaching pros feel it is better for weekend players to use this serve as a second serve rather than the American twist, because this does not differ too much from your first serve. Many top-flight players make their second serves not too much easier than their first serves. Similarly, you should try to hit your first and second serves with not too much difference in speed.

However, first try for more spin and better placement on your second serve. A shallow second serve that bounces close to the net gives your opponent a chance to come up and crack it. Serve within a couple of feet of the service line, and keep him back.

To lengthen your serves, pretend you are throwing your racket farther back in court (the baseline); this will make the ball go farther.

Remember, snap your wrist as you serve.

Aim for your opponent's backhand corner most of the time. In the deuce court, this will cut down his angles, for if you serve an easy ball wide to his forehand, he can then crack it down the line or way across court to your forehand. You will find it hard to defend these two widely separated areas. But if you serve to his backhand and he runs around it, he can't make a wide angle on you.

This applies in the ad court also. For if he runs way around his backhand, he will have to score a winner, or he will be so far out of court that you can start chasing him to the other corner.

After you learn to serve regularly to the backhand, try serving to the forehand side. This may catch your opponent unaware and keeps him from crowding too far over to cover up his backhand. This will also give you practice for serving against lefthanders.

How often should you serve to your opponent's forehand? You should ask yourself: 1. How well does he hit easy balls on his forehand? Some players can hammer back fast drives off their forehands but fall apart on soft returns. Serve a couple of second serves early in the match to find out how he handles them. Serve 20 percent as a rule to the forehand.

2. You may already possess an unorthodox but highly effective second serve. Some players manage to sneak over low, bouncing, skidding second serves that trouble opponents far more than the usual higher bouncing spin serves.

Ozzie Nelson of "The Adventures of Ozzie and Harriet" TV show fame used to serve a slow, low-bouncing second serve in doubles and then dash to the net. The normal reaction of most opponents in his class was to slam the return with all their might —at Ozzie, who would block it back past them. Ozzie had fast reflexes and could manage to return most balls above his waist. Thus his second serve, when aided by his net-rushing tactics and quick reflexes, proved more successful than most others. It could be that your present second serve stands up better than most in your league. If it does, let it alone and work on weaker shots.

Double faults. If you serve weakly to the pros, you might as well start walking back to pick up the ball. They will consistently hammer it away for winners. But against the average player, you may win more points serving a floater than a fast ball. So never give him a free point with a double fault.

Once you serve an easy ball inside, your opponent feels an overwhelming pressure to kill it. Sometimes he will. But many times the ball floats over so slowly that he has time to try to second-guess you.

Perry Jones, former Davis Cup team captain, often says, "Thinking during a point is fatal. Don't think—hit the ball!" Of course, he means trying to second-guess your opponent while swinging at a ball.

Your opponent will often start out aiming his return at your backhand, change his mind to aiming for your forehand, and end up hitting it right back to you. Or into the net. The next time he will feel an even greater pressure to prove that this time he will correct his error and really blast the ball. The odds have to be at least 8–5 that he will miss it also.

Naturally, you shouldn't depend on soft serves against all opponents. A smart one won't get mad or blast the ball but will simply return it away from you and force you into an error.

But always give your opponent a chance to miss. Make him earn the point. Get that second serve inside.

Court position. In singles you should stand close to the center service mark. The closer you stand to the court, into which you are serving, the easier it is to keep your hard serves inside. Your opponent has less time to move toward the ball, and it is also easier to serve straight down the line into the corners.

Frank Sedgman and Bobby Riggs would serve several feet from the center to force their opponents way out of court. Frank would rush the net on these serves and volley the returns for winners.

However, Frank and Bobby could pinpoint their serves, so they never served an easy one their opponents could move in on and kill. The average player just doesn't have the control to place the ball from farther over and thus leaves himself wide open for his opponent to crack the ball to the opposite corner.

Some players claim they have to stand way back of the baseline or far to one side to get their serves in. They are simply handicapping themselves, as though carrying an anchor. To keep their serves in, they should come down more on the ball, turning the face of the racket to put more spin on the ball and making sure to follow through.

Some players also like to stand way over when serving to the backhand court, but this makes it harder to surprise your opponent with an occasional serve to his forehand.

So if you stand near the center, you will do better. Tournament players can serve from different positions, because they can adjust their serves for longer distance and more spin. But if you don't play every day, why handicap yourself with trying to learn these various positions?

In doubles, when serving into the deuce court, the server usually stands in the center of his half of the court, which is nine feet from the center service mark. However, there are all kinds of exceptions, depending on your ability to place your serve, your speed of foot, and your tactics.

Many tournament players stand within three feet of the center service mark to serve more effectively to the opponent's backhand. See the chapter on tactics in doubles for the reasons for serving like this to the backhand.

Some players stand next to the service mark, as though in singles, to make sure of serving down the line to the backhand. However, the closer you stand like this, the more you will have to run over to cover any shots in your alley. You might try standing from three to six feet over to see how well you cover shots to your alley. If it is a strain running over, stick more to the middle of your court.

Still another place from which to serve is way over, twelve to fifteen feet from the center service mark. But you may find yourself serving continually to your opponent's forehand. If he wields a powerful crosscourt drive, he will wallop your serves to put you on the defensive. Or he could lob over your partner's head as you rush in, and then you would find it hard to cross way over to cover the lob.

Darlene Hard, a great women's doubles player, would purposely stand way over in serving, in both women's and mixed doubles. She told me she did this "because the idea is to make holes." She wanted to force her opponent way off court and thus leave the middle open. If the opponent blasted a forehand return, Darlene expected to volley it to gain the offensive.

Of course, Darlene's partner, Maria Bueno, would cover her own lobs, volley with precision, and poach like a hungry panther on a luckless gnu. Darlene could then concentrate on her own area and purposely serve to her opponent's strong side. Also, since Darlene was a great volleyer, she could handle sizzling returns.

The main premise of Darlene's serving wide is that women usually cannot win points merely by blasting the ball through their opponents. They have to force them out of position first, then hit for the opening.

However, some men prefer to serve way over from the side. Chuck McKinley said he preferred this position because he felt he could cover the wide-angle return as well as any lobs over Denny's [Ralston] head. He could also serve his second serve to his opponent's backhand.

Chuck actually did not have to cover too many lobs as he rushed in because his tremendous smash deterred much lobbing. If he had had an erratic overhead, his opponents would naturally have lobbed much more.

The value of serving wide to an opponent depends also on how alert your net man is. If he can poach well and if your opponent is slow-footed, the odds favor you.

Thus when weighing the merits of serving wide, ask:

1. Can you cover the lobs over your partner's head? Or can he cover them himself?

2. Can you volley the wide-angle return most of the time?

3. Can you serve occasionally to your opponent's backhand to keep him off balance?

4. How good is your opponent's forehand?

5. How fast is he at running wide?

When serving into the ad court, most players stand from nine to twelve feet from the center service mark. Some stand closer to slam a serve once in a while down the line to an opponent's forehand. This is a good idea, because some players return cross-court better with their backhands than with their forehands. Also, you may have to serve to a left-hander in that court sometime and this will give you practice in serving down the line.

Try serving to the forehand as well as to the backhand to see how well your opponent returns your serve.

What if your opponent stands way over to cover up his backhand? You may feel like serving mostly to his forehand. But you must be able to serve into the corner, for if you merely serve to his forehand, he can then step into it.

Most strategists feel it is better to serve mostly to his backhand to force him to run around it and thus out of court. Occasionally, serve down the line to his forehand. If he belts a hard forehand, make sure of getting your first serve in.

Don't forget: Serve 70 percent of your first serves in, or cut down your speed until you do.

The Forehand

If your forehand is your best shot, leave it alone!

Work first to improve your weak shots and/or tactics before you tinker with your forehand. It is far easier to win matches if you possess a well-rounded game than if you boast a strong forehand and a glaring weakness.

Also, you won't mind working to improve an erratic serve or backhand if you can rely on your forehand to win points. But if you start changing your forehand and go through a transition period when you can't count on it, you may lose to inferior players. Which is tough on the ego.

But if you have a shaky forehand, let's consider how to improve it. If you have played for years and years and get out only once or twice a week, you have probably formed habits and wouldn't have the time to spend on drastically changing your forehand.

However, if you're young or can practice an hour a day, you can try to remold your forehand.

Otherwise, you should merely try to modify your swing: If you take a big roundhouse swing now, try to cut down the arc. If you poke at your forehand, try to start your swing sooner so you can take more backswing, and then try to follow through more to c-a-r-r-y the ball longer on your racket.

Actually, most top-flight players today hit their backhands more soundly than their forehands. So do not try to copy exactly some favorite tournament player on his forehand, or you may be copying his mistakes. And lack the lightning quick reflexes to make up for it.

The Eastern forehand grip is the most popular. Hold the racket perpendicular to the ground and shake hands with it, the fingers spread apart, so that the V between your thumb and forefinger is exactly in the middle of the top plane of the handle.

Ready position. When awaiting the ball, face toward the net and point your racket (holding the forehand grip) at your opponent, your knees bent a little and resting lightly on the balls of your feet, your back almost straight. Some players hunch over like the Hunchback of Notre Dame, but it is harder to hit from that position.

At first your feet and legs may feel tired from leaning a little forward on the balls of your feet. But if you practice this way, you will start faster and reach balls that now elude you.

Remember, the main idea in all your strokes is to move your weight into the ball. All champions regardless of their strokes transfer their weight as they hit. Billy Johnston weighed only 135 pounds and wielded the hardest forehand of his day. Pancho Segura, weighing 145 pounds, pounded his forehand harder than much bigger Pancho Gonzales.

Your footwork, then, is merely a means of enabling you to step into the ball. If you fall toward the net and put your weight into the ball, you will do better than if you stand like a soldier at attention and merely poke at the ball with your arm.

When the ball comes, step forward with the left foot and turn so that your feet are roughly sideways to the direction in which you want to hit the ball. Your left foot is pointed diagonally and your right foot is parallel to the net when you want to hit down the line. This is the perfect stance, but of course you can only approximate this when you are running for a ball. The fact is that you will see lots of pictures of experts facing the net and making good returns, but they did this because they didn't have time to turn partly sideways.

When you want to hit crosscourt, you face more toward the net and hit the ball a little more ahead of you than when hitting down the line.

As you hit into the ball, step a little forward with your left foot toward the net so that your feet are about fifteen to twenty-four inches apart depending on your height; see Figure 9.

FIGURE 9 ════════════ NET ════════════

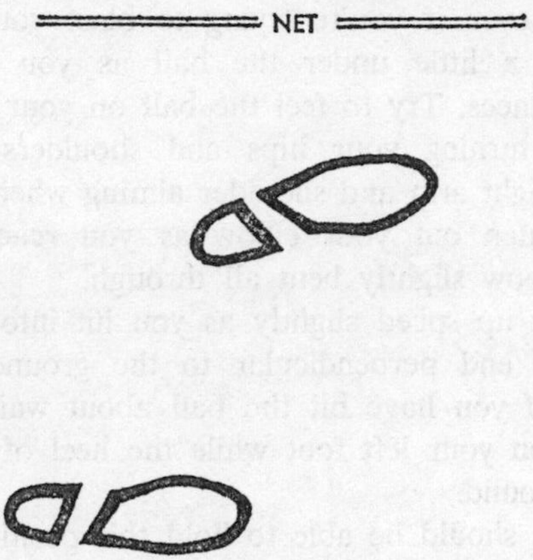

The left foot can be slightly ahead of the right. If you stick your left foot way ahead of the right with only a few inches between them in width, as in Figure 10, you will feel awkward because you cannot turn your hips and shoulders with the swing.

FIGURE 10 ════════════ NET ════════════

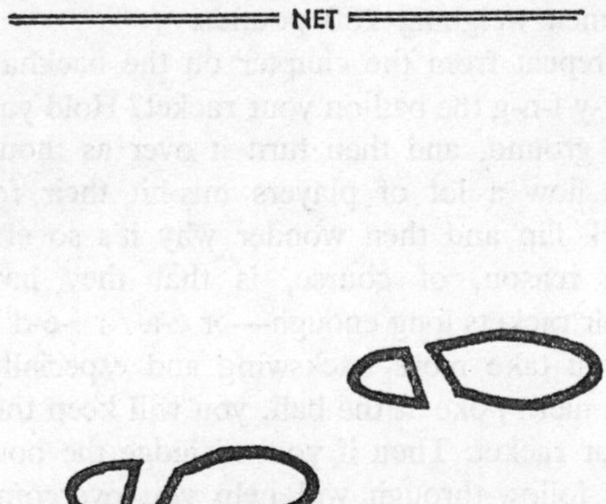

So keep your feet apart so that you can rock back and forth in balance.

When should you take your racket back?

The instant the ball crosses the net, and even before that, you know whether it's going to your forehand or not. Start your racket back in a slight arc (no higher than your shoulder) right away, for it is better to start too soon than too late. Swing back until the racket points to the back fence. You don't need any more backswing even if you're trying to blast your opponent off the court.

Lift a little under the ball as you come through, and bend your knees. Try to feel the ball on your racket by c-a-r-r-y-i-n-g it while turning your hips and shoulders so that you finish with your right arm and shoulder aiming where you want the ball to go. Straighten out your elbow as you reach for the ball, but keep the elbow slightly bent all through.

Pick up speed slightly as you hit into the ball. The racket face should end perpendicular to the ground and the top about eye level if you have hit the ball about waist high. Your weight now rests on your left foot while the heel of your right foot comes off the ground.

You should be able to hold this position as though posing for a picture. If you feel cramped and ready to fall over, you probably have your feet too close together, have the left foot stuck way out, or have extended your arm too rigidly, like an iron bar.

Your power comes not from the force of your right arm but from turning your hips and shoulders. That's why beautiful Beverly Baker Fleitz, weighing hardly 115 pounds, could hit harder than most men weighing 200 pounds.

To repeat from the chapter on the backhand: What is meant by c-a-r-r-y-i-n-g the ball on your racket? Hold your racket perpendicular to the ground, and then turn it over as though flipping a pancake. That's how a lot of players mis-hit their forehands—they give it a quick flip and then wonder why it's so erratic.

The reason, of course, is that they have not held the ball on their rackets long enough—or c-a-r-r-i-e-d it—to control it.

If you take more backswing and especially more follow-through than a mere poke at the ball, you will keep the ball that much longer on your racket. Then if you misjudge the bounce or the timing, the longer follow-through will help you overcome the mistake.

Can you think of all these things while you're playing? No—not unless you're a computer. So practice your swing before a mirror. Watch how far back you take your racket and how far you come through.

Swing easily. Most weekend players go from swatting the ball too hard to patting it back. Learn to swing through with a fair amount of speed and to place the ball as you will before you try to outslug your opponents.

When you start warming up on the court, think of only one feature at a time. Suppose you think about your footwork and keep your feet apart so you can swing from the hips. Think about taking little short steps as you hit a few balls.

Then think about taking your racket back sooner. Most players dash madly for a ball but don't start a swing until they reach the ball. Naturally, they swing late and mis-hit the ball. So start that racket back slowly as the ball crosses the net.

After that, think about following through and c-a-r-r-y-i-n-g the ball on your racket.

When you start playing, you can't think of all these things at once. But if you do only one or two of them, you will improve your forehand. If you bend your knees, for instance, you can't help getting your weight going into the ball better.

As you go over these features, you will find they become more and more automatic—such as learning to turn sideways has become.

High-bouncing balls. To hit a low-bouncing ball, you bend your knees, lower your racket in back below the ball, and lift up. Simple, eh? But a high-bouncing ball usually gives much more trouble. This stems from the player trying to run back to get the ball on a lower bounce around his waist line when the ball is already bouncing around his shoulder. Thus he is falling backward at the very instant when he should be moving his weight into the ball.

If you move quickly you may take some high-bouncing balls on a lower plane, but many of them you have to take around your shoulders. So you might as well learn how and thus add a greater threat to your game.

Bring your racket back as usual so that it is about waist high in back. Now, instead of trying to knock the ball down, thus sending it into the net or only to half court, lift under the ball and c-a-r-r-y it upward. Your racket should end up, not in line with your eyes as on the ordinary drive, but above your head. This will lift the ball two racket lengths over the net and deep into your opponent's backcourt.

If your opponent has stormed the net on a high-bouncing serve, see the chapter on the return of serve.

If your opponent has rushed up on a high-bouncing ball to your baseline, you should lob. See the chapter on the lob.

Most of the time, however, your opponent will be way back

on his own baseline when he sends over a high-bouncing ball. So you can aim the ball over by two racket lengths with little fear of his volleying it. For you must return deep or he will step into your short return and crack it.

The Continental grip. Another grip that is widely used is the Continental grip, which is used for both forehand and backhand. You hold your racket perpendicular to the ground and slide your hand, the fingers spread apart, so that the V between your thumb and forefinger is on the forward or leading ridge of the top plane.

Thus, using the Eastern grip, you turn your hand about three-eighths of an inch to put more of your hand on top of the handle. This difference doesn't sound like much, but it does make a difference in how you hit the ball.

In fact, the controversy raging between the two schools (Eastern and Continental) at times assumes that of a religious war. Admittedly, I must confess a distinct prejudice in favoring the Eastern grip.

It is harder to put topspin with the Continental, which requires much more practice because you have less margin for error. If there is one thing the weekend player needs, it is more margin for safety rather than less. He can't practice endlessly as Karel Kozeluh did and end up as Bill Tilden described him: "the human backboard." Nor like René Lacoste, who could hit a ball fifty times into the corners with seemingly no effort all day long.

The Continental grip is adapted to hitting low balls, but if you play on anything but grass, you will find that this grip handicaps you in dealing with high-bouncing balls. Players with this grip tend to run back from the net to take the ball on a lower bounce. The farther they run back, of course, the harder it is for them to make a forcing shot. High-bouncing serves also bother them more than a little.

If you play an opponent with the Continental grip, give him some high, deep balls and rush the net. When he runs back to take the ball on a low bounce he cuts down his chances of passing or surprising you with his choice of shot.

Some players favor the Continental grip because they claim they don't have time to change grips for hitting backhands. Actually, if you have time to turn sideways, you have time to change your grip. It is merely a matter of developing the habit of changing grips as you turn to the other side.

Consider how Pancho Segura changed grips—he would actually slide one hand over the other to grip the racket with two hands —and this while facing Gonzales' hundred-mile-per-hour serve!

Changing your grip from one side to the other is a matter of educating your hand to hold the racket in a particular way. This is a habit, like tying your shoelaces. When you first tried it, you had an awful time. So if you practice holding your forehand and backhand grips, you will become used to them and later never even think about changing them.

The big question about changing your grip from Continental or Western (to be discussed later) to the Eastern depends on how the rest of your forehand compares. If your footwork is slow, if you start your swing way too late, if you poke at the ball instead of swinging through—then you should work to correct those features first.

Certainly if you take the ball on the top of the bounce with your weight moving forward and c-a-r-r-y the ball on your racket in following through, you will do far better than with a so-called perfect grip and falling away from the ball.

If you do keep your Continental grip, you will find yourself with lots of company. If you become a champion, hordes of players will automatically change their grips to conform with yours. But the odds favor the fellow with the Eastern grip reaching the top.

The Western grip. If you place a racket flat on the ground like a snowshoe and pick it up, you will be using the Western grip. This grip in tennis compares with the Model T in autos.

Back in the days when tennis balls did not last one-third as long as today's, you either had to chop them heavily with underspin or drive them with lots of topspin to keep them in court. The Western drive enables a player with a strong wrist to flip up and over the ball so that it takes a nosedive over the net and bounces up high.

Amazingly enough, Rod Laver, who uses the Continental grip off both sides, hits the ball with so much more topspin than usual that when it bounces, it acts somewhat like the Western forehand. The ball crosses the net higher than most other pros hit against a net rusher, but it dips like a diving duck. This comes because he flips his wrist when hitting the ball.

Most coaches would shriek with anguish at pupils flipping their wrists like that, but Rod rules the world, so who can argue with him?

Meanwhile, back to the Western grip, it does have a great nuisance value. Most players favor your hitting a medium-paced ball that bounces waist high. If you use the Western drive, you bother your opponents with high bounces around their shoulders and the exaggerated topspin.

One of the last living exponents of the Western drive is the likable California pro, Carl Earn. He works so hard on his drives that a spectator will get tired just watching him. It seems a wonder that he can ever finish a match, let alone win one. But he even knocked off Bobby Riggs during a tour once with his crazily bouncing drives.

The big disadvantage of the Western drive is that you have to work so hard to put any real pace on the ball. Yes, it is true that little Billy Johnston hit the most powerful forehand of his day by swinging his racket like a warclub above his head. But as he came down, he stroked his racket perpendicular to the ground and c-a-r-r-i-e-d the ball in a groove for a few inches before he flipped his racket over.

Another disadvantage is in trying to hit low balls with this grip, especially on grass.

You can modify your Western by not brandishing your racket way above your head on the backswing. Cut down the big loop, but keep the rhythm. Also, try to hold the ball longer on your racket by following through and away from your body before you flip the racket over.

If you are young, aiming for the tournament circuit, or have time, you should mend your ways. Learn the Eastern grip so you won't handicap yourself. You'll hit the ball better and find it easier to volley at the net.

The Return of Serve

Returning serve rates almost as important as serving itself. Don Budge captured the Grand Slam by dominating with his lethal strokes and chopping up opponents with the greatest return of serves ever. Ken Rosewall met Arthur Ashe in the Pacific Southwest Open when Arthur was riding high after winning twenty-five straight matches and the National Open in 1968. Ken's admittedly weaker serve didn't work too well, but he made mincemeat of Arthur, 6-3, 6-2 by returning the latter's booming serves with precision.

You can improve your own returns by following these guidelines:

1. Watch the ball until you see it hit the strings of your racket. Forget about your opponent. Watch the ball!

2. Lean forward on the balls of your feet and start moving the instant you determine where the serve is going. Take short, skipping steps to move into the right position. By starting sooner, you increase the area you can cover and get set to swing sooner.

3. Start your racket going back right away. A common fault is to wait until the ball bounces and then hurriedly to slash at it. When running wide, make sure to take your racket back as you run.

4. If the server is firing cannonballs, shorten your backswing, but be sure to follow through, to c-a-r-r-y the ball longer on your racket.

Did you ever notice that when you try to return a fast serve safely by merely tagging the ball, it will sail into the fence? But when you know the serve is out by a mile, you swing freely and belt it back into court for a perfect return. This stems from your relaxing as you hit a ball you know is out. But mostly you made a good return because you c-a-r-r-i-e-d the ball on your racket and followed through more.

You should usually stand on the baseline for the first serve and then move in a couple of feet for the second. When facing a very hard first serve, try standing back a couple of feet from the baseline. However, the farther back you stand, the more of an angle the server gets on you and the more he forces you out of court with a wide-breaking serve.

The late Rafael Osuna of the Mexican Davis Cup team told me that when he beat Frank Froehling, III in the 1963 Forest Hills finals, he purposely varied his receiving position to combat Frank's hurricane serves. At times Rafe stood six feet back of the baseline and sent back returns of high, deep lobs. At other times he stood inside the baseline and chipped his returns just over the net. Rafe felt these tactics upset the rhythm of Frank's serve and enabled him to win in straight sets.

Once in a while, try moving inside the baseline against a cannon-ball server. The server will usually increase his efforts to ace you for daring to stand in so close. Thus tensed up, he will swing with all his might, and by trying too hard, serve faults.

5. Many servers telegraph the type of serve they will use by their preliminary motions. They will face around differently, throw the ball in a different spot, and swing in a different manner. Watch the server, especially in doubles when he is serving to your partner, to see if you can detect which motion he uses for different serves.

Some servers always serve wide to the forehand; you should then stand over farther to that side. A rule of thumb states that the farther a server stands from the center service mark, the farther toward your own doubles alley you should move. If he stands way over by his singles alley line to serve, for instance, you should move over to your own singles alley line.

Many times the server will first look at the corner to which he intends to serve. Great. This can tip you off to where to expect the serve. Never remind a server that he is serving all the time to one place nor that you have guessed where he is aiming.

6. If your opponent serves a wide-breaking ball with a hop, try taking it on the rise. This requires better timing, but if he is rushing the net, you can return the serve sooner and perhaps hit the ball at his feet. He will then try to rush in faster and/or to serve harder than he is capable. Either way you put pressure on him.

Also, you should vary your returns of serve with occasional lobs. If the net rusher knows he will volley every time, he will charge in closer than if he fears an occasional lob over his head.

7. If your forehand is stronger than your backhand, stand a little over on your backhand side so you can take more on the forehand side. Pancho Gonzales liked to stand like that, and then when the server delivered his second serve, Pancho would run around his backhand to crack his forehand. Pancho didn't do this all the time and thus kept the server guessing.

This trick works better when receiving in the deuce court, because by running around your backhand you will end up in the middle of the baseline. If you try this in the ad court you may find yourself running so far around your backhand that you will end up on your singles alley line.

Most opponents will prefer your returns to their forehands, but sometimes their backhands are steadier. Return to both sides to see which side your opponent prefers.

When returning against a net rusher, hit mostly through the middle, where the net is lower. However, in returning on your backhand in the ad court, hit mostly crosscourt to his backhand, because even if the ball sails high over the net, he will find it harder to deal with than a high ball on his forehand.

Returning lefthander's serves. Usually the lefthander serves a ball that breaks to your backhand. If it breaks slowly and you are quick-footed, you may run around it and take it on your forehand. But if the ball breaks sharply or you are slow-moving, take it on your backhand.

You may protest that your backhand is your weak shot. Even so, it is much easier for anybody to hit a ball that is breaking away from him than a ball that is breaking into him.

When facing a heavily topped or sliced serve, *be sure to follow through.* The ball spins so much that if you merely poke at it, the ball will slide off your racket and plop into the net.

When facing an unusual serve in singles, do not try for the sidelines or wide angles. Play it deep and toward the center to give yourself more margin of safety. Then as you become more accustomed to the serve, you can tell how much leeway to allow yourself in aiming for the sidelines.

Remember, once you have returned the serve deep, the odds in favor of the server vanish. You are now both even.

When facing an unusual serve in doubles, hit to the backhand side right at the server rushing in. It will cramp his stroke until you get used to placing the ball away from him.

8. In doubles, you want to keep your return lower than in singles because the net man may poach. See the chapter on poaching for hints on how to deal with net men seeking to kill your returns.

Otherwise, you should hit crosscourt away from the net man with a fair degree of speed. Mainly, you should strive to get the ball into play to give the opposition a chance to miss. Forget about making sensational returns for placements.

If the server stays back, return deep and hurry to the net. Then you put pressure on him to produce a good shot, because if he puts up an ordinary shot or lob, the odds favor your team.

If your serving opponent comes up to the net, toss up a lob once in a while to keep him off balance.

Watch the ball instead of the opposing net man. If you make a good return crosscourt, he will only upset his partner by making futile lunges.

Calling the serve. The unwritten rule in calling serves is that if you do not actually see the ball land outside, you should play it. Or if you did not return it, give the point to your opponent.

This attitude of fair play and sportsmanship lifts tennis above sports like baseball, where the players think it smart to hoodwink, influence, or bulldoze an umpire to decide in their favor.

Some players make a habit of asking the server to serve close balls over—especially ones they could not return.

It is tough to call a ball against yourself, but your opponent faces the same problem. Asking to play close ones over time and again is violating the chivalric code of tennis, because your opponent has to exert himself needlessly.

If your opponent keeps asking to play balls over, you may feel like asking if he has had his eyes checked lately or commenting that he never quibbles over balls that he returns well. However, a better answer is to ask that he decide one way or the other "to keep from delaying the game all the time."

44

You may add in a firmly polite voice that you hate to waste so much time replaying points.

A difficult opponent may ask, "But actually, what did you think the ball was?" Of course, he wants to put you in the position of feeling you shouldn't be taking the point.

"It looked good to me," you may say. He then says, "Are you sure it looked good? I mean, from my angle, I thought perhaps . . . tell you what, take two more." He speaks like a king generously donating bread to the peasants.

The purpose in tennis is not to conduct a parliamentary debate on points. The ball is either in or out, and play shall be continuous. To avoid these discussions, simply state, "You call the balls on your side and I'll call them on mine. Then we can keep right on playing."

This puts it up to your opponent to decide to incur suspicions that he is cheating or to give you the point. If he is way out of court and you are close to the line and he asks your opinion, you should give it and then announce the score.

The worst part of your opponent calling good balls out is not so much the actual point but the resultant effect on you. If you let it rankle you, the annoyance may upset your timing and stroking for the next games. You should assume that your opponent is honest until proved guilty by repeated bad calls.

Some opponents do not know any better and apply the tactics of sandlot baseball to tennis. When you thus straighten them out, you are doing the game a service. Naturally, you yourself have to set the right example. You can't condemn tactics in others that you employ yourself even in a lesser degree.

If you have to call some close ones against yourself, you will watch the next serves far more carefully. And this will improve your return of service.

Some players make it a point to be very generous in their calls in the opening games. They feel their opponents will then classify them as Sir Galahads and will overlook calls made later strictly on their merits.

Giving extra serves. Your opponent serves a first serve close to the line but out. You hit the ball back into his court, calling, "Fault."

Is your opponent entitled to the first serve over again?

Some servers believe that the slightest interference with their rhythm of delivering one serve right after another entitles them to an extra serve. Many players on seeing the server frown at the interruption, say, "I'm sorry. Take two, please."

Know what the server usually does then? He hauls off and serves a cannonball. If he gets it in, he usually wins the point. If he doesn't, he still is better off. Because the next time he serves a close one, you're likely to let it go so as not to disturb the server by returning it. And you'll see too late that some of the close ones land in.

Anybody allowed to serve three balls instead of two will always serve better. Sometime try giving an inferior player three serves instead of two on every point and see how hard you have to struggle to beat him.

The concept of giving an extra serve is an outmoded fashion from the days of ankle-length skirts for women. I have played against national champions who were in no danger of losing unless struck by lightning. If anybody could afford to be generous and/or polite, these champions could. Did they give me extra serves if they happened to knock a ball back?

No. Not one single solitary extra serve.

Why not?

Because among tournament players giving an extra serve is like allowing two bounces. It just simply isn't playing by the rules.

Any receiver is expected to chase after all balls that land near the line and return them. If he wants to run after balls a mile out, that's all right, too. He is just wasting energy he could use later to chase back after a lob.

If the server serves a ball just when another ball from the next court bounces onto his court, he should get the serve over. Or if there is an interruption from outside that causes a whole minute's delay, he may get an extra serve.

Some servers, whether unconsciously or deliberately, try to intimidate the opposition into giving them extra serves. When you return a close serve, calling it out, they frown and scowl. Some receivers feel that perhaps they miscalled the ball so they hastily call, "I did think it was out, but play two more."

Stick by your decisions. If you thought it was out, say so. Don't give the server something he doesn't deserve.

Suppose that it bothers you when somebody belts the ball back into your court on first serves? If you were playing with your boss, you wouldn't get upset. You can train yourself to pause, get into position, and serve your second ball. Millions of tournament players have trained themselves to do this, and you can also.

During the 1969 Pacific Southwest Open, one player I watched as a linesman would return every single ball served to him that landed within eight feet of the lines. That's right, every single ball. He didn't let one ball escape him, for he wasn't going to take a chance on missing a good serve. The player: World Champion Rod Laver.

Tell your opponents that if Rod Laver feels he should play every serve back, that you feel you should do the same.

In line with this, you cannot return a ball, wait to see if it landed good, and then seeing it was out, call the serve as out. This violates tennis etiquette and the spirit of the game.

If your opponent keeps doing this, ask him to call the balls as soon as he hits them so you'll know whether to play it back.

Serving the second ball too soon. Occasionally you have to chase after a close but out serve. You are still way out of position when the server delivers his second serve.

What should you do?

1. Struggle to return it? No.

2. Concede the point and next time try to hustle back faster into position? No.

3. Make no attempt to return it. Say you are not ready.

You should ask him to serve *one* ball (not two) over. The server must wait until the receiver is ready. So long as the receiver makes no attempt to return the ball, he is within his rights in calling he was not ready.

Usually, the server has fallen into the habit of firing one serve after another, and no opponent has ever corrected him. So when you ask the server to serve the second ball over, he may pause between the first and second serves for a while. But since it is a habit, it will reassert itself and soon he will start firing one serve after another.

One means of slowing him down is to drift back into position while still watching the first ball sail by you into the fence. The server can then see that you are not ready. He may scowl to show that you are "breaking his rhythm and ruining his serve." Let him scowl. You are under no compulsion to rush back into position merely because the server has developed a pernicious habit of firing serves one after another like a machine gunner.

Some players feel that the quick second server does it purposely to gain an unfair advantage. Most of the time the quick second server does not realize this, so you will have to educate him by repeating that you are not ready.

The Volley

Volleying is shooting the rapids, hunting tigers, and betting the long shot. It's riskier than playing it safe from the baseline, but you can apply more pressure on your opponent and end points sooner.

Volleying can lift your singles game to new heights, but it is possible to win many matches on clay by volleying only rarely. But in doubles, whether on clay or a fast surface, you must usually volley and take the net to win.

In singles on clay, you must rush the net with discretion, because the slower surface favors the steady retriever over the volleyer. But grass, wood, cement, and asphalt all favor the net rusher, because the ball takes off faster after bouncing.

In fact, Gardner Mulloy told me that to make a champion of a boy, he would train him on a cement court to encourage him to build an offensive game.

Another factor determining your volleying is your temperament. Are you a gambler at heart? Do you want to crush your opponent?

Next, how tall are you? The taller you are, all else being the same, the easier for you to cover the net and lobs. How quick are your reflexes? If you are agile and light-footed, you will volley better than a slow-footed slugger.

Does this mean that if you aren't tall, fast, and courageous, that you should remain chained to the baseline? That you should avoid the net completely?

Not at all. The volley is a much simpler shot than the forehand drive. Most weekend players miss at the net primarily because they take great big backswings while standing flat-footed and facing the net—not because they aren't agile like mountain goats.

Anybody can learn to punch a volley and to move his feet. And to use the percentage plays that give the volleyer the edge on his backcourt opponent.

Footwork. You should face toward the net, your racket pointing at your opponent, your heels a little off the ground, your weight on the balls of your feet, your back slightly bent. If you bend way over like the Hunchback of Notre Dame, you are limiting your area of action.

When the ball comes to your forehand, you turn *half* sideways or diagonally, as in Figure 11.

FIGURE 11

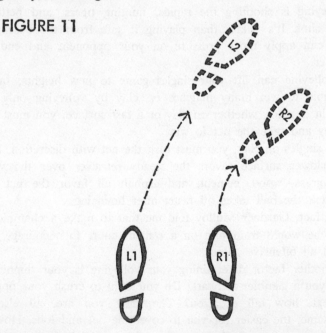

Forehand volley. Don Budge has suggested that when facing half sideways, put out your right hand as though a traffic policeman signaling "Stop." Then hold your racket in that position. By hitting your volleys in front diagonally, you hit the ball sooner and at a higher level. Best of all, you can make better angles that way.

The difference between a drive and a volley is the difference between using a sledgehammer and a tackhammer.

You punch at the ball with very little backswing and a very short follow through, hardly a foot. You don't need a big backswing, because the purpose of a volley is not to send the ball back with hurricane force but to deflect and guide it. The harder your opponent hits the ball, the less need for you to add any power of your own, for your racket will act as a wall to ricochet the ball away from him.

Think of thrusting your weight into your volley. By transferring your weight to the front foot, you punch the ball with your weight rather than your arm alone. You should bend your elbow slightly in volleying. Do not extend your arm straight out like a crowbar to reach balls.

Racket face angle. You tilt your racket back slightly from a perpendicular position—"opening the face" so that you can either get under low balls or volley high ones just as well.

You chop downward to put underspin on the ball to hold it in court. If you merely block the ball, it will fly off your racket. Chopping into the ball enables you to control it much better. Pancho Gonzales would heavily undercut his volley against hard-hitting opponents to keep the ball in court.

Another way to improve your volleying is to aim higher over the net.

Most volleyers miss by volleying smack into the top of the net. Some even stand right on top of the net and manage to volley into the bottom of the net. All volleyers tend to come down too much on their volleys.

So to increase your winning percentage, punch more forward and not so much downward. As I said before: *Always give your opponent a chance to miss the ball by returning it over the net.*

If your volleys now go out by a mile or do not feel "solid," you are probably opening the face of the racket too much and thus slicing the ball too thinly. Close the face more by tilting the racket more toward the perpendicular.

On low balls be sure to bend your knees, and get down to the ball. Generally, it is better to return these balls deep instead of trying for sharp angles.

Keep your wrist firm or locked when volleying. If you flick your wrist, you will put only the power of your wrist into the stroke instead of your body.

Watch the ball! It's amazing how many players look away just before hitting the ball to check their opponent's position or to see if the lines of the court are still there.

Watch the ball until you see it hit the strings of your racket. Your opponent is either in position or not. If he's out of position, you need not worry if you make the volley. If he's in position, you should make all the more certain that you volley correctly.

One reason photographers try to take pictures of a player striving for a hard shot is that his face reflects his intense concentration. But on an easy shot, he is relaxed and perhaps looking away.

The lesson in this derives from your watching a hard-to-get ball much more than you watch an easy one. The easy balls give you so much more time to think that you tend to look up on them —which is why you miss so many of them that you shouldn't miss.

Also, be sure to stroke through, as the ball itself will have no pace.

Backhand volley. It is easier to make backhand volleys than forehand volleys if you turn half sideways to put your weight into your volley. On the backhand side, you aren't as likely to take an unneeded big backswing nor to follow through too far.

See Figure 12 to show how you turn half sideways.

You keep your elbow down and your racket ahead of your body so that you volley out front and not at your side.

You chop into the ball the same way as on the forehand, with your weight going forward onto your right foot.

Most players tend to undercut the backhand volley too much by tilting the face of the racket too far backward from the perpendicular. If you keep popping balls up into the air or too far, you are probably tilting the face backward too much.

Remember, you take no backswing (except on high balls) and a very short follow-through.

High backhand volley. To hit a high backhand volley, you should bring your racket about a foot back, keeping the wrist firm, and lean into your stroke with your weight going forward. Since most of these balls will carry little pace, you must apply the power yourself.

Players usually miss this shot because they flip the racket with a

FIGURE 12

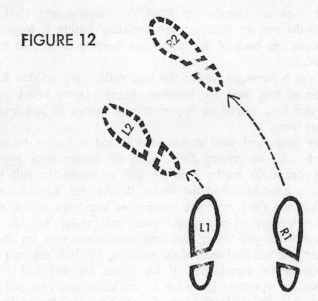

loose wrist and end up dumping it into the net. So be sure to put your weight into the shot.

If you are moving forward and within five feet of the net, you may try for a sharp angle. But if you are retreating or stand back a ways from the net, you'll do better to play the ball really deep, preferably to the backhand.

If you have to run backward for a high backhand volley, be doubly sure to aim much deeper than seems necessary, because it is harder to get your weight into the shot.

Most players hit this shot into the net, because they underestimate the distance the ball must travel. Because it is harder to slug a high backhand volley than a high forehand volley, common sense dictates playing the ball deep until you get another ball that gives you more chance to angle.

Volleying in singles. The No. 1 volley to learn on your backhand is the volley deep to your opponent's backhand. It is a more natural shot than the volley to his forehand, and the backhand is usually his weaker side.

Besides, by angling the ball to the side instead of straight ahead, you force your opponent more out of court.

First volley. The first volley you make on either side is the hardest. You are running up from the baseline and can't come close to the net, so that you are probably hitting it from fifteen or eighteen feet back of the net. From there, it is hard to make a sharp angle.

Play the percentages. Make the first volley deep so that it lands a couple of feet from the baseline. Many players volley only to the service line, where an opponent can charge in and whip the ball past them.

Volley deep, and your opponent will find it harder to surprise you with a lob or passing shot. Also, the farther back you force your opponent the harder it is for him to return the ball low or to make a good lob. And the longer it takes for the ball to leave his racket and reach you, the more time you have to size up the shot. Then move in and angle your next volley for the point.

At first when you volley, you can concentrate only on the ball. But later you will find that while watching the ball you can notice your opponent's movements. If he plants his feet and takes a big swing, he will most likely try to crack the ball past you. Once you spot this, move closer to the net to take his shot higher than by staying back.

If your opponent retreats and takes a short swing, the chances are that he will lob. Usually we all hit our lobs with easier, shorter swings and relax more than when trying to slug the ball. When your opponent thus takes a short swing, get ready to back up.

By thus anticipating your opponent's shots, you will get a jump on him.

Favorite shot. Most weekend players use the same favorite shots against a volleyer time and again. If forced wide on the forehand, they will crack the ball crosscourt. If forced back on the backhand, they will lob.

Try to keep track of your opponent's favorite shots—see how many times he goes for a down-the-line forehand, how many times he prefers crosscourt. On his backhand, does he chop short at your feet or usually lob?

You can see why it pays to concentrate on your own match instead of idly gazing at other courts and wondering how their matches are coming out. The more you think solely about your own match, the more and sooner you see the pattern in your opponent's game.

When you determine his favorite shots, start breaking for that spot he is aiming for. He may not realize you are anticipating his shot and will try to make it better by shaving the line closer or lobbing deeper. This added pressure can destroy his most powerful weapon.

Never remind your opponent that he is using the same type of shot over and over again. Lots of times he never realizes he is always hitting his shots to the same place.

Sometimes your opponent will realize that you are handling his best shot effectively and will try another. But if he rarely hits a forehand down the line in other matches, the chances are that even if he tries it against you, it may not work too well. So then he'll switch back to his dependable shot: the crosscourt.

Stop volley. This is a volley that demands greater touch than the usual volley and should not be tried until you can place your volleys at will.

You cut in close to the net and when volleying, pull your racket *backward* instead of punching through. This causes the ball to drop dead over the net.

You should be within two or three feet of the net and volleying a ball of average speed or less. Otherwise, against a fast ball, you may hit the ball back to the service line or too short—into the net.

If you delight in punching all your volleys, forget about this delicate shot. But if you possess a feel for varying the pace of your volleys or want to experiment, try this against weaker opponents. Using this stop volley at times will add to your attack by discomfiting your opponent at the baseline.

Variety of attack. In doubles, you should try to rush the net all the time on your serve unless:

1. Your opponents keep lobbing over your net man's head.
2. You can't get in past the service line to make your first volley.
3. You tire too much physically from the exertion.

Then you should wait until you can make a forcing shot against your weaker opponent before rushing in.

In singles, a lot depends on the surface, as I said before. Even more depends on your speed of foot and physical condition. The pros can rush the net all the time on their serves, but they boast the best condition of any athletes and could run a major league baseball player into the ground while carrying a bucket of water.

Another reason for not rushing the net continually is that your opponent will groove his returns to drop them either at your feet or to lob over your head. But if you stay back once in a while, he will hit short and give you an easy approach shot, because he thought you were coming in. The next time you come in, he may think that you are staying back and will hit higher over the net for added depth—where you can volley it easier.

Usually, you should volley to the other side of the court away from your opponent to make him run. Once in a while, volley to the place he left—especially if it is to his backhand. Then he will have to stop, turn around, and hurry back.

Then the next time you volley, he will hesitate about running to the other side, and when you do hit there, he will start a little late in running that way.

This tactic works well against the rabbit-footed player who covers court with ease and starts off so fast that he reaches the ball in plenty of time. These players love to run, so that merely chasing him around the court doesn't upset them. Try volleying where they left.

Just as ham goes with eggs, the volleyer must possess a dependable overhead. He need not kill the ball with his smashes, but he must smash consistently. Sooner or later, when your opponent finds that you are volleying his drives for points, he will switch to lobs. If your smash is erratic, he will forget all about passing you and start lobbing you to death. You will then hesitate to come up even on short balls, and your net game will disappear faster than a cold drink down a parched youngster's throat on a hot day.

Practice. Footwork is of the essence in volleying. Many a pro finds that a pupil who complains about missing volleys is actually stroking the ball correctly but moves like an elephant in a swamp. So the pro spends time drilling the pupil in starting and moving toward the ball when the pupil could be doing that on his own.

The easiest way to practice taking little short steps is to bounce a ball on your racket and purposely make yourself go forward, backward, and to the side. You can do this nearly any place, and you can make the exercise as mild or as vigorous as you please.

A better exercise is to skip rope. Never mind if you can't whip the rope over your head at first and pick up your feet. Keep trying, because if a child of six can skip, so can you. Build up the length of time gradually. It is far better to skip two minutes a day every day than to try skipping ten minutes once a week. Don't make work out of it—someday you'll put it off because it will seem too strenuous, and the next day also, and then you'll give it up.

The Australians, who go at their training programs like junior executives aiming to become president of the firm, all skip rope industriously. American champions have also. In fact, one day, a member of the Los Angeles Tennis Club noticed that Pancho Gonzales was borrowing my skipping rope.

"What does a champion like him who's so fast need to skip rope for?" he asked.

"Because he wants to stay fast," I said.

Certainly, Pancho has been one of the best-conditioned athletes of his age and has retained his speed long after others who were younger have faded. He used to stand at the service line when his opponent fired a drive, and charge in so fast he would end up practically at the net in volleying for the point.

This brings us to the next step: Lean forward on the balls of your feet, and have a partner throw or hit a ball to one side. Then dash into the net to volley it as soon as possible. Go all out to burst forward toward the ball. This will speed up your interceptions.

Try to volley deep, within a foot of the baseline.

Next, your partner should drive balls of average speed about ten feet on either side of the middle. If he blasts the ball at you, you will only improve your ducking. Later, as you volley better, you can practice against hard hitting.

Aim your forehand volleys deep to the backhand corner, then to the forehand corner. Cut in to angle your forehand volleys sharply.

Volley deep from your backhand to the other's backhand corner, then to his forehand corner. Cut in to angle your backhand volley sharply.

High backhand volleys present a tougher problem. You have to remind yourself to overcompensate and aim deeper than seems necessary. Practice hitting them deep to the backhand, and only after you can do this, practice hitting them deep to the forehand. Lastly, cut in on high backhand volleys to angle them sharply. This requires sharper timing and touch, so leave it for last.

A fine exercise for speeding up your reflexes is often used by the Australians: Both players stand on the service line and volley.

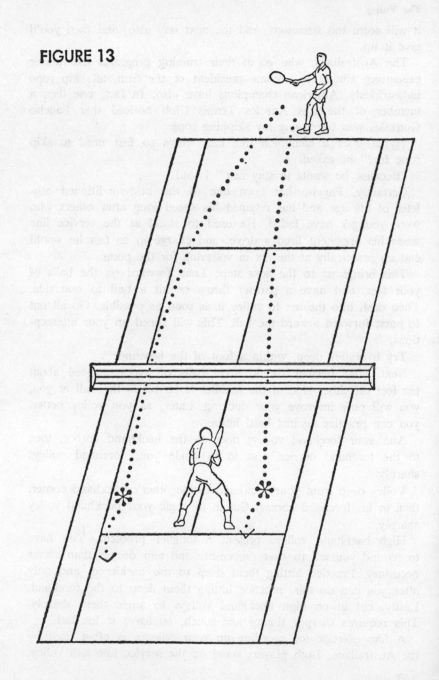

FIGURE 13

This cuts down on your backswing and makes you react faster and watch the ball better.

An even better exercise is to volley against two players on the other side. You really have to keep moving, because they can return the balls twice as well as you in covering half the court.

Position play in singles. If you hit the ball to the middle of the court while at net, you should station yourself on the center line to cover equal sides of the passing area. See Figure 13.

A few players purposely hit to the middle like this in using the center theory. The idea is that the backcourt player finds it harder to hit a passing shot because he has no wide angles to shoot for. However, the volleyer also has no wide angles to use, and so he must be a far better than average volleyer to make an angled volley and to put the ball away.

Thus, most players prefer to force an opponent way out of court and then volley for the point to the other side.

When the volleyer hits the ball to the backhand corner, he should shift over about a foot toward his right to cover equal sides of the passing area. See Figure 14.

The symbol V indicates the position of the volleyer. You can see that now he can cover both sides equally well. He doesn't have to worry about shots landing close to the net on his backhand side, because the backcourt player just can't hit it there with any speed and keep the ball inside the court.

When the volleyer hits the ball to the forehand corner, he should shift over about a foot from the center line toward his backhand side to cover equal sides of the passing area. See Figure 15.

The symbol V indicates the position of the volleyer. As in Figure 14, the volleyer can cover both sides equally well. He need not worry about shots going way wide on his forehand close to the forehand alley line, because the backcourt player can't hit them there with any speed and still keep the ball inside the court.

Position at net in singles. Your base of operations should be about two feet inside the service line and in the middle of your court. From there, you move forward to cut in on the ball. As shown in Figures 14 and 15, you vary your position according to where the ball is in your opponent's court.

However, you should also vary your position according to how often your opponent lobs. Some players think it is a sign of weakness to lob, and thus they rarely lob. Fine. Come in four or five feet

FIGURE 14

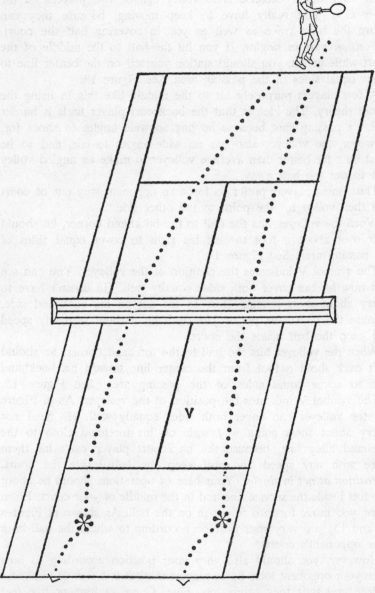

closer to the net, and the instant your opponent hits the ball, move in. You will then take the ball higher and closer to the net and can make sharper angles.

Remember, never remind an opponent that he is not lobbing, or he will correct this oversight and start mixing lobs and break up your net game.

If your opponent is smart enough to mix up lobs with drives, you should hold your position until you can see where the ball is coming.

If he lobs practically all the time, it's usually because he can't hit hard enough to break an eggshell and so can't pass you. You should retreat to the service line so you won't have to run back so far to smash. Then after smashing his first lob, get ready to move in to take his usually weaker return.

The half volley. Sometimes the ball comes at you so that you can neither volley it nor drive it. You then stroke through with your racket to trap the ball just as it is coming off the ground. This is the half volley.

At its best, it is as good as a well-placed volley, and at its worst, it is a defensive shot.

At the net it is always better to rush in closer to volley the ball at a higher level, but sometimes you cannot help yourself.

In making the half volley, be sure to bend your knees to get down to the ball. Use a shorter backswing and shorter follow-through than on your drive. You should lift up and c-a-r-r-y the ball on your racket with medium speed. If you try to slug a half volley, you will knock it out.

Making a half volley requires greater touch and feel for the ball than a volley. Your margin of safety is lower, because you are stroking the ball below the height of the net and have to lift it rather than come down on it.

If you find yourself making half volleys in the backcourt, it is because you are not moving quickly enough to get back into position or away from the ball, or you are caught in no-man's-land.

Practice. Enlist another player to hit balls around your feet, and practice taking them as they come off the ground.

Be sure to bend your knees and to watch the ball.

The lob volley. The lob volley is a volley used to lob the ball over your opponent's head while he is at the net.

You lift under the ball on your volley, and instead of chopping downward, you chop upward.

FIGURE 15

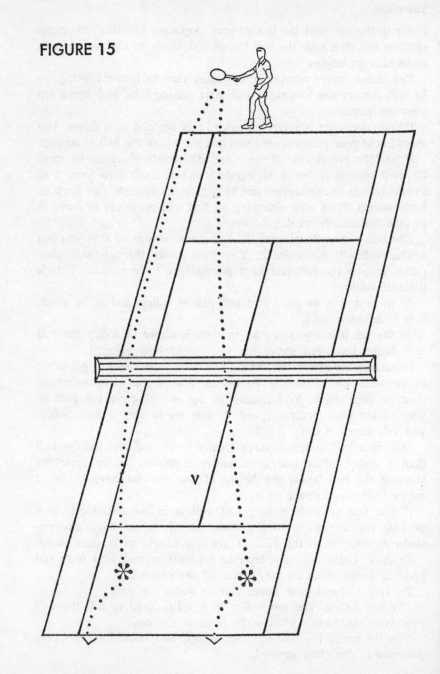

A good lob volley catches your opponent by surprise, and can go over his head for a point. If he does run back for the ball, you then assume command of the net, and the pressure is on him to bring off a good shot—not easy when he is running backward.

The lob volley requires a fine sense of touch. If you slam your volleys and depend on your power instead of touch in volleying, you should forget the lob volley.

This shot is for gamblers, because if you lob volley too low, you are giving your opponent an easy ball that he can smash for a kill.

The lob volley is not often used in singles, because if you can volley the ball, you can find an opening past your one opponent. In doubles, however, when your opponents are closing in at the net and you can't find an opening past them, you may lob volley over their heads. This drives one of them back to retrieve it and breaks up their formation at the net.

If you are closer to the net than your opponent, you can hit downward more than he can and should then avoid using the lob volley. But if you are back at the service line and he commands the net, you may use the lob volley.

Practice. Stand about two feet inside the service line while another player crowds the net. Have him hit volleys to you and practice lifting under the ball and over his head. Explain that he can then practice his overhead on your shorter lob volleys and that thus you can both practice together.

The Smash

Most players would vote the smash as the most soul-satisfying stroke in tennis. Swinging your racket with all your power and crashing the ball past your helpless opponent's feeble stab must surely please even the most gently inclined of players.

The music of the finale of Beethoven's Fifth, the sound of a bat cracking a home run ball, the roar of a football stadium crowd at seeing a ninety-yard run are all minor melodies compared to the resounding boom of a decisive smash.

For there is nothing to compare with the delight in smashing a ball solidly, feeling the ball crunch in the middle of the strings, and hearing the deep note of a well-hit shot.

To the gallery, a cleanly hit smash represents the triumph of virtue over the sly and tricky forces of evil, the perfect tag line to a lengthy exchange of stroke dialogue, and the final note of a crescendo.

An opponent may quibble that your winning drop shot was lucky, that the wind carried your lob over his head, that he misjudged your angled backhand, or that he missed a sideline drive by an inch. But when you smash for the point, you destroy any alibi of your opponent. There is no rebuttal to killing an overhead ball, no disputing your slamming the door of Fate in his face.

This probably explains why nearly all players smash not wisely but too hard. They kill one ball and hit the next three on the wood or into the bottom of the net. They exert every ounce of energy as though swinging a sledgehammer, and the effect is often as though they were—at a bumblebee.

They waste enough power to build another Hoover Dam, and after starting a match by slamming harder than a champion, they often end up poking their overheads back as fearfully as a miser forking over a dime for a bus ride.

Our old friend Shakespeare said that when we are sick in fortune, often the result of our own misbehavior, we blame our disasters on the sun, the moon, and the stars. Similarly, the smashers blame their errors on the sun, the wind, and their rackets.

Certainly, there are few things more frustrating than swinging assuredly at a puny lob and then knocking the ball into the net while your opponent grins at being let off the hook.

Yet there is a simple way to improve your smashing right off: *Swing about three-quarters as hard.* You'll be less tense and more relaxed, and you'll swing through more smoothly.

After all, you don't get any more points for smashing a ball a hundred miles an hour than you do for killing it at fifty miles an hour.

Is that all there is to smashing well?

Ah, would that it were, for we would all have overheads like the pros.

But swinging about three-quarters as hard is a good start. For most players it would greatly improve their batting average. But there are other ways to increase your kills.

Let's consider the swing itself. Lots of players think the smash should be just like the serve except that your opponent is tossing the ball up high for you.

They are partly right. You should take an overhand swing. But where do most smashers hit the ball when they miss the shot?

Out by a mile?

Rarely.

Smack into the net?

Yes. Decidedly yes. You will see a player standing right on top of the net and smash a lob—down into the bottom of the net. He couldn't do that if he purposely tried for a week. Yet many players smash there time and again.

This overwhelming percentage of most bad smashes going into the net means that players are hitting down too much into the ball—the way they serve.

The Smash

When you serve, you are trying to keep the ball *within* twenty-one feet of the net (the service court).

But when you smash, you should be trying to keep the ball deep —*outside or beyond* twenty-one feet from the net (service court). Except, of course, when you are trying to angle your smash toward a side fence. Otherwise you should smash deep.

One reason for smashing deep is that it is harder for your opponent to return a smash at his feet than a smash that lands in the service court area. In the latter case, your opponent can back up and manage to return a good number of your smashes. Also, by smashing deep you are giving yourself more margin of safety, because even if your smash is going out, your opponent will be tempted to play it anyway, or the ball may brush him or his racket.

Therefore, in smashing you should swing *up and over* the ball rather than downward, as in serving.

A good way to remember the difference in swings of a serve and of a smash is this: Think of throwing a ball into a bushel basket ten feet away. You would be throwing mostly *downward,* wouldn't you? Well, that's the way you serve—as though throwing your racket *downward.*

Now think of throwing a ball into a bushel basket eighty feet away. You would throw *upward* more, wouldn't you? That's the way you should smash—as though throwing your racket far into the distance.

Also, be sure to follow through so that you will c-a-r-r-y the ball on your racket.

Another reason for hitting smashes into the net is that your opponent may be putting a heavy undercut or chop on the ball, especially on his backhand lobs. This undercut tends to pull your smash into the net.

So when facing an opponent who heavily undercuts his lobs, be sure to aim your smash back a lot farther into his court than you usually would.

Still another reason that players smash into the net is that they tend to hit the ball too far in front. So try to hit a lob a little farther back than where you would hit a serve.

Placing your smashes. You have probably marveled at how experts not only crack their smashes hard but also place them so well —while you may be smashing hard but right back to your opponents.

Actually, it is more important to place your smashes than to slug

FIGURE 16

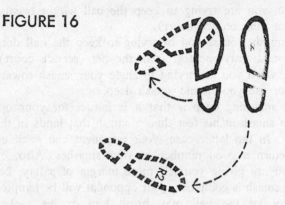

them. Ken Rosewall can kill a lob when standing way back on his own baseline, because he places it either in the forehand or backhand corners. Yet he really doesn't crack the ball as hard as many lesser players.

Thus another way to improve your smashing is to place them into the openings, away from your opponents. When you serve, you snap your wrist as though throwing your racket in that direction. You do the same with your smashes. Snap your wrist in the direction you want to aim your smashes, and see the improvement.

Footwork. You advance toward the net in moving toward most shots, but in the smash, you almost always retreat from the net. So the footwork differs in that your first step should be backward. However, since you are trying to take the lob on your right side,

FIGURE 17

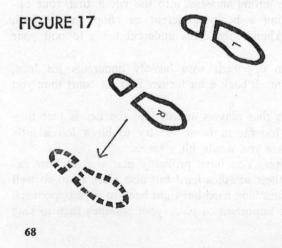

you should always pivot on your left foot and swing your right foot behind your left, as in Figure 16.

In retreating, draw your right foot back first from ten to fifteen inches, as in Figure 17.

Now draw back your left foot, keeping it about a foot or so apart from your right foot so that you can smash at any instant, as in Figure 18.

FIGURE 18

If you will practice this pivoting and retreating, you can't help improving your smashing. Many players miss smashes simply because they are off balance and can't get set to swing at the ball.

So when a lob sails toward you, pivot right off, and draw your racket back of your head.

Advance warning. If you watch your opponent, he will sometimes warn you beforehand that he intends to lob. This has been covered in the chapter on volleying, but it won't hurt to repeat:

Most players intending to drive a ball tense up, turn sideways, and get set for a big backswing. But when intending to lob, they take a shorter backswing, remain more relaxed, and don't bother to turn sideways.

Also, many players develop patterns of lobbing regardless of their opponents' ability or position on the court. They will always lob when forced back on the backhand side but will rarely lob on the forehand.

They will always lob to your backhand side even though you are standing on your backhand sideline and would be vulnerable to a deep lob to your forehand corner.

When you discover your opponents' pattern of lobbing, you can profit by being forewarned. As I said before, never joke or tell your opponent that he lobs the same way all the time or to the same place or under the same circumstances—as when some players always lob when served to their backhands. He may play the whole match without realizing his mistakes and thus enable you to gain a victory.

Which lobs should you hit on the fly and which on the bounce?

Generally, when your opponent sends up a sky-high lob, you should let it bounce. Otherwise, the wind may deflect it a trifle or the sun may temporarily blind you and thus throw you off. Also, it requires better timing to judge a sky-high lob than one that has bounced.

Experts take many more lobs on the fly, since they do not want to be forced way back from the net, and because of the axiom that usually the closer a player is to the net, the easier it is for him to win a point because of the better angle afforded and the decreased time available to your opponent to prepare for the shot.

If the lob is skimming over your head, be sure to smash it on the fly, for once the ball bounces, you'll rarely catch up to it again.

If your opponent mis-hits a lob or puts a lot of sidespin or underspin on the ball and it floats not too high, you will do better to smash it in the air. Otherwise, when it bounces, it may take an erratic hop that you can't handle.

Smashing in the sun. Your opponents keep lobbing into the sun just over your head, as is their privilege. Just as you swing at it, you are blinded by the sun, so you literally can't see the ball. Yet experts can smash well in the sun. What should you do?

You can stay way back on the baseline.

You can make remarks about lobbing into the sun as being unsportsmanlike—which it isn't. Besides, this will prove a boomerang when you change courts and you want to lob balls into the sun against them.

The answer is to look at pictures taken of experts. Lots of times the player isn't even looking at the ball. Yet he makes a good return. Why?

Because he swings the same way all the time and c-a-r-r-i-e-s the ball on his racket. He watches the ball until he lines it up to within three or four feet of him, and then he swings through on it. As said before, experts groove their swings so that they consistently swing the same way every time, whereas the average player will sometimes poke at the ball, sometimes follow through like an expert, and sometimes wind up and blast at the ball—three different swings.

So if you will swing your overhead at a ball in the sun and c-a-r-r-y it on your racket by following through (instead of using a feeble poke) and aim deep—you will improve your returns. Be sure to aim deep, and don't try to make a sensational smash. Keep your smash deep, and their next lob may be really short.

Missing easy smashes. More players miss easy smashes than any other type of shot. Usually it's because:

1. They tense up and hit much harder than necessary.
2. They look away from the ball to see if their opponents haven't left the court for a soft drink and/or if the lines are still there.
3. They change their minds in the middle of the swing.
4. They are squeamish about hitting an opponent only a few feet away.

Regarding No. 1: As stated before, ease up slightly when smashing with the feeling that if you really wanted to, you could hit harder.

Concerning No. 2: Either your opponents are in position or they are not. If they are in position, then you had better concentrate on smashing well. If they're not in position, then any halfway decent smash will win the point.

The lines won't change no matter whether you look at them or not, so you can forget about them.

But you will ask, "What about this business of not always having to look at the ball when you hit it?" That's right—if you're an expert with a grooved smash. If you are inconsistent, then you should concentrate on the ball.

On No. 3: Another reason for watching the ball is that when you look at your opponents, you are subject to that strange disease known as Changing Your Mind in the Middle of Your Swing. This disease ruins more setups and causes more nervous tension within a player and between partners than indigestion.

You have an easy lob to kill and decide to smack it between your helpless opponents. You sneak one last glance at their quivering bodies and change your mind: You will instead try for an angled smash to the backhand.

This is fatal. You have set your body into lining up the ball for down the middle and have started a swing. You may not look like a champion, but your smash there will crash through to win the point. What else matters?

But when you change your mind, you find yourself cramped for smashing to the backhand, so you try to adjust your swing at the very last tenth of a second. Only a champion can do that, and he not always. So you don't swing through either way, and the ball plops into the net or off the wood.

Once you decide to smash someplace, go ahead and smash there. If your opponent is waiting, you may win the point anyway. If not, then next time aim for a different place.

In this connection, some players will tap an easy lob just over the net to catch their opponents unawares. This is fine about twice in a set in doubles. You may use it more if your opponents are notoriously slow-footed or if you have great touch. But otherwise, any kind of a drop shot should be used very sparingly in doubles.

The trouble with an easy tap over the net is that you may unknowingly be standing ten feet back of the net and try the shot— and give your opponents a setup to belt past you.

Nearly all the time, either angle your smashes or hit with a fair amount of speed and deep.

About No. 4: One might say it is a tribute to the finer instincts of tennis players that they miss easy smashes for fear of hitting their opponents.

In most other sports, like basketball or football, the temptation to knock over, smash into, or mow down the opposition with no penalty would prove overwhelming. And in fact often does—even with a penalty.

But we tennis players evidently are a nobler breed. Our code frowns on deliberately trying to hit a player with a ball. Thus even the most sadistic of players who enjoy blasting the ball at a helpless opponent feel compelled to apologize after each incident.

Yet time and again you'll get an easy lob (especially in doubles) and start smashing only to realize halfway that an opponent is standing right in the path of your intended smash. You don't want to hurt him, so you ease up and hit halfheartedly—smack into the net.

Does your opponent thank you for saving him a painful bruise? Does your partner hail you for your humanitarian act? In both cases, no. You have thrown away an easy point and feel cheated.

Should you purposely hit an opponent?

No. In self-defense, he will hold up his racket and thus may deflect the ball right back past you for the point. Also, you may bruise him so he'll have to quit—and then where will you get a suitable fourth to finish the match?

Or he may smash one himself right at you—twice as hard.

You should aim for an opening and let fly. *It is up to your opponent to get out of the way.* He should either scamper to the sidelines, turn his back, or retreat to the baseline.

It is entirely up to your opponent to note on how well his partner is lobbing, and when he sees that the lob will float short, he should quickly retreat to the baseline.

Actually, if you did hit your opponent not too severely, you would be teaching him a lesson: Next time he will hurry back to the baseline, where he can defend against a smash, or he will turn away. Thus one small bruise could result in his keeping much more alert during the rest of the match.

Where to direct your smashes in singles: When fading back on your backhand side of the court to smash, you should play the percentages by smashing mostly to your opponent's backhand. Surprising an opponent is always desirable, but this is one time when you should keep smashing to his backhand whether he anticipates it or not.

The compelling reasons are:

1. You will be smashing to his weaker side.

2. High-bouncing balls off your smashes discomfit an opponent much more on his backhand than on his forehand.

3. When you hit the ball to his backhand, you will be sending the ball across the net at its lowest point—the middle.

4. You can hit harder with more margin of safety by smashing diagonally along the longest distance in the court.

5. You will be forcing your opponent more out of court with an angled smash to his backhand than smashing down the line to his forehand.

If your opponent lobs to your forehand side, you may elect to smash down the line to his backhand or crosscourt to his forehand.

The rule of thumb on this choice is: If your opponent is lurking way over on the backhand side of his court and the lob is short (within the service line), angle your smash to his forehand.

If your opponent is standing in the middle of the baseline and has lobbed deep, smash down the line to his backhand.

Of course, once in about twenty smashes, you may smash contrary to where you have been aiming just to confuse your opponent. But only once in twenty times. Too many points are lost by players trying to outsmart their opponents by going against the percentages.

Angling your smashes. A rule of thumb about trying to angle your smashes into the side fences is that the closer you are to the net, the easier it is for you to make the shot. The farther back you are, the less you should try for a sharp angle. Generally, if you are taking the lob on your service line, be content to smash deep rather than to try for a sharp angle.

In this connection, if you have been angling your smashes wide to your opponent's backhand and you notice that he is drifting way over to protect that side, then occasionally smash down the line to his forehand. Especially if his lob has fallen short.

Where to direct your smashes in doubles: It is a lot harder to put your smashes away in doubles than in singles, so the usual idea is to split your opponents apart and then smash for the opening.

However, if one opponent is weak and the other is strong, smash to the weaker one, even if to his forehand. Then if the strong opponent starts hogging the weaker one's court, smash to the strong one's court.

Assuming that your opponents are about the same, you can start by smashing deep to the backhand side. Then smash the return through the middle. If the opponent on the forehand side tries to cover the middle, smash to his forehand side.

Remember. When smashing you dominate the net, and you should feel no compulsion to kill the ball right off. Just smash deep, and sooner or later your opponents will lob short, and you can then kill it.

Once in a while you will run into a team that will call needlessly to each other from the baseline just as you are about to smash. The sound of "Stay over—I'll cover this side" sometimes disturbs smashers, who then miss. Yet they can't complain, because the defenders are permitted to call to each other.

Or the defenders will murmur sadly, "Oh, oh" in distress at lobbing so short.

It is amazing how well these defenders can time their remarks at the exact split second when you are smashing.

What can you do?

If you protest, the defender will apologize profusely and perhaps offer to play the point over. But if you accept, Heaven help you when he is smashing and you so much as flutter your eyelashes and he misses. Because he will then protest that your foot-shuffling or deep breathing or racket swinging disturbed him as much as his previous "Oh, oh" disturbed you.

So all you can do is concentrate on your smashing in spite of the comments of your opponents. It could be worse. Back in the days of coal-burning locomotives, I used to play at Chicago's Hamilton Park, near a railroad station. One player was notorious for waiting until a train started to leave the station to lob. So just as his opponent would look up to watch the ball, a shower of cinders would come down like manna from Heaven—except that it was manna for the lobber. Because once the opponent got a cinder in his eye, he would either stop trying to smash or would ruin his concentration by trying to get the cinder out.

Thus, if your opponent mutters or groans at putting up a short lob, attribute it to the natural distress of a sure loser.

If one opponent is halfway up at the net and the other is defending from the baseline, smash through the middle. The net opponent may touch the ball with his racket, he may swing at it and miss and thus disrupt his partner's timing, or he may let it go and then tell his partner, "I thought you were going to hit it."

If you are smashing from way backcourt and both opponents are at the net, smash through the middle. If one habitually hangs over in the middle, you may smash down the line, but remember that the net is higher there. Besides, you are giving him a wide angle if he can volley it.

If you smash from way backcourt and one opponent at the net is a vigorous poacher while the other lingers in the backcourt, smash well over into the side of the backcourt player.

Practice. Along with the lob, the smash is the least-practiced shot in tennis. A player will go out to hit hundreds of drives and volleys but not one single smash. Yet the smash can be practiced alone if necessary.

Here are some exercises for practicing alone:

1. Always warm up gradually when smashing, just as a baseball pitcher never throws his fast ball right off.

Throw or bounce the ball so that it will go up high as a lob. Let it come down and bounce, and then smash it.

Smash eight balls in which you concentrate entirely on one feature only, such as footwork. Then smash another eight while thinking of smashing deep, bringing your racket back sooner, or nearer to the backhand corner.

Remind yourself to smash with some energy in reserve, because you want to develop a steady, well-placed smash—not a hard but erratic overhead.

2. Standing way over on your backhand side, smash the ball at a sharp angle for singles. Then for doubles.

Smash the ball down the line to your opponent's forehand corner.

3. Standing way over on your forehand side, smash the ball at a sharp angle crosscourt for singles. Then for doubles. Then down the line to your opponent's backhand corner.

4. Bounce the ball so that you have to race backward to the baseline to smash the ball. Aim for the backhand corner. Then aim for the forehand corner.

All these exercises you can do while waiting for your partner or opponent to show up. The more you practice smashing, the more you sharpen your judgment as to how hard to smash to keep the ball inside and how high over the net. Also, by smashing in practice, you will be more relaxed and will see how effortlessly you can kill a ball by getting your weight into it.

Practice with another player:

If nothing else, when rallying with your opponent before starting a match, ask him to give you a couple of lobs. Then offer to give him some lobs. The pros and top-flight tournament players always practice their overheads in their warm ups, and they don't need the practice as much as weekend players do.

The best way to practice with another player is to take the time to practice ten or fifteen minutes, with each one taking turns at smashing and lobbing. Thus you both practice your shots at the same time.

1. Your partner should lob high and short at first, with you letting the ball bounce and then smashing it. A couple of these easy lobs

will warm you up, and then he can lob high and deeper, with you letting the ball bounce first.

2. Your partner should lob floaters just over your racket so that you have to back up and take them on the fly. After a couple of easy floaters, he should try to lob deeper.

Change off after ten smashes. And to practice your lobbing, have your partner at the net hit a ball way to one side so that you have to run way over to try to make a real lob over his head.

Footwork practice. Many players miss smashes simply because they are still facing the net when they swing. They haven't trained themselves to pivot backward the instant the ball floats over the net. Thus not only are they off balance, but in facing forward they can't help smashing to their opponent's forehand.

So to improve your smashing right off, practice pivoting and backing away from the net. You can do this any time, any place— at home, in the back yard, in an office, in a schoolroom or gym.

See the diagrams on pages 68 and 69. If you'll pivot ten times a day, you'll make such a habit of it that later on you won't have to think about it at all on a court. Then you'll pivot automatically, get into position better, and kill your smashes.

Alex Olmedo, who helped bring back the Davis Cup for the United States, ranges about the court like a hungry leopard closing in for a kill. Part of this skill in moving well is undoubtedly his native inheritance but a lot of it derives from his constant drilling on footwork.

I have watched Alex practice for years at the Los Angeles Tennis Club on skipping rope, bouncing up and down, running backward, and jumping as high as he can. Alex has developed unusual spring in his legs, so that on jumping for lobs he seems to take off from the ground like a jet plane.

For you to get more bounce from your ounces of weight:

1. Skip rope two minutes a day. As I said before, the idea is to skip a little every day rather than to wear yourself out once a week with ten minutes.

2. Jump straight up and down. Bend your knees to get a better takeoff, and swing your racket as you reach upward.

3. When playing doubles and waiting for the ball to be served to your partner, bounce up and down on your toes a couple of times. This will remind you to poise on your toes during actual play, and when a lob soars over your head, you will start that much sooner.

The Lob

The lob is the poor relation of tennis. Most players feel that winning a point by blasting the ball rates hearty applause, while winning by lobbing ranks as underhanded work of the devil.

Actually, a dependable lob is like money in the bank, the unexpected Christmas bonus, or the tidy little inheritance of high-quality stocks. A good lob not only can dislodge your opponent from ruling the net but can also wear him down physically from smashing strenuously and force him to desist from his victorious net-rushing forays by upsetting his confidence.

One good lob can change an entire match. Dennis Ralston was leading 2–1 on his own serve against Fred Stolle in the Davis Cup match at Cleveland in 1964. Dennis rushed the net, and the Australian threw up a high lob over the American's head. Wanting to save his strength, Dennis let the ball go because he thought it would sail out. Instead, the lob dropped right on the line.

Dennis lost his serve for 2-all and from then on, Stolle took command and won the match to take back the Davis Cup for Australia.

If a good lob works like a slingshot against top-flight players, it becomes a deadly machine gun against average players. Top-flighters are used to running back for lobs, but chase your weekend opponent back six times for lobs over his head and you blunt his attack for the afternoon.

The simplest way to improve your lobbing is to lob too far rather than too short. *Think deep.* Notice that usually point-losing lobs drop short to be killed. Very few lobs sail out.

Bobby Riggs, perhaps the greatest lobber ever, cut down Don Budge in their pro tour largely because of his pinpoint lobbing. Bobby consistently lobbed too far rather than too short. Ken Rosewall, another great lobber, follows this example.

When you aim higher and deeper, you won't be giving your opponent overhead practice on shallow lobs. For if you give him some shallow lobs, he will groove his swing, and when you finally send up a deep one, he'll fade back and swing with confidence.

Why do most players lob too short? Consider that on other shots, you are running toward the ball, and thus the momentum of your body tends to propel the ball faster, in addition to your swing. But in chasing after balls that force you to lob, you are usually running backward and falling away from the ball.

Thus you tend to pull away as you hit the ball, and you send it at less speed than you thought.

Another factor that makes you lob short is that the length of the lob from the baseline that would sail over an opponent's head is too short from ten feet back of the baseline. So you must lob deeper the more you retreat.

Another way to improve your lobbing:

Make a real stroke instead of a poke. Your opponent blasts his serve and charges in like a thirsty rhinoceros toward a water hole. You have tried to drive past him, and you have only hit the ball right to him, where he kills it. This time you decide to lob. You tag the ball in a short, fearful poke and see the ball soar into orbit toward the fence.

The ball sails because it didn't stay long enough on your racket, so you must c-a-r-r-y the ball on your racket. Think of taking a short backswing—not as much as on your drive—and c-a-r-r-y the ball as you follow through.

Backhand lob. It is best to chop into the ball to hold it longer on your racket. This underspin will help you to guide it better and thus c-a-r-r-y the ball. Also, the underspin tends to make the smasher hit into the net, where most smashers' errors go.

If your lobs go straight up and too shallow, turn the face of the racket more toward the perpendicular or "closed face." Then you will hit the ball more squarely.

When running after a ball, start your swing going so that you will take a real swing instead of a poke at the ball.

If you are down love–40 and your opponent rushes in, try to lob. Even if you lose the point, you have made your opponent work harder by running back and smashing.

Of course, you should lob mostly to your opponent's backhand, because a low lob there causes him more trouble than a high one on his forehand side.

Try to make your lob resemble a drive as you prepare to hit it. A lob that catches your opponent off balance wins many more points than a deeper lob that is telegraphed ahead of time.

Bobby Riggs and George Lott, one of the greatest doubles players, both were masters at pretending to drive and instead lobbing with the same motion.

Also, as you perfect your lob, you will find that when you spot your opponent fading back ahead of time, you can then change your stroke and drive the ball at his feet.

Forehand lob. Some players disdain lobbing off the forehand, but they are limiting themselves. Once an opponent realizes this, he will simply crowd ever closer to the net when the player starts to hit a forehand.

Also, by trying a series of attempted passing shots against a net rusher, you will sharpen his volleying to a groove so that at last he cuts in and makes a winning volley. Tossing up a lob breaks up his rhythm and keeps him from volleying from close in.

As on the backhand lob, try to make your lob look as much like a drive as possible. Turn sideways, take a back swing, and lift into the ball. C-a-r-r-y the ball on your racket, and be sure to follow through.

A few tournament players put lots of spin on their lobs so that when they bounce, they take off beyond reach. Ted Schroeder and Vic Seixas both used this type of lob, but it is risky, because the ball is not held on the racket long enough for safety. In fact, most forehand lobs fail because the lobber flips his wrist and the ball skids off the racket.

The best lobbers keep the wrist firm and c-a-r-r-y the ball in a long follow-through to guide it. Try this on your forehand lobs and watch the improvement.

Types of lobs. The defensive lob is used when you are forced way out of position against an opponent who is dominating the net; it is hit high and deep. This gives you plenty of time to return to position, take a deep breath, and prepare yourself for the oncoming smash.

If you lob high and deep enough, you may force your opponent so far back that he cannot smash effectively and may return to the middle of your court. Or he may even have to lob the ball back.

Usually, however, this lob does not surprise your opponent, and it is intended only to give you a respite and to stabilize the rally on equal terms.

The offensive lob is a lob that floats on a shallow trajectory over your surprised opponent's racket. It pays instant rewards, because the ball should bounce so low that he cannot get back in time to retrieve it. You take a chance that he may leap up and kill the ball. But nothing is better to keep your opponent from crowding the net than an occasional shallow lob.

The lob volley is a volley that you lift up above your opponent's head to catch him off balance. See page 61 for an explanation. If well done, it should win the point because of the surprise. If it is short, you are handing him a free point. This volley takes more skill than the usual volley or lob.

To add another trick to your collection, try this against weaker opponents when they hit the ball with medium speed close up. If they hit hard, volley as usual. If they hit easily, be sure to put your body into your lob volley, because the ball will have no pace on it and you must add the pace yourself.

Lobbing in doubles. Top-flight players do not lob as much as formerly, when the Kinsey brothers demoralized their opponents with persistent lobbing. One reason is that players today are taller and harder to lob over; another is that because they rush the net so much more today, they must learn a competent smash.

However, the smash remains an erratic stroke in the realm of the weekend player. He doesn't like to run back (who does?), and he tries to kill every lob. Compare him with Gonzales and Laver, who smash just hard enough to put them away.

Thus, if you can lob effectively, you can break up your opposition, especially against a team with one player right on top of the net. See the chapter on tactics in doubles.

When playing against a team of a righthander and a lefthander, watch for the occasions when the lefthander is playing the ad court and the righthander the deuce court. Then when both are at the net, lob through the middle. Neither will be quite sure who should take the lob, because it is coming on the backhand side for both.

If one opponent smashes much more erratically than his partner, you should lob to him even on his forehand side rather than to the backhand side of the consistent smasher.

You should lob primarily to take the net away from your opponents and to enable you to assume command there. If you stay back and keep lobbing all the time, your opponents are bound to improve their smashing or will grow more cautious and merely return the ball deep and stay at the net.

Mix up drives with lobs. If your opponent smashes short and lingers in a no-man's-land, you should pounce on his returns and drive the ball at his feet.

Psychology. All opponents dislike your using a shot that is beating them. They especially dislike having to run back for lobs and missing their smashes. So they will try to make you quit lobbing by remarking about your soft game as though this is an illegal method. Or they will comment about how hard it is to smash when facing the sun.

This is akin to saying a player shouldn't serve or drive hard when the wind is at his back. You take turns facing the sun, and if he hasn't learned how to return lobs yet, it is high time he started learning. You are thus giving him a free lesson.

Tournament players make use of the sun and the wind at every opportunity and accept the changing moods of nature as a challenge.

Jack Kramer, former world champion, has told me that a player should accept difficulties as part of a match. Whether the opponent hits too easily or too hard; lobs all the time or rarely; dawdles around the court or hurries into position; beguiles the gallery into favoring him instead of you, or uses outmoded strokes that discomfit you more than clean, hard-hit drives—all these difficulties should challenge you to surmount them. When you do, you demonstrate your superiority.

Practice. Players will practice forehands and backhands for hours but never think of practicing lobs. The easiest way to practice lobs is to take some balls and, tossing them to one side, back of the baseline and low (since you make most lobs off low-bouncing balls), lob to the backhand corner.

Find a youngster who likes to smash the ball. Ask him to stand at the net and hit some balls to one side so you have to run. Then lob. Youngsters like to smash more than older players and don't mind running back. If possible, alternate positions and go to the net while he lobs. Make a game of it by seeing who scores the higher percentage.

If the other is competition minded, make a real game: The smasher gets a man on base by smashing so that the other touches the ball but does not return it. If the smasher kills the lob without the other touching the ball, he gets a two-bagger. When the smasher hits enough smashes to send the men around the bases, he scores a run. Thus, the smasher can hit four singles in a row and send one man home, leaving the bases loaded.

If the smasher does not win the point, it is an out. If the lobber sails a lob out, it is a base on balls. Three outs and the two players change sides.

If this game sounds too complicated, merely change sides after each has smashed seven times.

Practice lobbing against inferior opponents or easy servers, for they permit you to remain relaxed so you can think about the mechanics of lobbing.

In warming up before a match, ask your opponent if he would like to try a few smashes. Then after he does and you practice lobs, ask to try a few smashes yourself.

The Drop Shot

If the serve and drive are the steak and potatoes of tennis, the drop shot is the celery and olives. Since a drop shot is a soft ball purposely hit to drop close to the net, you may go through a whole match without using it once. Against a net rusher whom you wish to keep from the net, you would refrain entirely, but against a heavy-footed baseliner, you could win a match with occasional drop shots.

If you watch the pros, you will rarely see a drop shot. They roar to the net so quickly and can reverse themselves so adroitly that it is hard to catch them off balance. Ken Rosewall may drop shot a couple of times in a long match, but the other pros consider it only an ornament.

However, using a drop shot against a weekend player is another situation entirely. Many of them dislike the net, especially on clay, and a drop shot forces them into unfamiliar territory. The change of pace disturbs their steady driving game, and they can't put away a drop shot many times even when they do reach it.

The drop shot works best on grass and clay. It is effective on cement against veterans, but is never used on wood. Thus, the faster the surface, the less you should use it.

As will be stressed in the chapter "For Ladies Only," the drop shot can become a devastating weapon for women to draw an opponent to the net and then follow with a lob. Maria Bueno and

Darlene Hard, superlative volleyers, have used the drop shot to befuddle their opponents and mix up their attack.

To make the drop shot, you take a short backswing and chop under the ball to lift it about a foot over the net. The chop or backspin on the ball will tend to slow down the ball's forward impetus and thus keep it closer to the net.

You aim a foot over the net as though making a miniature lob to give yourself more margin of safety than if you chopped straight through to the ball. Be sure to follow through on your drop shot to control the ball better by c-a-r-r-y-i-n-g it on your racket.

Try to plant the drop shot within five feet of the net. If you hit it ten feet back, you are simply presenting an easy ball for your opponent to knock off for the point.

Use drop shots against medium-paced or slow drives rather than fast drives. Do not try the drop shot from the baseline because 1. It will take longer to reach the net and thus warn your opponent, and 2. It is harder to keep it close to the net.

Try to disguise your drop shot to catch your opponent by surprise. Drop shot mostly to the backhand, because if the ball does bounce high, your opponent can't kill it as easily as on his forehand.

A typical use of the drop shot is shown in Figure 19.

Notice how far the opponent, Player A, who has just made a forehand drive crosscourt, will now have to run to get the drop shot.

Player B has the option of either following his drop shot to the net or of retreating to his baseline to await A's return. Usually, B should retreat to his baseline so that when A rushes up and returns the ball, B can then lob over A's head.

Remember, your opponent is at a distinct disadvantage when coming in for a drop shot since he tends to keep running forward after retrieving it. Thus he will have to stop and then run back for your lob.

As stated before, it is easier for all of us to run from one side to another than to run up and then back. So in pulling your opponent in and then forcing him back, you are making him exert himself much more than in a baseline exchange of drives.

Another advantage of the drop shot is that you break the rhythm of your opponent. Did you ever notice that in exchanging drives in practice from the baseline, and at about the fourth ball you find yourself hitting better? This is because you get used to the ball coming back at the same pace, and you groove your drives.

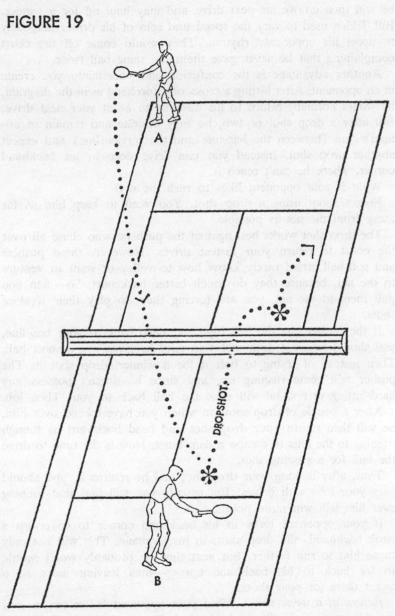

FIGURE 19

A

DROPSHOT

B

So if you hit four balls back at the same pace to your opponent, he will then groove his next drive and may haul off for a winner. Bill Tilden used to vary the speed and spin of his drives purposely to upset his opponents' rhythm. They would come off the court complaining that he never gave them the same ball twice.

Another advantage is the confusion and uncertainty you create in an opponent. After hitting a crosscourt forehand as in the diagram, he would normally return to his baseline to await your next drive. But after a drop shot or two, he may hesitate and remain in no-man's-land (between the baseline and the service line) and expect another drop shot. Instead you can drive deep to his backhand corner, where he can't reach it.

What if your opponent likes to rush the net?

Forget about using a drop shot. You want to keep him as far away from the net as possible.

The drop shot works best against the pushers, who chase all over the court to return your fastest drives. However, these pushers and soft-ball artists rarely know how to volley or want to venture to the net, because they do much better backcourt. So when you pull them to the net, you are forcing them to play their weakest shots.

If the pusher hits the ball high and deep back to your baseline, you should return it deep and wait until he gives you a short ball. Then instead of trying to belt it for a winner, drop shot it. The pusher will come rushing up, and since he doesn't possess any hard-hitting drives, he will ease the ball back to you. Then lob.

After a couple of drop shots in which you have lobbed over him, he will then return your drop shot and head backward as though running to the hills to escape a dam burst. Now is the time to drive the ball for a passing shot.

Thus, after making your drop shot and he returns it, you should vary your lobs with drives. But usually you will find that lobbing over him will win more points.

If your opponent lurks in his backhand corner to cover up a weak backhand, aim drop shots to his forehand. This will not only cause him to run farther, but next time he probably won't scuttle so far back to his backhand corner—thus leaving more of a target there for your shots.

Return of a weak serve. When your opponent ladles up an easy second serve, you will probably feel like cracking the ball. But lots of times you find your opponent pulling back to get set for your mighty drive.

Break him up by drop shotting the easy serve once in a while. Your opponent will be going backward and have to reverse himself to dash up for your short ball.

Better yet, by mixing occasional drop shots with deep drives, you will be confusing your opponent. This will put more pressure on his second serve and cause him to serve more doubles.

This stratagem works best in singles. But in doubles you should avoid bringing your opponent to the net, since the team that dominates the net usually wins.

Forehand or backhand drop shot? Most players take a big, healthy swing on their forehands and rarely chop. Some find that trying to change from hitting a powerful topspin forehand to chopping an underspin drop shot is too much of a problem. They start to drive, decide to drop shot in the middle of a swing, and end up lifting a high soft ball that lands in the middle of the court and which their opponents kill.

If your forehand swing and the drop shot stroke are too different for you to change on the spur of the moment, forget about using the drop shot during rallies. Instead, use it only on drop shotting weak serves where you can decide ahead of time when to change your swing.

Most players chop their backhands, and thus it is easier for them to modify this swing into a drop shot. Also, since the change is less, your opponent will find it harder to detect the difference and to guess when to expect a drop shot.

A favorite backhand drop shot is shown in Figure 20, where your opponent drives his forehand down the line to your backhand. Note that you should be standing ten feet inside the baseline and not back of the baseline when you try this drop shot.

Also, do not try a drop shot against a slugger, since then it would be much harder for you to control.

In Figure 20, the drop shotter would retreat to his baseline to await his opponent's next shot. If the opponent makes a fair return, the drop shooter should lob over his head to make him run back. If the opponent hits short, the drop shotter should come in quickly to try for a passing shot.

To reap the full benefit of a drop shot, you should make your drives correspondingly deeper—way back to the baseline, so that

FIGURE 20

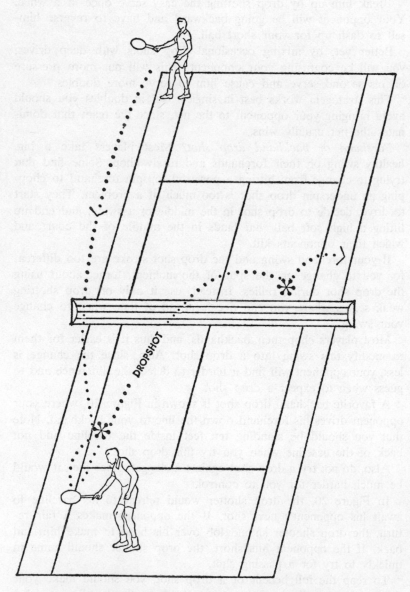

DROPSHOT

there is a wide difference between your drive and the drop shot. If your drop shot is merely a shorter and higher-bouncing version of your midcourt drives, you won't fool your opponent too much.

Remember also that any opponent may force himself to race up to the net for your first couple of drop shots, just as he will for the first couple of lobs over his head. If you will keep tossing in a drop shot now and then, you will find his determination and his legs weakening.

Also, like any opponent who is being outmaneuvered (by your lobbing afterward over his head), he will try to end the point right away by slugging your drop shot or trying for a winner. This pressure will cause him to lose more points than if he tried to place his return better.

The drop shot in doubles. The court for each player to cover is much smaller, and a drop shot should be used very sparingly. You are trying to force your opponents *away* from the net instead of trying to lure them to it.

Sometimes a heavy-footed opponent will be hanging back while his partner is at the net, and you can then drop the ball short, in the former's territory—provided you are standing inside the service line and have an easy ball to handle.

But lots of points are lost by players trying to be too clever in this regard. If you have an easy ball in doubles, you should usually hit it between the two opponents or angle it.

The psychological aspect. The first successful drop shot you pull off on your opponent may cause him to shake his head or smile at your lucky shot. But after the next couple of times when he has had to scurry up for a soft drop shot and then rush back for a lob, he will begin to lose his composure.

He may frown or scowl or complain that "he always used to get those easy shots" and can't understand how he can miss them. And he will keep complaining, either by muttering to himself or murmuring aloud about the easy putaways he's missing.

Of course, they aren't easy at all. As stated before, it is much easier to run sideways for a ball with pace and take a good swing and hit the ball seventy feet into the opposite corner. Then you have lots of margin of safety.

But running forward is more cramped than running sideways, and a soft ball is always harder to hit than one with pace. Hence it takes better timing and control to hit them moderately than to slug back a fast ball.

But most players do not consider this. They feel that all soft balls are "sitters" and easy marks and should be killed. They also tend to feel that anybody who hits a soft ball is *ipso facto* a weaker player than a slugger.

And since we all hate to play against the type of game that we can't handle, most players try to stop this so-called weaker player from using his shots. They murmur that it is a sissy way to win points—forgetting that Pancho Gonzales could chop his backhand so feather soft that it plopped just over the net at his opponent's feet. In fact, Pancho could hit the ball easier than any of us and control it better.

But the average player will try to make you quit using drop shots by any means he can think of. The usual way is to appeal to your sympathy. He will come puffing up to the net after futilely trying to return your drop shot and he will pause and shake his head. The more histrionically inclined will pat his chest as though to allay heartburn, pull out a handkerchief and wipe his face, and pant like a dog in hundred-degree heat.

If you have an ounce of human kindness in your heart, you will feel that the poor fellow is ready to keel over and that you are taking unfair advantage of an obviously worn-out player. So you quit using the drop shot and he pulls ahead and wins and hurries back to the locker room to scare up another match.

Far from feeling sorry for an opponent who huffs and puffs on the round trip from the baseline to the net for your drop shot and then back again to the baseline, you should realize that you are doing him a favor. He has taken up tennis to get strenuous exercise, not the mild cakewalk of a bowler, and he will feel deprived if he doesn't run around.

Thus the exercise he performs at your bidding will tire him physically so that he can sleep untroubled and relaxed. There are no insomniacs among tennis pros, ditch diggers, and ballet dancers.

Running will stimulate your opponent's circulation, and the bending down will help reduce the unhappy accumulation of flesh around his middle and strengthen his muscles. Besides, when running he won't be able to worry about various troubles: His income tax, his daughter wanting to stay out late on date nights; the mortgage falling due or his inability to secure a parking space when shopping.

All these troubles he will forget while chasing madly after your drop shots. In fact, after a session with you, he may consider that his other troubles are light in comparison.

As stated in the chapter "For Ladies Only," the drop shot is a lethal weapon against other women. The victims will thus complain longer and perhaps more bitterly, but this should not deter you. You are saving money for your opponent. Instead of her having to pay for reducing salon treatments, you are giving her a free session, and the money saved can be spent on more worthwhile objects such as new dresses.

Defense against a drop shot. What if your opponent is fiendish enough to use a drop shot against you?

Johnny Hennessey, former National Doubles champion, told me how he once solved this problem—whimsical, fun-loving Johnny, who had celebrated too thoroughly the night before was playing an opponent who was drop shotting him to death. The score mounted against him.

Finally, he called his opponent over and asked if he knew there was a ban that season against drop shots. The other became flustered and quit using them, and Johnny's game improved. Later, his opponent checked and protested that there was no such ban.

Johnny smilingly agreed and said he had only been joking. His opponent tried to drop shot again, but he had lost his touch, and Johnny easily ran out the match.

However, just in case you don't possess Johnny's wit, you might consider these methods of defense against the drop shot:

1. Watch to see if your opponent telegraphs his shot by shortening or changing his usual swing for a drive and by not bothering to get his feet into position to hit hard.

2. Run as fast as you can to the drop shot. The sooner you reach the ball, the higher the bounce and the more chance you can handle it easier.

3. Hit your drives deeper to make it harder for him to make a drop shot from the baseline.

Where should you return a drop shot to your backhand?

The late Rafael Osuna, 1963 national champion, told me he just ran up and hit the ball to give his opponent the most trouble. A very fast man, Rafe could race up, see where his opponent was heading, and then flip his return to catch the other off balance. This is great if you can sprint as Rafe did and possess his fine

FIGURE 21

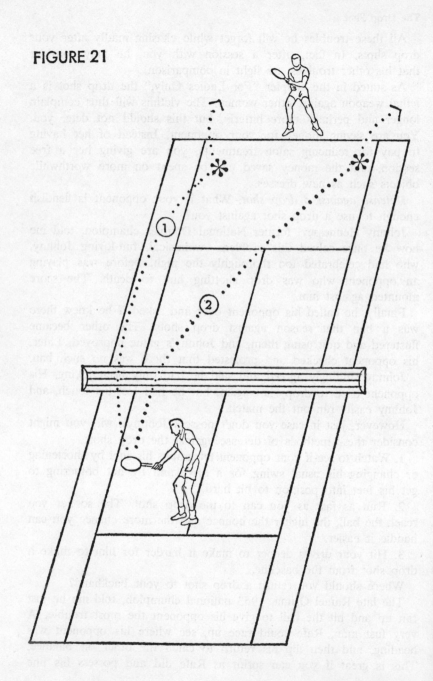

touch and control. Otherwise, let's consider the standard answers to a drop shot as shown in Figures 21 and 22.

1. The favorite return of the pros is shot No. 1 in Figure 21. Pancho Gonzales especially liked to chop his backhand down the line deep to his opponent's forehand corner. Then he moved to about a foot or two this side of the center service line to cover either a down-the-line or crosscourt return. The pros like this shot because they have to move only a short distance to get into the right position at the net, and this gives the opponent less chance of passing since he doesn't have a big angle to shoot for.

The big question only you can answer is whether you can hit your backhand down the line into the forehand corner. If you merely hit the ball six feet from your opponent's forehand alley line and he thus doesn't have to run far, you are setting up the ball for him. You must hit deep and close to the sideline to make this shot work—unless your opponent lumbers around like a truck toiling up a steep grade.

However, you may try this shot once in a while "just to keep your opponent honest" and to make him stay in the middle of his baseline instead of crowding way over to cover up his backhand.

2. The favorite return of Frank Sedgman, the Australian wizard, was to chop really deep to his opponent's backhand corner as indicated by shot No. 2 in Figure 21. He would hit a sliding chop that seemed to hang in the air as it drifted deep; this gave him more time to move to about two feet to the other side of the center service line to cover an opponent's down-the-line shot.

This deep chop to the backhand corner is the easiest return for you to make, because you are hitting the ball through the middle of the net where it is lowest and you have a greater area to aim for. Another advantage is that you are usually playing to an opponent's weakness.

The disadvantage is that your opponent can return either crosscourt or down the line, and you have more area to cover at the net. Remember: When you come in on a wide-angle shot, you are giving your opponent a wide angle at which to fire back. Keep track of whether your opponent can make a backhand down the line; if he can't, then use this shot more and expect the crosscourt return.

3. If you like to take a chance and if your opponent crowds way over to his backhand corner, use shot No. 3 in Figure 22. You drop shot him right back over the net. This shot pays double,

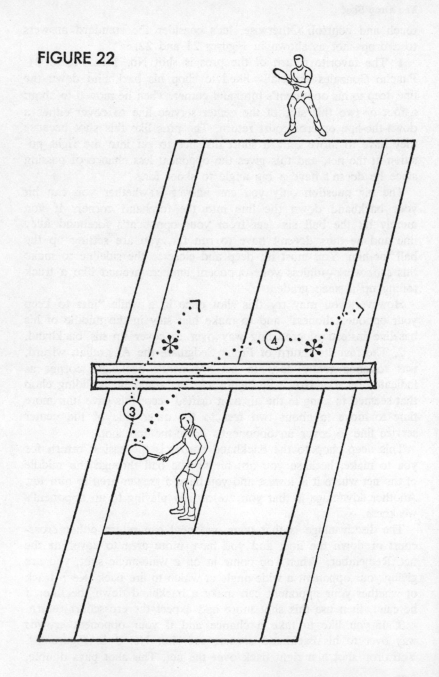

FIGURE 22

not only in winning the point but also in giving keen satisfaction at beating your opponent at his own game.

As you come up, you chop the ball gently, making sure to follow through and c-a-r-r-y-i-n-g the ball on your racket. The underspin you impart to the ball helps make it come back to you and slows down its forward impetus.

This shot demands a fine touch. If you are a slugger whose easiest effort cracks the ball like a rocket, forget this shot. For if your drop shot bounces too high or near the service line, you are giving the point away.

Practice this shot against an inferior opponent when you can relax and think how to make it. When you learn it, you will move your game up another notch.

4. If your opponent's drop shot lands close to your backhand alley line, you can make use of the sharp angle available by angling sharply crosscourt to his backhand. See shot No. 4 in Figure 22.

Generally, the more the drop shot lands toward the center, the more you should use shot No. 2 in Figure 21. The closer the ball lands toward your backhand alley line and the more your opponent hugs his backhand corner, the more often you should use shot No. 1 in Figure 21.

Another valuable aid in coping with drop shots is to keep track of what returns work best against your opponent. Some opponents will always lob their backhands because they can't hit hard enough off that side to break a window, let alone pass you. Then you should get ready to fade back for a smash. Other opponents nearly always go for the crosscourt off their backhands.

To heighten your game, practice all four shots against inferior opponents, because sometime you may discover an opponent who can't handle one particular shot.

If your opponent drop shots to your forehand, see Figure 23 for the three returns.

1. The typical safe shot is to hit deep down the line to his backhand, as in shot No. 1. This should be one return you should practice to increase your accuracy. You force your opponent way back so that the pressure is on him to make a good shot.

2. To disconcert your opponent and to gamble on winning the point outright, drop shot him right back, as shown in shot No. 2.

3. If you can take the ball higher than the net and your opponent is lurking in his backhand corner, hit the ball crosscourt

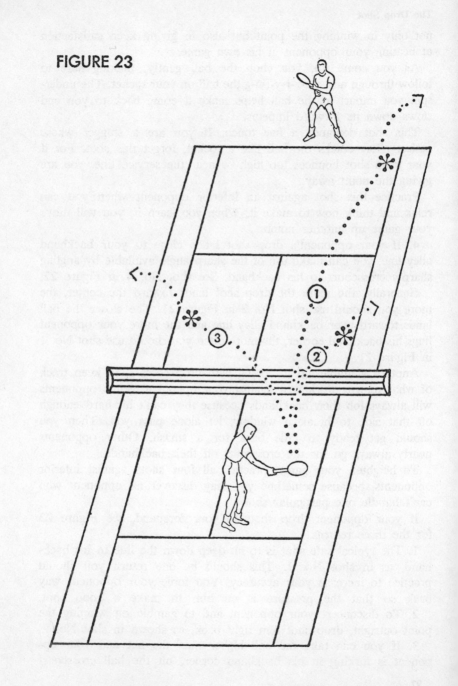

FIGURE 23

as shown in shot No. 3. This is a go-for-broke shot, because if you don't make a wide enough angle, your opponent can come roaring up and crack your return with his forehand for a winner.

However, you might use shot No. 3 occasionally to keep your opponent off balance so he can't know for sure where you will return his drop shot.

If you cannot practice much, concentrate on shot No. 1. Frank Sedgman used this shot nearly all the time to lay the ball smack into the backhand corner. If you keep practicing, you can learn to do the same, since this takes no special skill or lightning reflex.

The psychological aspect. Most players show less resentment over an opponent blasting them off the court than being trapped into errors on deft strokes. Thus, if an opponent keeps winning points by drop shots, you may feel like muttering and scowling more than usual. This display might influence a soft-hearted opponent into letting up on you, but a real competitor would recognize that this meant you couldn't handle drop shots—and he would therefore use even more of them against you.

A classical answer to an opponent's winning shots is to praise them lavishly. He may then become dizzy with success and try to make even better ones closer to the line or the net. When he starts to miss, you remark on how well he has *previously* been hitting them. You are then appearing to be sportsmanlike in praising his good shots while actually undermining his confidence.

Another classical answer is to show no concern whatever. You pick up the balls and play the next point with no outward sign of distress. You then concentrate on how to counteract his winning shots.

In the long run, the second approach is better, because all the praise in the world won't enable a beginner to beat a champion.

The Approach Shot

How many times have you forced your opponent into making a feeble return in half court, but you missed the approach shot?

If you're average, you miss a lot more of these soft shots that land halfway up than you do harder drives.

FIGURE 24

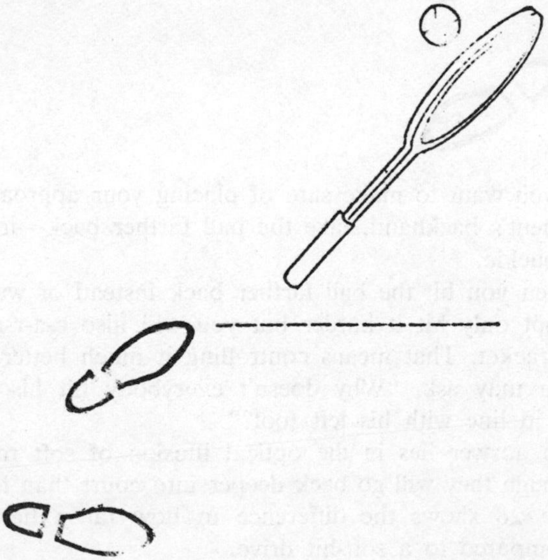

Yet there is no other shot like the approach shot in which you can improve so quickly with such little extra effort.

First of all, most players just do not run up far enough to hit the ball properly. They hit the ball way in front of the left foot, as shown in Figure 24.

The result is:

1. The ball is flicked rather than c-a-r-r-i-e-d on the racket, so it is hard to guide or control.

2. Since you're hitting the ball at the end of your swing, you put little or no pace on it.

3. It is very hard to direct the ball to your opponent's backhand, since taking the ball way in front pulls it to his forehand.

To control your approach shot better, you should hit in line with your left foot, as shown in Figure 25.

FIGURE 25

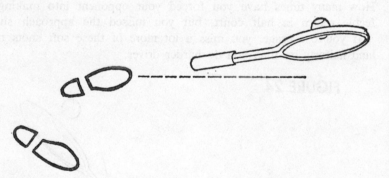

If you want to make sure of placing your approach shot to your opponent's backhand, take the ball farther back—in line with your belt buckle.

When you hit the ball farther back instead of way in front, you will not only hit it harder but you will also c-a-r-r-y it longer on your racket. That means controlling it much better.

You may ask, "Why doesn't everybody hit his approach shots more in line with his left foot?"

The answer lies in the optical illusion of soft returns that look as though they will go back deeper into court than they actually do. Figure 26 shows the difference in how far a hard-hit drive will go compared to a soft-hit drive.

FIGURE 26

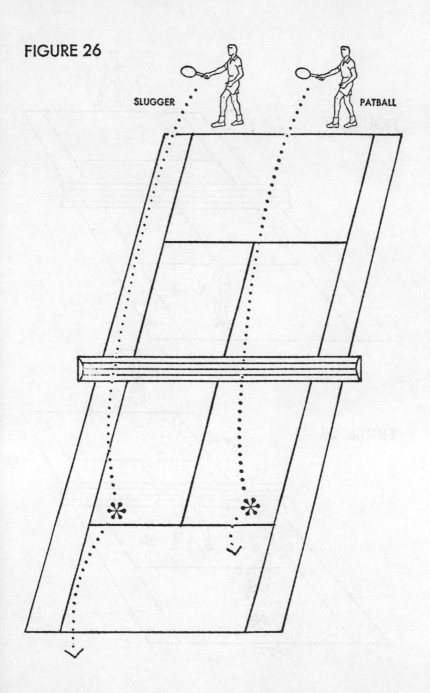

SLUGGER

PATBALL

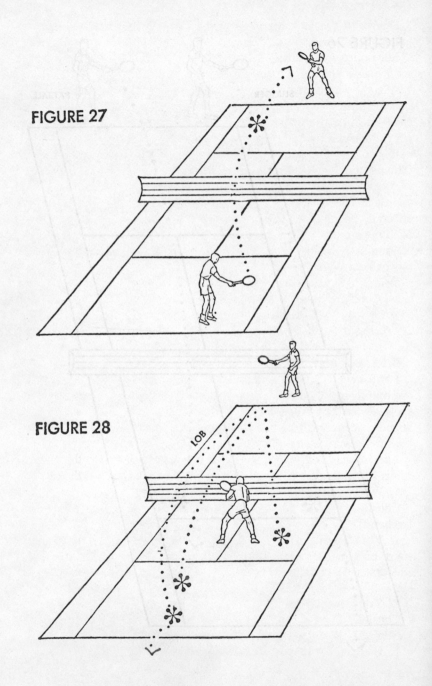

FIGURE 27

FIGURE 28

LOB

Slugger A cracks a hard drive, and although the ball bounces on the service line, it still travels all the way to the baseline, waist high.

But notice that Patball B hits a soft drive that will bounce on the service line and then travel hardly a few feet more.

A good way to tell if you are getting up soon enough is to make sure of hitting the ball on the top of the bounce. Then it's much easier to hit it harder and keep it inside the court. Also, your opponent has less time to reach it.

If you hit the ball on the falling bounce, you are loafing in running up and will find it harder to make a forcing shot.

Watch the ball! Everyone has a tendency to look up in making an approach shot to see what his opponent is doing. Remember: Either he is in position or he is not. If he's out of position, he can't handle your shot. If he's in position, you should concentrate on making as good an approach shot as possible. In either case, watch the ball until you see it hit the strings of your racket.

Swing. As you come up to the ball, draw your racket back slowly but not quite as far back as your usual drive. Then as you step into the ball, come through a little faster.

Try to hit the ball with medium pace. The object of an approach shot is to put your opponent on the defensive, not to blast the ball for a winner.

I will never forget hearing Jack Kramer, then world professional champion, coach Kurt Nielsen, Danish Davis Cup star, on approach shots at the Los Angeles Tennis Club. Jack kept emphasizing that nobody, including himself, could slug his approach shots the way he did his backcourt drives.

The forehand approach shot. Your opponent waits in the middle of his baseline after hitting short to your forehand about the service line. Where should you hit the ball?

Consider Figures 27 and 28, if you, player A, hit to player B's forehand:

1. Your approach shot to his forehand does not pull him out of court but actually sets up the ball where he can easily trot over and crack his forehand three ways: down the line, crosscourt, or lob.

2. You are playing to his strong side.

Consider Figures 29 and 30, if you, Player A, hit to player B's backhand:

1. He can try to pass you crosscourt.

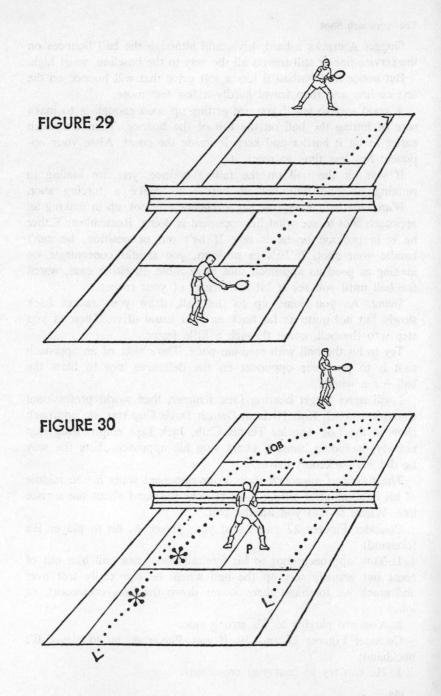

FIGURE 29

FIGURE 30

2. He can try to lob over your head.

3. He can try to pass you down the line. However, in contrast with his forehand down the line, which every player can make, he will be an exceptional player to consistently hit his backhand down the line to pass you. The net is higher there than in the middle, and it is a much riskier shot: If he misjudges your approach shot the least bit, he is either hitting the ball right to you or out in the alley.

Thus you really only have to guard against two shots when you go to the net on the backhand: a crosscourt drive or a lob—and the added fact that his backhand is usually weaker than his forehand.

Jack Kramer told me that he used to hit 90 percent of his approach shots to his opponent's backhand. This enabled Jack to groove his approach shot by constant practice so that he could make it with mechanical perfection.

If you keep practicing this approach shot deep to your opponent's backhand, it will become a habit. You will then avoid the indecision characteristic of many a player. He rushes up, decides to hit to the backhand but changes his mind at the last instant and aims for the forehand—but he then hits the ball right to his opponent in the middle of the court. This trying to outguess your opponent also tends to make you look up instead of concentrating on the ball.

If you play an opponent who scurries way over to his backhand corner every time, you should "keep him honest" by hitting once in eight times to his forehand corner. Then he'll stick closer to the middle, and you can hit to his backhand.

Keep your approach shots *deep* to his backhand, since most players find it harder to hit a high backhand than a high forehand. Bobby Riggs sometimes used to loop drive his approach shots high to his opponents' backhands and then leisurely stroll to the net because he knew they couldn't do too much with high-bouncing balls on their backhands.

What if you are forced wide to your forehand on an approach shot? See Figure 31 for one possibility.

You can try for a winner by hitting wide crosscourt. But you must hit way wide, if you return the ball merely to the center of the court, you're dead.

Regardless of how well you hit your crosscourt shot, be sure to

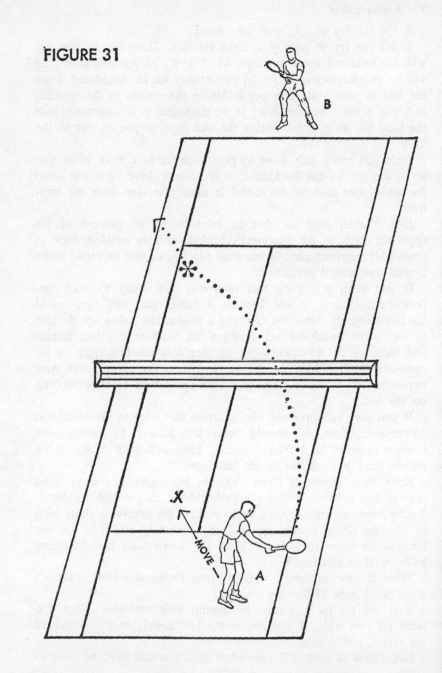

FIGURE 31

run in to the net about two feet past the center service line on the left court side and about twelve to fifteen feet back of the net. The arrow shows the position, X, that you should take. Then you can cut off any attempted passing shots of your opponent if he happens to reach your crosscourt drive.

Another possible approach shot is shown in Figure 32.

You can hit down the line to your opponent's backhand. Be sure to hit really deep, because if you hit short, he can come in fast and pass you with a backhand crosscourt shot. Also, hitting deep gives you more time to move into position No. 2, as shown in Figure 32. This spot is about two feet inside the center service line on the right court side and twelve to fifteen feet from the net.

One advantage in this shot is that you are hitting to his weak side. The disadvantage is that he will anticipate your hitting it there and put on steam to reach it. However, the pros favor this shot, because the net rusher gets into position much more easily.

The odds favor your using this shot nine out of ten times and the crosscourt forehand the other time to catch your opponent going the wrong way and to keep him guessing.

The backhand approach shot. If forehand approach shots present problems, backhand approach shots seem to double the trouble. The weekend player at least swings on his forehand, but he merely pokes at the ball on his backhand, so that even when it goes over, it doesn't bother his opponent.

One reason is that the weekend player doesn't run as well on the backhand side as on the forehand and so loafs even more in going up for short balls. Also, he hesitates in going up because he feels he can't put much pressure on his opponents from that side. Actually, he can put more.

We all know that the easiest way to make a winning volley is to force your opponent way wide and then angle his return way over to the other side. When you hit a forehand from the middle of the court to your opponent's backhand, you can't make half as good an angle as you can from your backhand to his backhand. See Figure 33.

Notice how much farther you force your opponent out of court with the backhand shot.

However, there is one catch to forcing your opponent wide: He may use the angle to pass you.

The saying, "One good angle deserves another" means that when

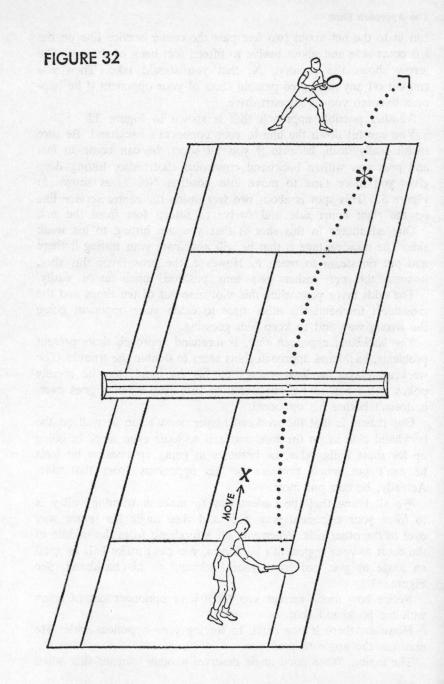

FIGURE 32

forced wide, your best shot usually is to angle right back. Thus, your opponent, when forced wide on his backhand, may elect to drive crosscourt. This is one of the hazards in going to the net, but if you force your opponent to run wide, he should find it more difficult to get set for a passing shot.

To improve your backhand approach shot, first make sure of getting up to the ball in line with your right foot, which is facing diagonally to the net. Then take a real swing instead of tagging the ball.

The backhand drive. If you have a good backhand drive from the backcourt, use it on balls that are short and high. This is a harder shot to make than the backhand chop, but if you like to gamble, you will win more points outright.

Tony Trabert hit his backhand drive with topspin very effectively, but most pros prefer to use a chop, because in running forward, a chop is easier to control. Also, in driving your backhand from far back, you will not have as much time to come up as on the slower chop.

The backhand chop. The backhand chop approach is used much more because it is easier to place, easier to hit on the dead run, and if hit low, it forces your opponent to hit up on his return.

Frank Sedgman executed this shot so superbly, you'd think he had invented it. He would come gliding in on cat feet to a short return, take back his racket and, c-a-r-r-y-i-n-g the ball, would chop it deep, not hard, into the backhand corner. This was the wand of Merlin enchaining his opponent back of the baseline, unable to ward off the magic. If the luckless one tried to lob, Frank drifted back and smashed deep. If he tried to drive back the approach, Frank cut into the net and volleyed deep or for the point. The odds favored Frank better than the house percentage on a slot machine.

None of us can attain his perfection, but we can all improve this shot, since it demands no great reflex action, no blinding speed, and no power.

Let's repeat in this section how to hit the backhand chop:

1. Watch the ball! Many players look up to see if their opponent is still there or is trying to erase the lines. The easier the ball, the more you should glue your eyes on it.

2. Be sure to follow through as you hit. C-a-r-r-y the ball on your racket.

3. If you keep hitting your chops too high or too far, tilt your

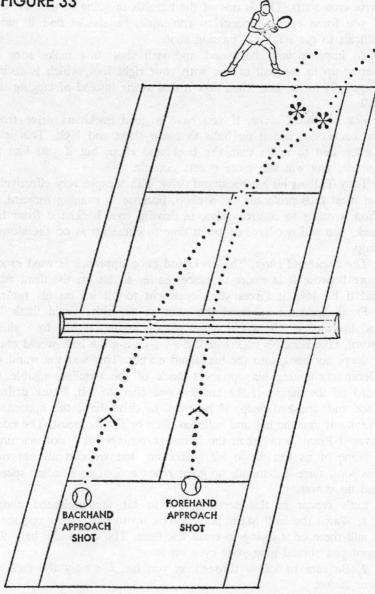

FIGURE 33

BACKHAND
APPROACH
SHOT

FOREHAND
APPROACH
SHOT

racket more toward the perpendicular. Everyone tends to open the face of the racket too much. The result is that you hit the ball too much of a glancing undercut so that the shot neither sounds nor feels solid.

4. Keep your racket lower as you take it back so you won't hit downward too much into the net.

5. Aim to hit too far rather than in the net. Give your opponent a chance to miss the ball.

Where should you hit your backhand approach shots?

You can hit down the line to his forehand, as shown in Figure 34. The player then goes to position A to cover the return shot.

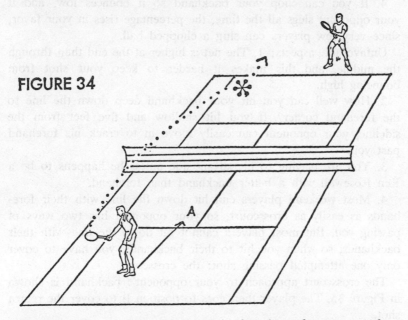

FIGURE 34

Experts often use this shot because the player has to go only a short distance to cover the return. Also, if the approach shot is chopped, the ball bounces low, and this makes it harder for your opponent to run over and crack a fast drive. Then too, the experts dislike giving an opponent a wide angle when it takes longer for the former to get into position at the net.

Should you use this shot? Favorable aspects:

1. If your opponent tends to hang way over to cover up his backhand, this shot will force him to run much farther. The next

time he will more likely remain in the middle, and then you can hit to his unprotected backhand.

2. You don't have to run as far to cover his return.

3. Your opponent may never lob off his forehand, or he may lob poorly because he uses this shot so little. If you don't remind him that he never lobs, he may spend the whole afternoon trying to pass you. Since you know he's not lobbing, you can crowd the net and thus make better volleys.

Some players encourage the nonlobbers by murmuring occasionally like a funeral director that he's having tough luck on his forehand that day.

4. If you can chop your backhand so it bounces low, and if your opponent slugs all the time, the percentage rises in your favor, since very few players can slug a chopped ball.

Unfavorable aspects: 1. The net is higher at the end than through the middle, and this makes it harder to keep your shot from bouncing high.

2. How well can you hit your backhand deep down the line to the forehand corner? If you hit shallow and five feet from the sideline, your opponent can easily move in to crack his forehand past you.

3. You are playing to his strong side unless he happens to be a Ken Rosewall with a better backhand than forehand.

4. Most weekend players can hit down the line with their forehands as easily as crosscourt, so your opponent has two ways of passing you. But most players cannot hit down the line with their backhands, so when you hit to their backhands, you have to cover only one attempted passing shot: the crosscourt.

The crosscourt approach to your opponent's backhand is shown in Figure 35. The player then goes to position B to cover the return shot.

There are many advantages:

1. It is far more natural to hit crosscourt off your backhand than down the line.

2. You are usually playing to your opponent's weak side.

3. If you make a sharp enough angle, you may win the point outright.

4. If you practice this shot, it will become mechanical and so grooved that it will take away any indecision on your part.

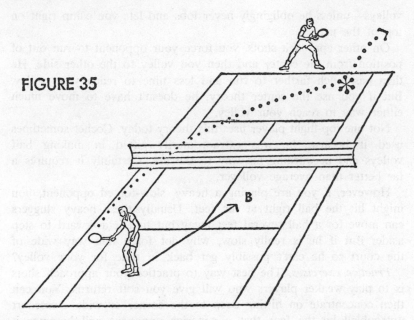

FIGURE 35

5. The net is lower in the middle, where your crosscourt shot passes.

6. If you angle well, you will force your opponent way out of court and thus make it easy for you to volley his return for a putaway.

The disadvantages:

1. If you hit short, your opponent can come in to drive the ball past you before you get into position.

2. As said before, "one good angle deserves another." If you angle sharply on your opponent, he can angle back just as sharply.

3. Your opponent may be able to bother you more with lobs if your overhead is shaky than by hitting hard against your excellent volleys.

The center theory. Another approach shot is to hit the ball down the center near the baseline. This center theory cuts down the angles at which your opponent can pass you.

This outmoded theory is like the football diagrams that look better on paper than in reality. If it is hard for an opponent to pass you, it is even harder for you to make a winning angle on your

115

volleys—unless he obligingly never lobs and lets you camp right on top of the net.

On other approach shots, you force your opponent to run out of position from the center and then you volley to the other side. He then has much farther to run and less time to reach your volley. But if you use the center theory, he doesn't have to move much either way to reach your volley.

Not one top-flight player uses this theory today. Cochet sometimes used it because he was extraordinarily gifted in making half volleys and in working his way to the net. Certainly it requires a far better than average volleyer.

However, if you are playing a heavy, slow-footed opponent, you might hit the ball right at his feet. Usually these heavy sluggers can move for a ball several feet away but find it awkward to step aside. But if he is really slow, why not force him way wide of the court so he can't possibly get back in time for your volley?

Practice exercises. The best way to practice your approach shots is to play weaker players who will give you soft returns. You can then concentrate on hitting deep to the corner or wide crosscourt untroubled by the fear that a superior opponent will hammer it back past you.

In practice rallying, ask another player to hit easy balls that bounce inside the service line. Start from the baseline and dash toward the ball to take it on the top of the bounce. Think of only one feature for about six balls: getting up to the ball in time. Then think about another feature for another six balls, such as hitting really deep.

Your opponent can meanwhile practice retrieving your shots or making replies to them. You can then reverse roles and let him practice his approach shots while you try to defend yourself against them.

If no opponent is available, stand ten feet back of the service line and toss a ball forward so that you have to run up five feet to hit it. Toss the ball at varying heights and varying distances for variety.

Remember, developing a dependable approach shot comes largely from patience, moderation in hitting, and practice. It takes no great talent, and it can well lift your game to a higher level.

Lefthanders

Lefthanders are a special breed who are commonly believed to be born to swing hard and erratically. Maurice McLoughlin did revolutionize the game with his booming serve and net rushing, but many other lefthanders display guile rather than power. Norman E. Brookes, the Australian wizard, Jaroslav Drobny, and Art Larsen used their rackets as a cabinetmaker does a tool to produce a work of art.

Lefthander Seymour Greenberg, once ranked No. 5 nationally, proved steadier than a downpour in a Congo rain forest. A story goes that a spectator at a Greenberg match in the National Claycourt left the stands, went to buy a cola, finished it, and returned to find the same rally going on. Seymour was not a human backboard; he just played like one.

Certainly, if you are a lefthander, you possess a built-in advantage over righthanders. You play righthanders all the time and become accustomed to their shots, but your opponents do not to yours. Their shots are grooved to bombarding a righthander's backhand—which is your forehand. Your left-handed serve curves the opposite way—the wrong way, according to righthanders—and upsets opponents.

But lefthanders should play even better than they do. Only world champion Rod Laver combines speed, power, agility, and a well-rounded game. The other lefties may possess outstanding serves and net games, but they are held back by mediocre strokes and lack of determination and concentration.

The reason may be explained by a favorite story of Paul Lukas, the esteemed Hungarian actor. He said Metro-Goldwyn-Mayer movie studios posted signs: "It is not enough to be Hungarian. You must also work."

Similarly, it is not enough to be a lefthander. You must also work to improve your game. Here's how:

1. Never mention to an opponent that you are lefthanded. He may play a whole set before finding out. The less you remind him, the more likely he will forget it in times of stress and hit smack to your forehand. Or lob to your forehand side.

2. Get 70 percent of your first serves in. You have read this message time and again so far, and I hope to implant it a dozen more times before the last chapter.

Lefthanders feel they must blast their serves at least one hundred miles an hour or they won't count. Tennis coaches totter on the brink of sanity from pleading with left-handed pupils to cut down the speed and quit serving doubles. But the pupils seem to think that if 10 percent is good enough for movie agents, it's good enough for them. Or that some day they will suddenly start getting all their first serves in at faster speeds than Gonzales'.

The magic number is 70 percent. Not 10 percent or 40 percent but 70 percent.

Roy Emerson has said that in doubles when he and Fred Stolle have gotten over 60 percent of their first serves in, they have never lost a match as amateurs. Sometimes they have gotten 77 percent of their first serves in. But when their percentage dropped to 50 percent or 40 percent, they lost, regardless of how their other strokes were going.

If your shots are like Roy's, then 60 percent is fine. Otherwise, 70 percent. If you put anything on your serve at all, you will still bother your opponents more than a righthander serving much harder.

3. A southpaw should *never,* repeat *never* serve doubles. Even an easy spin serve may upset your opponent because he can't make up his mind on which side to take it.

Eight out of ten points are won on errors. Get your serve in and force your opponent to make a winning shot.

O.K., let's make it one double fault a match. Any more are tax-free gifts of points.

4. Learn to place your serve. Southpaw Johnny Doeg won at Forest Hills in 1930 mostly on his serve, which he could drill down the line into a corner or crack it curving wide.

Many lefthanders concentrate only on serving to their opponents' backhands so that the latter stand way over to chop it back because they can get set for it. But if you learn to serve into both corners, you make your opponent stand more in the middle, and by thus mixing up your serves, you keep him from getting set.

5. Some southpaws who find that their opposite spin serves bother opponents will then put more and more spin on their serves. However, this cuts down on your speed and gives your opponent more time to reach the serve.

Develop more than one kind of serve. Mix up your speed serves with slow, high-bouncing twists.

Keep track of how well your opponent returns your serves on his backhand. Lots of righthanders return serves better with chop backhands than harder-hit forehands.

Occasionally serve right at a righthander. From force of habit, he will step away to cover up his backhand and thus the ball will break into him.

You should strive to develop a wide-breaking serve in the ad court to the righthander's backhand. Right-handed Herbie Flam, the 1950 Forest Hills finalist, known for his superb control and retrieving ability, recounted to me the devastating effect of Rod Laver's wide-breaking serve to the ad court in their Wimbledon match:

"No matter how carefully I tried to return serve with my backhand, the balls would veer into the alley. Rod was varying the speed and break on his serve so well that I couldn't groove my returns."

When you force your opponent way off court, he may return:

1. Short to your backhand. You should then crosscourt your backhand to force him far over on his forehand, as shown in Figure 36. You should then take the net to cut off his return, and proceed to position A, about a foot or two on the other side of the center service line.

The more your opponent returns to the singles alley line on your backhand side, the more you should use the angle to crosscourt. Even though you are hitting to his forehand, he still has to run way over for the ball.

2. If he returns short to the middle, try to take it on your

FIGURE 36

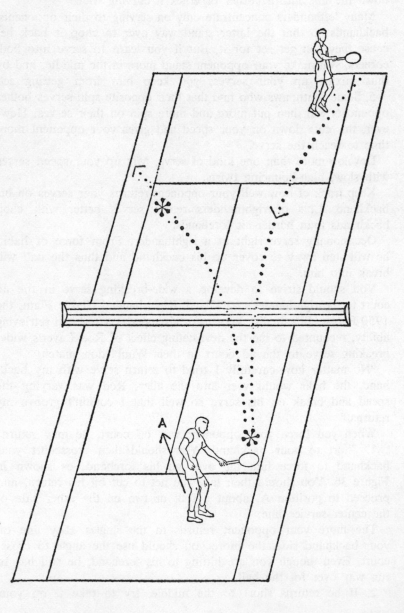

A

forehand. You then have the option of hitting your forehand to his forehand, or if he has run back to the center of his court, then crosscourt your forehand to his backhand.

If his return lands short to the middle on your backhand side, the odds favor your chopping your backhand down the line to his backhand. It is harder for a player to reverse his direction (for example, starting to run back to the middle and then back to his backhand corner) than to run much farther in one direction.

3. If he returns midcourt to your forehand, you should usually drive down the line to his forehand. You must drive deep, for if you drive short, he can come in fast to crack a crosscourt forehand to your backhand. See Figure 37.

Once in a while, if your opponent rushes back toward the middle, hit your forehand crosscourt to his backhand. If you can make a sharp enough angle, you may win the point outright.

If he returns deep to your forehand and you are forced back of the baseline, you should crosscourt your forehand, for from that distance you can't put as much pressure by hitting down the line as when he returns short.

Even if you crosscourt your forehand, you are starting a duel between your forehand and his backhand, which favors you. In fact, all matches between righthanders and lefthanders usually resolve themselves into who can take more balls on his forehand and drive them crosscourt to the other's backhand.

Net rushing. Most southpaws like to play net even on clay; this is not as effective as on concrete. This stems partly from lefthanders' serves bringing forth weak returns on which they can pounce. Also, righthanders find it hard to lob down the line off their backhands to a lefthander's backhand because 1. It is inherently a harder shot than lobbing crosscourt, 2. There is less margin of safety, and 3. Habit makes them lob automatically crosscourt to the lefthander's forehand side, where he can easily smash. Besides, when a lefthander smashes, he naturally curves the ball to the righthander's backhand.

Thus, if you excel at all at the net, you should rush in at least occasionally when serving wide to the backhand in the ad court. You have a greater percentage in your favor than a righthander coming in on that serve, for your opponent's natural return off the backhand is crosscourt to a righthander's backhand, where the latter finds it harder to make winning volleys.

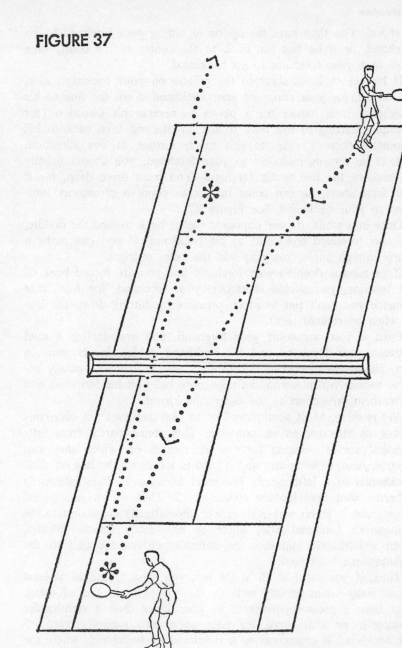

FIGURE 37

But this backhand crosscourt return would go to your forehand, and if it sails high over the net, you should put it away faster than your opponent can say, "Good shot."

Thus your opponent would then have to thread the needle after that—try to pass you down the line on his backhand. Tournament players find this shot hard to make, and weekend players should find it ten times harder. If the ball sails high over the net to your backhand, you should angle it off as shown in Figure 38.

Backhand. A lefthander's weakest shot is usually his backhand. He will push or poke it back somehow until he gets a chance to run around it or rush the net. He may get by in the lower echelons, but higher up, a shrewd righthander will hit wide to your forehand to open up the court and then bombard your backhand.

Certainly you should first work to develop a steady chop or slice backhand. When returning serve in the deuce court, you usually must take it on your backhand or be forced way out of court. So you should first learn to take those curving serves on the rise and chop them down the line to your opponent's backhand or deep to his forehand corner. By chopping you give yourself more time to return to the middle, and if he rushes the net, you can return the ball low and at his feet.

In doubles, taking the ball on the rise pays dividends, because it gives the server less time to get close to the net.

You should especially practice chopping down the line from your backhand to his backhand, since few righthanders use this shot against other righthanders. In a duel of this kind, the lefthander should win most of the time in placing the ball more accurately and more steadily to the corner.

When forced way wide on the backhand, some lefthanders try to poke the ball back to their opponent's backhand down the line. This gives your opponent a chance to crosscourt his backhand and put you at the end of a pendulum.

See Figures 39 and 40 for what happens to lefthander L who, when forced wide on his backhand, returns to the backhand of righthander R. Notice how this gives player R a chance to hit what is known as the "deadly diagonal." Pancho Segura comments that when L is forced wide into his doubles alley, he must hit crosscourt or he's dead.

Figures 41 and 42 show the entirely different situation when L returns crosscourt to R's forehand. If R hits down the line to

FIGURE 38

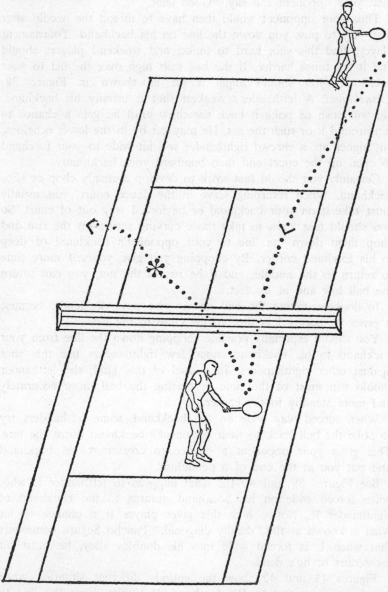

L's forehand, L can crosscourt with a "deadly diagonal" that forces R far out of court.

Of course, R's best shot would be to hit deep right back to L's backhand to start a duel to see which player hits short first or gives the other a wide crosscourt opening.

The backhand drive. You should thus use the chop to return fast serves, to aim closer to the lines, and to give yourself time to get back in position by hitting a slower-moving ball.

But you should also learn to drive the ball besides merely chipping it back. When an opponent storms the net on your backhand, you should be able to rifle a passing shot through an opening. Thus passed, an opponent will feel he should cut in closer to the net next time—thus leaving himself open to a lob. Or he may stay back to play defensively.

Many lefthanders slice their backhands because they use Western grips or heavy topspin on their forehands and then don't bother to change grips. Rod Laver uses the Continental grip for both sides and manages to put heavy topspin on his backhand as well by flipping his wrist. However, he is the exception, for few players possess his exceptional timing or have practiced endlessly, as he has.

If you use a forehand grip on your backhand, you are bound to undercut the ball too much. Try changing your grip a little away from your forehand and toward the backhand grip, as shown in the chapter on the backhand. The grips shown are for righthanders, but you can reverse the instructions. Or tilt the face of the racket more toward the perpendicular when hitting the ball. This gives you more of a flat hitting surface.

Practice hitting high-bouncing balls, because that makes you tilt your racket more toward the perpendicular. Practice, or rally with easy opponents to get used to changing grips.

By adding power to your backhand, you increase the range of your game and lift yourself up another notch.

Playing another lefthander. When you play another lefthander, you realize how righthanders feel when facing you. This is a new type of opponent, against whom you rarely play.

1. Never remind your opponent that you are left-handed. This may seem useless, but your opponent has grooved his shots against righthanders, and the more he forgets he's facing a southpaw, the more likely he is to hit and lob to your forehand.

FIGURE 39

FIGURE 40

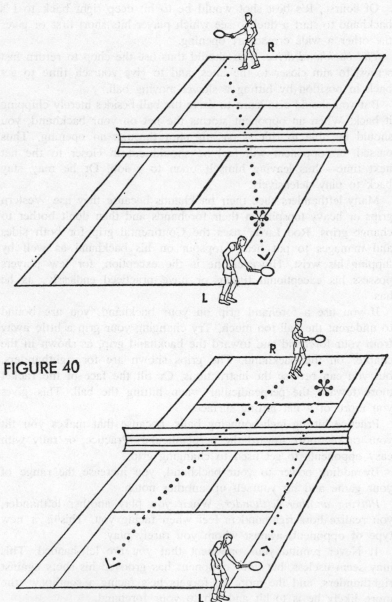

2. Keep reminding yourself silently that your opponent is left-handed and where to hit to his backhand. Especially remind yourself that if he comes to the net, you will lob down the line on your forehand, crosscourt on your backhand.

3. Try serving wide to his backhand in the deuce court. He may forget about the spin breaking into him the opposite way from a righthander's.

4. Serve wide to his forehand in the ad court. He won't be used to running that far on his forehand in that court, since righthanders usually try to serve down the middle to their opponents' backhand.

5. Test both his forehand and backhand. If he proves steadier on his backhand than on his forehand, shift your attack to the latter side.

Choice of court in doubles. From which court in doubles should you return service when playing with a righthander?

1. Some lefthanders prefer the deuce court, because they can return serve better on the backhand at an angle. Similarly, a right-hander can usually return service on his backhand better from the ad court than in the deuce court. It is easier for both players to hit a backhand crosscourt with a natural follow-through than to hit a backhand halfheartedly to keep from pulling it to the net man.

Also, if the righthander definitely rates as a better player, he would then prefer facing an opponent's serve on the most important point of the game, the ad point.

2. However, most lefthanders prefer the ad court, because they can stand way over to cover up their backhands and return serve on the forehand. Then they can make devastating crosscourt returns on the server's backhand side.

The right-handed server is torn between the desire to serve wide to the lefthander's forehand or to play it safe by serving down the line to the latter's backhand. However, to make sure of serving down the line, the server has to stand closer to the center service line, and this leaves his backhand side wide open.

Thus the percentages favor the southpaw receiving in the ad court, since he can usually do more to break down the server's morale.

The team then can cover both sides very well but must watch for balls down the middle. The player with the stronger backhand should take the ones in doubt.

Defense against lefthanders. Having counseled lefthanders about

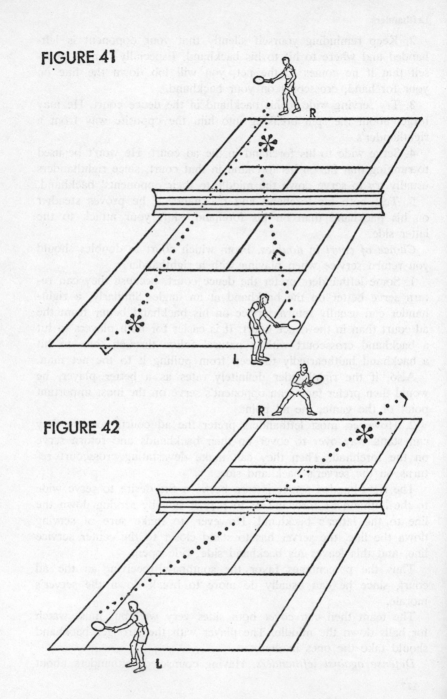

FIGURE 41

FIGURE 42

capitalizing on their unique abilities, it is only fair to point out how righthanders can counteract them.

First off, a lot of tricks that lefthanders pull on righthanders can be reversed by the latter.

Return of serve. In many matches, the righthander covers more ground than a marathon runner in running around his backhand to return serves with his forehand, which is stronger.

This is a great idea, but it collides with the axiom: It is easier to run three steps *toward* a ball than to back one step *away* from a ball. It is far easier to put your weight into a shot as you run toward a ball than to back away and then step into it.

Thus if you try to run around your backhand, you had better emulate Jack be nimble, Jack be quick when facing a lefthander's serve. A great deal depends on how much of a break or curve the serve has. If it comes with average speed and a gentle spin, you can easily step around to take it on your forehand.

If the serve comes blasting at you with a wide break, forget about running around your backhand.

Another factor depends on whether you are returning serve in the deuce court or the ad court. In singles, if you run around your backhand on the deuce court, you will end up in the middle of the baseline in perfect position. If you run around your backhand in the ad court, you may end up at the side fence and leave your court wide open for his return. Not so good.

In doubles, you can take more chances in running around your backhand, because you have less court to cover.

Want to know one big reason righthanders miss service returns against lefthanders? They poke at the ball instead of hitting through. Because of that reverse spin coming at him, a righthander must make doubly sure that he follows through and c-a-r-r-i-e-s the ball on his racket to offset this uncommon break.

If the serve breaks consistently into your backhand, you might as well take it there and chop it back. If he always serves to your backhand, you will become accustomed to the spin and return better as the match progresses—unless you are playing Rod Laver.

If your returns go wild, aim for the center of the court to give yourself more margin of safety. If your opponent stays back, play the ball high over the net to keep your return deep.

If your opponent rushes the net on a puzzling serve, still aim to get the ball back over the net rather than to pass him. Then he still

FIGURE 43

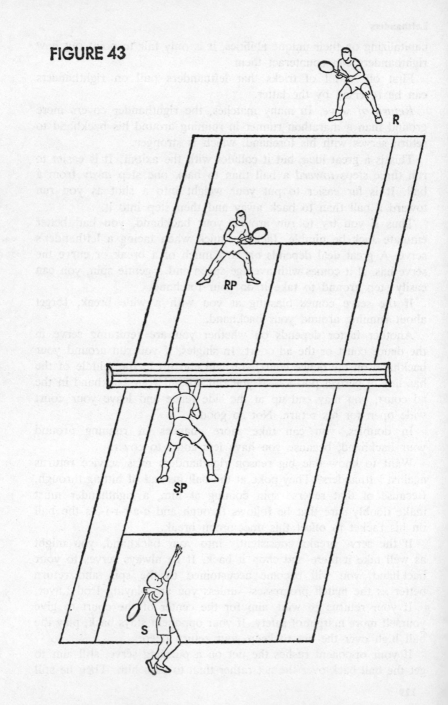

has to make a winner off his volley. Otherwise, if you keep vainly trying to pass him, you will be throwing points away. If he serves wide to your backhand in the ad court, your best return is crosscourt. As said before, one good angle deserves another. You can make a better angle in return than off a ball in the middle.

If your opponent serves wide to your forehand in the deuce court, your best return again is to crosscourt your drive. The net is lower in the middle, and you can aim lower as a result.

Naturally, you should try to vary your returns with occasional down-the-line shots or lobs when he rushes the net.

If the portsider serves a high-bouncing ball breaking wide to your backhand in the ad court, try to take the ball on the rising bounce. If you let it break wide and take it on a lower bounce, you will find yourself forced way out of court.

The Australian formation. The Australian formation in doubles is an unusual serving formation designed to break up the left-hander's devastating return of serve off his forehand in the ad court.

The usual serving formation in the ad court is for the server to stand midway between the center service mark and the doubles alley line and for the server's partner to stand halfway between the net and the service line and three feet from the singles alley line.

But when a righthander serves to a lefthander in that court, he finds that if the latter takes the ball on his forehand, he can easily crack it crosscourt to the server's backhand side. Since most left-handers develop a tremendous crosscourt drive as their next best shot after their serves, the righthander finds himself at a disadvantage.

Hence, the Australians came up with the idea of blocking the lefthander's crosscourt return by posting the net man in the way. See Figure 43.

The server, S, stands close to the center service mark while his partner, SP, stands on the same side, halfway between the net and the service line and about three feet from the center service line. The lefthander must now hit his forehand or backhand down the line, away from the net man.

After serving, the server runs to the position shown in Figure 44.

The left-handed receiver tries to hit his returns away from the net man, SP, but it is now harder for him to score winners if the serve goes to his backhand. If his backhand return goes high

FIGURE 44

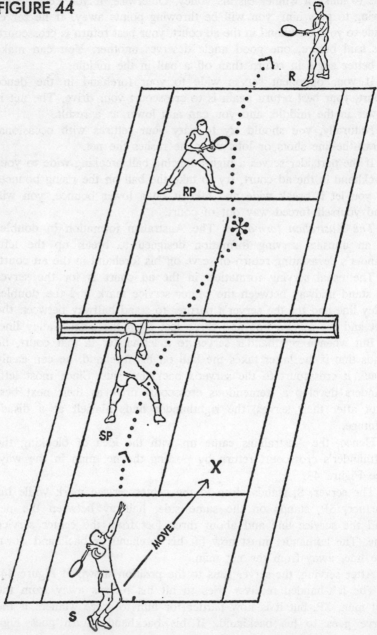

through the middle, the net man can poach (see the chapter on poaching) and kill it, as shown in Figure 45.

Unless the receiver can keep his backhand return low, he faces trouble if the server attains the net and makes a successful volley. While it is true that many lefthanders can hit down the line in returning serve, most still prefer the more natural crosscourt return. Thus you are forcing your left-handed opponent to make a less favored return.

Tony Trabert and Victor Seixas, former National Doubles champions, used this formation in combination with signals for poaching. Keep the receivers guessing, they figured, by presenting varying situations on the serve.

Alex Olmedo and Ham Richardson used this Australian formation in the 1959 Davis Cup match against Mal Anderson and Neale Fraser. Left-handed Fraser dominated the first three sets with his booming serves and slashing forehands, and the Aussies led 15–40 on Richardson's serve for two match points. They took the first two sets 12–10, 6–3 and dropped the third, 14–16.

During the rest period, the American board of strategy suggested that the United States team use the Australian formation to break down Fraser and attack his comparatively weak backhand. This they did and kept changing formations to prevent Fraser from grooving his returns. They won the last two sets 6–3, 7–5 and brought back the Cup for America.

Marty Riessen and Clark Graebner also use this formation in conjunction with poaching, because they believe it puts more pressure on opponents than using the same formations all the time.

Admittedly, the Australian formation has some defects. If the left-handed receiver can step around his backhand to crack his forehand down the line, he can mow down the server, for the server has to run farther to reach volleying position. Also, the receiver can lob more easily over the net man's head to the backhand corner than if the server came in from his usual position.

In fact, such widely varied exponents of tennis as Dennis Ralston, Gene Mako, Manuel Santana, and Rod Laver all told me they regarded the formation with little favor. (This contrasted with Pancho Segura, who thinks highly of it.) Laver pointed out that the receiver could put topspin on his backhand return to send the ball at the server's feet. It so happens that Rod has a fine topspin backhand and can return equally well off both sides.

FIGURE 45

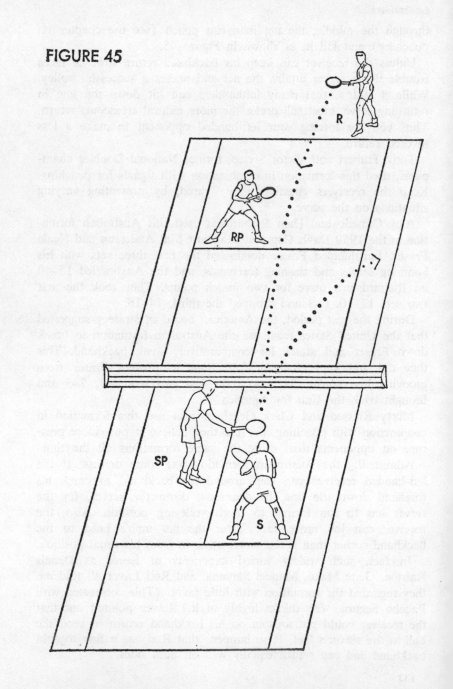

Lefthanders

Thus the better the player the more easily he can adapt his return of service to hit either down the line or crosscourt. But many players who return service the conventional way often find it hard to adjust to a different type of return. Bill Crosby, formerly ranked No. 2 in National Doubles, could return all day like a machine off his backhand crosscourt in the ad court. But against the Australian formation, he would run into error.

Hence, if you face a righthander with a superb crosscourt backhand return, try the Australian formation. He can't hit his backhand down the line any better, and it might be a lot worse. Also, by switching formations at times, it may break up the groove of his backhand returns.

Again, in mixed doubles, if your feminine partner finds that her male opponent in the ad court is crushing her with returns to her backhand, try the Australian formation. Your male opponent will be hitting to her forehand now, and she may do a lot better.

If nothing else, the Australian formation can produce a nuisance value because it disturbs the even tenor of the receiver's returns. Try it for variety at times. It may uncover a weakness in your opponents and change the match in your favor.

Serving to a lefthander. When serving to the deuce court, the classic method is to serve wide to your opponent's backhand, force him way over, and if he returns weakly or short, drive to his forehand. Thus, keep him on the run.

Try this first and then test his forehand. He may prove to hit more steadily, if less harder, on his backhand than on his erratic but slugging forehand.

Usually, it pays to serve wide to his backhand in this court since you can get a natural wide angle that forces him out of position.

Try to vary your serve by serving right at him. He may try to run around his backhand and thus find himself way out in the doubles alley when returning your serve.

Suppose you serve wide to his backhand and he returns down the line to your backhand. Where should you hit your next shot?

Most players are tempted to hit right back to his backhand, which may be weaker than his forehand. However, since most nontournament players can't run all day, many times you will do better by crosscourting your backhand way wide to his forehand. He will then have to run from one sideline to the other. If you

135

can make him run back and forth like this a few times, you will cut down his energy, put more pressure on his trying to make better service returns, and cause him to try for winners with his forehand when running at top speed.

When serving to the ad court, stand close to the center service mark to make it easier to serve down the line to his backhand. He may crowd way over to protect his backhand but still serve mostly to that side.

Once in a while, "to keep him honest," serve wide to his forehand. But not too often (say once out of eight times), for you are courting double jeopardy:

1. You are serving to his strong side.

2. He can easily hit a crosscourt drive to your weaker side, which starts the rally off with you on the defensive.

If your left-handed opponent proves to hit more effectively off his backhand, serve more to his forehand.

It is far more important to get your first serve in on the ad court than the deuce court, because if your second serve doesn't hook to his backhand, you will be providing an easy ball for him to run around, take on his forehand, and crack to your backhand. When serving to the deuce court, however, it is not too hard for you to place your second serve to his backhand side.

To practice serving down the line in the ad court, play some easy right-handed opponent and aim your serves to his forehand. This will make the match more even and will give you a great chance to improve the control of your serve.

Doubles

Doubles differs greatly from singles, and you should consider these differences to improve your game. Doubles requires less effort, more skill, and calls for a greater variety of shots. You can win at singles by condition alone and without venturing to the net once, however, in doubles, two seniors who mix up their shots but can't run around the block will often beat a pair of energetic youngsters who slug every ball.

You can keep improving your doubles game as you grow older, but regardless of the shots you learn in singles, after a while age catches up at seventy and you may lose to a boy merely because he can outrun you.

If you learn the fundamentals of doubles and avoid the sucker shots, you can lift your game well above your present equals'. If you are going to school, you may earn a letter at doubles by using your head, since most juniors know little and care less about doubles. If you are older, you can increase your enjoyment, climb the ranking ladder, and make it easier to get games.

Playing doubles is a battle of serves, for the scores are much closer than in singles. Thus you should concentrate on the two most important strokes: the serve and the return of serve.

Read the chapters on those two shots. To repeat, get 70 percent of your *first* serves into the court. Allow yourself one double fault a set. Any more presents a free gift of a point.

137

1. Always give your opponent a chance to miss. No matter how easy a ball you hit over the net, he still has to put it away.

2. Generally speaking, the team that captures the net wins the match. There are exceptions, to be noted later. Don't throw away your advantage when at the net by missing ordinary volleys. Make your first volley deep instead of trying to put it away. The percentages then work in your favor.

3. Hit your shots through the middle between your opponents until you have a chance to put the ball away at an angle.

4. One-eighth of doubles is teamwork. Make an effort to get along with your partner and to discuss strategy with him. Expect that he as well as you will miss some shots.

5. Develop two types of lobs: the kind that skims over your opponents' heads and the high skyscraping type that enables you to get back into position from way off court.

6. Use your lobs to drive your opponents from the net and to vary your service return. If you never lob when returning service, the net man will edge closer to the net and start making remarkable poaches.

Many opponents will set up an instant wailing wall when you chase them back for lobs. They murmur that only weaklings or frail girls lob and that you lack the strength to play a real man's game: driving hard right to them at the net where they can volley it easily for the point.

As said before in the chapter on smashing, we all hate to run backward for lobs. It takes more effort and wears a player down faster than twice as much running sideways. Your opponents will not crowd the net when you keep lobbing, so you should then mix up your lobs with drives at their feet.

Never remind your opponents that they are not lobbing to you.

7. The most popular position nowadays for doubles players is to have the receiver's partner stand on the service line while the receiver remains on the baseline. See Figure 46.

The reason is that when the receiver returns the serve past the server's partner, SP, the receiver's partner, RP, will move in closer, about halfway between the service line and the net. The receiver's partner will then be able to cut in on balls through the middle to put them away. His just being there will also put pressure on the server to keep the ball away from him and thus play it too close to the net or knock it out on the other side.

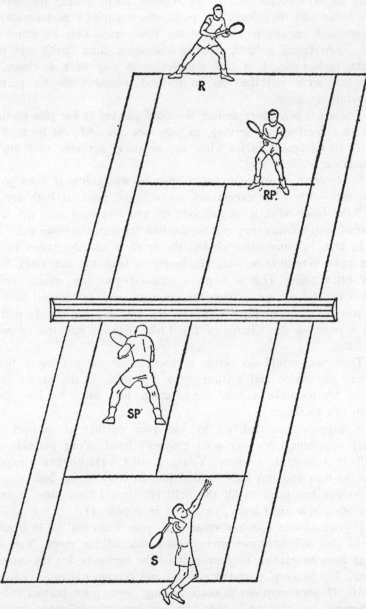

This is a great idea, but first the receiver must hit the ball past the server's partner. If the receiver keeps hitting the ball to the latter and thus loses the point, the receiver's partner should stand back on the baseline for the first serve. Lots of teams do this when facing a hard, reliable first serve. Stan Smith and Bob Lutz, ranked No. 1 in U.S. doubles, each stay back at times for the first serve and then go up for the second while his partner is returning serve.

The usual procedure among weekend players is for one partner, whether receiving or serving, to play one up and one back. This leads to backcourt rallies while the opposing net men each try to poach on a likely shot.

8. However, it is easier for a team to win points if both go to the net—with a few exceptions, to be noted later. If both are up and the other team is playing one up and one back, the net team should win, because they can hit the ball between the other pair.

In fact, in tournament circles, the receiver usually rushes to the net upon returning service. He hopes to take the net away from the other team. This is a great idea—if you can return service low over the net, away from the net man, and can hustle right in. If you are slow or return high over the net, you are merely putting on a rerun of the Charge of the Light Brigade into the cannons' mouths.

Then you would do better to concentrate on making a better return of service and mixing up a few lobs. If the server stays back, try to make a good deep return, and when he hits short, then run to the net.

9. Suppose you rush up to join your partner at the net and your opponent lobs over your partner's head. Your partner then calls in a loud, clear voice, "Yours, partner." He obviously expects you to turn and run back behind him to retrieve the ball.

So you run back to hit the ball. He should then cross over to the other side right away, as shown in Figure 47.

If your partner does not cross over, your team will be in trouble, since you will have two men on one side of the court. You will then have to explain to your partner the necessity for his crossing over. Try to keep your voice down and remain patient.

10. If your opponents keep lobbing over your partner's head whenever you rush up to join him, you have the following options:

FIGURE 47

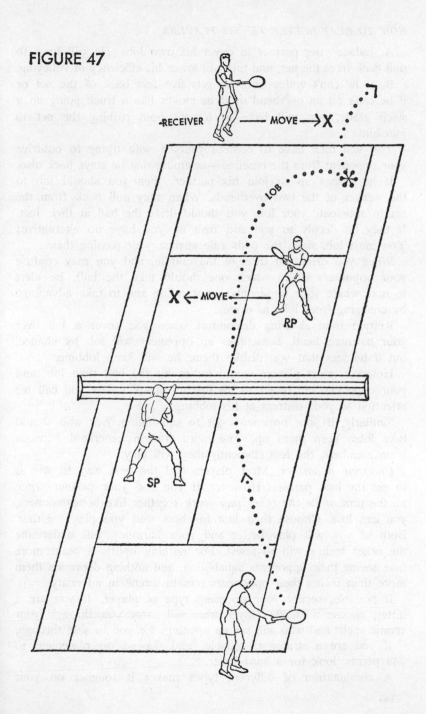

A. Induce your partner to cover his own lobs. He will have to pull back from the net, and this will lower his efficiency in volleying.

B. If he can't volley once he gets five feet back of the net or if he can't hit an overhead or if he moves like a truck going up a steep grade, you will have to forget about rushing the net to join him.

You will then have to content yourself with trying to outdrive your opponent from the baseline—assuming that he stays back also.

If he rushes up to join his partner, then you should lob to the weaker of the two overheads. When they pull back from the net to anticipate your lob, you should drive the ball at their feet. If they hit deeply to you and rush in, you have no alternative: You must lob, since the odds rule against your passing them.

When you drive, hit through the middle, and you may confuse your opponents as to which one should take the ball. Be alert to note where your opponents are standing and to take advantage by changing from lobs to drives.

Refrain from showing discomfort when you cover a lob over your partner's head. Sometimes an opponent will lob by chance, but if he sees that you dislike them, he will keep lobbing.

However, most players would rather hit the ball than lob, and your opponent will revert to his driving attack unless you call his attention to your distress at his lobbing.

Similarly, if your opponents get to squabbling over who should take lobs, keep them up. The more friction generated between team members, the less efficiently they will play.

Choosing a partner. Most players feel the best way to win is to get the best partner. However, if you and your partner argue all the time while the other pair work together like honeymooners, you can lose. Choose then first for how well you play together. Both of you will play better and your harmony will undermine the other team's will to resist. For nothing uplifts a team more than seeing their opponents squabbling, and nothing depresses them more than seeing their opponents remain serene in adversity.

If possible, secure your opposing type of player. If you are a hitter, choose a steady player who will carry you through your erratic spells and who will set up openings for you to slug through.

If you are a strategist, reliable, and depend on placement to win points, look for a hard hitter.

A combination of different types makes it tougher on your

opponents if one ball steams past them and the next dies softly at their feet. For your opponents can more easily accustom themselves to one kind of shot and develop a defense or attack to cope with it. But a continual change of pace demands greater flexibility to withstand it.

We all know it is easier to smash two overheads in a row or volley twice than it is to smash once and have to hurry back to the net to volley, especially when we don't know whether the next ball will call for a smash or a volley.

The best doubles teams always consist of a slugger and a strategist. Don Budge's hurricane backhand and net attack teamed with skillful Gene Mako's controlled angles to sweep the world's tournaments. Toto Brugnon, who created the openings for his partners, won Wimbledon four times and was runner-up three times with Borotra and Cochet. Yet the latter two paired together couldn't win half the tournaments.

Similarly, the late Rafael Osuna, a touch artist, formed a better team with Dennis Ralston than when the latter paired with another slugger, Chuck McKinley.

So try to choose a partner whose game will complement yours, but make allowances for his differing personality. Sluggers prefer aggressive, thunderbolt attacks, while the strategists are the accountants of the game, who count the cost of trying difficult shots or maneuvers.

The caste system. The caste system reaches its highest peak in doubles, not only in the making up of teams to oppose each other, but in the behavior of the higher-ranking player toward his lowly partner.

The better player seems to assume he should hit at least 70 percent, if not 90 percent, of the balls. This is a good system if he plays Davis Cup or you are betting your life savings, the balls, and the drinks on the match. Or playing with your boss or client. Otherwise, it's ridiculous.

If you let your partner hog the court, you'll cut down your hopes of improving. For you'll hit so few balls you won't get as much practice in three sets as in one set of singles. And practice is one feature that most weekend players need the most. They simply don't practice enough to learn new shots or improve on old ones compared with "tournament circuit" players.

In social doubles, as at a dinner party, it is bad manners for one player to hog the court. Your partner wouldn't try to eat off your plate at dinner, would he? Then why should he try to steal the tidbits from you on the court?

Another reason your partner shouldn't hog the court is he will most likely get so far out of position he can't get back to cover his own territory. But most important of all, to improve your doubles, you must play your share of the shots.

If your partner urges you to stand on top of the net to volley, you will never learn to volley ten feet back. You will never practice smashing, because you won't get any lobs you can reach.

Worst of all, if you become used to playing that close to the net, you will find that with an ordinary partner, you won't be able to keep up your own end, for you won't be used to covering so much more territory.

But suppose your partner insists you get up close because he claims you're missing too many shots playing back. You should disarm him with, "We're just playing for the fun of it, aren't we? It's just a game, isn't it?"

Your partner is trapped, since he can't very well insist that winning a mere tennis match is more important than landing a contract, selling a house, or healing the sick.

You follow up, "Since it's just a game, suppose you play your way and I'll play mine. After all, the pros play back, and if I'm going to learn to play like them, I should play farther back too, right?"

Keep repeating that tennis is only just a game. Your opponents may even believe it too and let up just enough for your team to win.

So stand halfway between the net and the service line as a starter and your opponents will send far more balls at you. You will relish the challenge of foiling their attempted passing shots or lobs, and you will enjoy the game much more than as a spectator close to the net.

If you are playing a pair of juniors who slug everything and never lob, by all means move closer, where you can volley better. But you should try to cover all the shots in your half of the court, and if they start lobbing, pull back to smash your own lobs.

What if your partner persists in hogging the court and crossing over into your territory?

You may feel like hitting him over the head with your racket. Never do this. You might splinter your racket or break the gut.

Aim at the seat of his pants and let go. Then apologize profusely. Every time he crosses over, swing at his rear end, and if possible, trip him. You should then help him up, ask solicitously if he's hurt, and apologize profusely. After a while he will cringe at the sight of your racket swinging through.

Partners like this magnify their own successes and ignore their many failures. They think that one sensational shot or poach counts more than six ordinary returns of yours that force errors. A point is a point is a point, and if he wins five points outright while you are forcing twenty-five errors, you are five times better than he is.

Coaching. The road to conflict between partners is greased with good intentions by the player who considers himself superior. He doesn't realize that unless he is a magician, he can't change a weak backhand into a Rosewall weapon with a few magic words. It is hard enough for a professional coach to improve a player's backhand in half an hour of concentrated effort let alone during a match, when the player never can get set to practice.

You may suggest that your partner lob more to a weaker opponent or serve more to the other's backhand or suggest that you both just try to get the opponents' serves back instead of trying for outright winners. You may offer one suggestion every other game at the most. Too little advice is far better than too much, which befuddles your partner so he doesn't know what to do next.

One of the game's finest strategists was Bobby Riggs. He knew more about his opponents' weaknesses after one game than others did after a whole match. He could mix accurate deep drives with feather-soft drop shots and change the pace like pressing a button.

He used to play many matches when paired with weak partners against supposedly superior teams of two equal partners. If anybody had a right to instruct his partner (especially considering the heavy stakes), Bobby did.

One might expect that Bobby would constantly impart a stream of advice to his dub partner in order to lift the latter's game to mere mediocrity. But instead Bobby would content himself with a word or two at the start, a rare comment or two during the match, and mention only praise for his partner's efforts. Not a harsh word or stern command ever came from Bobby. As he said later, he couldn't change his partner's game in a year, so why try to change it in one afternoon?

The result was that Bobby won so many matches with awkward, inexperienced partners that spectators preferred to wager on him instead of investing in General Motors stock.

Inevitably you will pair with a partner who considers himself your superior and therefore entitled to coach you continually. He will tell you to bend your knees, watch the ball, lob deeper, hit harder, return cannonball serves twice as fast, take more backswing, run faster than Tom Okker, smash harder than Dennis Ralston, and follow through more. Invariably he tries to make you pattern your game after his—except ten times better.

Every time you miss, he shakes his head and looks up to the skies to inform spectators what a horrible partner you are. He berates you as though catching you shoplifting, and Niagara's roar can't compare with the constant stream of his advice.

Meanwhile, this lovable character is missing all kinds of easy shots while occasionally bringing off a good one. He serves one ace and three doubles. But he sees only the errors you are making.

Sometimes you are warned ahead of time, since his kind are avoided like a man who has lost a battle with a skunk.

If warned, avoid all show of friendliness or delight at being paired together. Establish right off that you consider him your equal only if he plays way over his head. Never apologize at missing a shot, or he will take this as a green light to start coaching you.

Never applaud any of his good shots, for this only heightens his egocentric conception of himself as world champion. Some unsuspecting players allow him to make a suggestion or two right at the start because they want to be friendly. Nothing is more disastrous, for once started, this adviser makes more and more suggestions—especially if he himself begins missing shots.

The classic answer is, "If I could play half as well as you expect of me, I wouldn't be playing here. I'd be on the Davis Cup team."

You may counterpunch suggestions by making some of your own. When he misses a shot, you caution him to watch the ball more, run faster, or start his swing sooner. These are vague suggestions that he can't combat, whereas if you suggest he use the Continental grip, he may retort that the club pro teaches the Eastern grip.

A still more drastic remedy is the all-time riposte: A world champion was playing one time at the Los Angeles Tennis Club with his charming wife. The well-meaning husband was telling her where and how to play her shots, since if anybody had the right and knowledge, he did.

She didn't improve, but found herself playing worse. Finally, she said, "Honey, you play your half of the court your way and I'll play my half my way."

Tell your advice-giving partner the same, and he may become disgruntled and sullen but at least you can concentrate in peace on your own game.

Breaking up your opponents. Besides trying to further the good will spirit of your own team, you should also try to break down the teamwork of your opponents.

The easiest way is to direct your shots mostly at the weaker opponent. Just as you direct your shots mostly to the weaker side (usually a backhand) because the percentage works in your favor, so also your weaker opponent will give you less trouble with his returns.

But an added bonus is that the stronger opponent becomes upset over his partner losing points and will try to either take more of the latter's shots or will put pressure on him to improve. If the weak partner keeps missing his overheads, lob him to death. His stronger partner will try to cover them instead and will leave his own territory wide open. Then hit to the unprotected area.

Most of all, once your shots cause friction between partners, you need not play brilliantly. They will miss shots they ordinarily make because (a) the weaker partner tries too hard, and (b) when the stronger partner does hit a ball, he feels he has to kill it or the next ball will go to his weaker partner, who will miss it.

Another effective tactic is to hit through the middle. The first time both will try for the ball and almost hit each other. The next time both tend to back away in an excess of politeness. After that, balls through the middle will disturb both, because if they lose the point, each will tend to blame the other.

If the net man swings and misses the ball, the baseline partner will feel like telling him to let the balls go without swinging at them. So the net man lets a ball whistle by him and the baseline partner swings futilely and says, "That was your ball."

"But you said to let them go," retorts the net man. "So I did."

From there on, they will bicker and argue like a pair of fish-wives—and lose their concentration and the match.

Still another stratagem works on the theory that the better player in a team suffers from the delusion that his weaker partner is losing all the points. An opponent then catches the eye of the better player and shakes his head in sympathy when the weaker partner misses a shot. The opponent may even murmur, "Too bad you're stuck with him today. Not much you can do."

The better player usually assumes that since he is laboring under a heavy burden, he should take more of the shots. He will tend to overpoach and hog the court—which his weaker partner resents, either audibly or in silence. The results are a breakdown in teamwork and victory for the opponents.

Types of partners. Francis Bacon once said that some books are to be tasted, others to be swallowed, some few to be chewed, etc. Tennis partners should also be treated differently.

Here is a partial list and how they may be treated to bring out the best:

1. The bursting-with-energy youngster who slugs the ball: When you two are waiting for your opponents, suggest he hit a little easier, not baby the ball, but just a little easier. "You've got a great serve, but if you'll serve easier you'll get a lot more in. And still make it rough on them."

If you're a lot older, let him chase down the high lobs. Praise his placements but not his power—or he'll try to overpower your opponents even more.

Since he's young, he'll make a lot of errors mixed in with fine shots. He'll miss setups, but if you remain calm and play steadily, you'll make a good team.

2. The timid soul. He doesn't think he can beat anybody. You should praise his good shots and soften any criticism. Keep encouraging him, but don't expect him to make any brilliant shots. You'll have to do the forcing while he's the accompanist who keeps the ball in play.

3. The compulsive talker. This fellow rattles on like an endless string of boxcars at a railroad crossing. Don't bother listening or replying, since he's too wrapped up in his own speeches. After every shot, he comments aloud as though for a television program. Figure that although he bothers you with his incessant chatter, he's

actually helping your team—for he's bothering two players on the other side. That's a one-to-two advantage for your team.

Concentrate on the match and your own shots. Save your suggestions and breath, because he won't be listening if you talk anyway.

4. The sulker. He misses a few shots and decides he just can't play that afternoon. Avoid an outwardly determinedly cheerful attitude or he will cry, "How can you say I'm doing better? Look at all the shots I'm missing—shots I usually make all the time."

It does no good to point out that he rarely makes those brilliant shots. So temper your encouragement with occasional phrases, "That's a good one, partner. . . . Nice shot. . . . Now you're hitting them."

5. The jokester. He never takes anything seriously—at least, not on the surface. There you are slaving away over a hot net, chasing after balls, and he indolently slaps at the ball and idly notes the girls in shorts on the next court.

He makes all kinds of wisecracks, some of them funny, and seems to regard the match as merely an excuse to wear white. He tries trick shots, and misses until you feel like hitting him over the head for throwing away points.

Actually, he wants to win, but his nonchalant attitude covers up his determination not to appear a loser in a serious contest. Some years ago a nationally ranked player went through the same antics in tournament after tournament, but never made the grade to top-flight status. He feared to face reality, and by his acts tried to pretend that he wasn't really trying, so why should he be blamed for losing?

A long pep talk isn't going to change the jokester. You should avoid laughing at his quips, or you'll encourage him. Assume a business-like expression at the start and keep it. Don't let down, or you'll be relaxing the way he is. If you are serious, he can't help catching some of it too.

If you play against him, by all means laugh at his antics. But don't let up on your onslaught against him. Tell his partner that old jokester can't help it if he kids around—so the partner will feel what's the use of breaking his neck to win points when paired with a character like that.

6. The old-timer. He seems to have played way back in 1900, and his strokes haven't changed since. You shouldn't try at this date to improve his shots—or his manner of playing. He may seem to totter around, but somehow he manages to return the ball.

Don't try to rush him any more than you'd try to prod a mule into galloping.

His odd shots may give your opponents more trouble than your orthodox smooth strokes. Expect to cover a lot more court and to have to supply the punch. He'll probably play more conservatively than you do, so don't ask him to haul off and hit winners down the line.

He may even stand in no-man's-land (the area between the service line and the baseline) while you are receiving service. You may point out that he should stand either at the service line or the baseline, but he won't believe you. Not even if he sees the Wimbledon doubles champions in action. He figures he's always played that way, so why change?

Save your advice. Just concentrate on your own shots and pray that your opponents won't notice your partner's defenseless position.

Sucker shots. Some shots in doubles are called "sucker shots" that should rarely or never be tried because of the odds against them. Here are a few sucker shots:

1. You are forced way out of court, and your opponent on that side is standing close to the net. You try to pass him down the line, but he volleys your shot for the point. He should always win the point, since you are shooting for a very narrow opening.

You should hit through the middle, way crosscourt, or lob deeply. If both are at net, lob!

2. Your opponent backcourt returns the ball short, and you rush up to hit the ball and join your partner at the net. You notice your opponent's partner shifting around at the net and decide to trick him. You try to pass him down his alley. Invariably you will throw the point away, since he will volley the ball through or past you or you will try to keep the ball too low and hit the net.

This is the most inexcusable sucker shot. All you need do on this approach shot is to hit deep to your opponent backcourt. Then you and your partner will dominate the net and force your opponent to make a much better-than-average shot from backcourt.

3. Your opponent serves an easy second serve and stays back. You drop shot the return. He comes up, returns the ball deep, and now forces the pressure on you. As in No. 2, the player backcourt has to hit a deep lob or slam the ball through the middle—two tough shots to make consistently.

You should rarely drop shot in doubles, since it pulls your opponent to the net—which you want to keep him away from. Also, if your drop shot falls too short into the net or too high, where he can crack it, you have thrown away your advantage. Stand in closer on easy serves and hit deep through the middle or at an angle. Then go to the net and finish off his return.

4. Your opponent hits a ball that lands at about the service line. You rush in and try a lob. Your opponent reaches up and kills it. Only an expert can rush in short and throw up a lob over opponents' heads.

You should hit through the middle or right at your opponent, because he won't have time to get set for the shot.

5. You are standing ten feet from the net and have an easy smash. You decide to fool your opponents and smash gently to drop the ball dead over the net. At that distance, you will have greater luck picking the Kentucky Derby winner than winning the point. You will end up hitting into the net or give your opponents a chance to rush up to wallop the ball past you.

You should smash these easy lobs either at an angle, through the middle, or down the line. But smash them, don't baby them.

6. An opponent lobs a very high ball as you stand close to the net. You stick your racket out and push the ball back. Unless you make a sharp angle, you are returning the ball so easily that your opponents can deal readily with it. Also, by standing so close to the net, you may happen to brush it and thus lose the point. Then too, you may misjudge the ball when it comes from a great height, since a puff of wind may blow it off course.

You should let the very high lobs bounce so you can take a healthy swing at them.

Poaching

As you may know, poaching is crossing into your partner's territory in doubles to put away an opponent's easy return.

A typical poach is shown in Figure 48. The net man has left his own area to intercept his opponent's return of serve and to volley for a winner.

Like smashing an easy lob, making a successful poach appeals to the killer instinct. What joy to pounce on the ball and crash through your bewildered opponents as they stand helpless!

But besides earning a particular point, a good poach brings many fringe benefits: Your opponent will then feel the pressure to make a much better return next time. He may become undecided about trying to pass you down the alley through a narrow opening, known as "threading the needle," or to hit through the wide opening to your partner.

Your opponent's partner may remind him to keep the ball away from you at the net. Since your opponent is already trying to do this, he may resent this unneeded advice and concentrate even less on the ball.

Your own partner will feel less pressure in trying to ace your opponents and by relaxing, serve better. The fact is that a skillful poacher can practically win the serve for his partner. Think if you had Rod Laver as your partner at the net!

Indeed, as in many wage settlements, the fringe benefits may

FIGURE 48

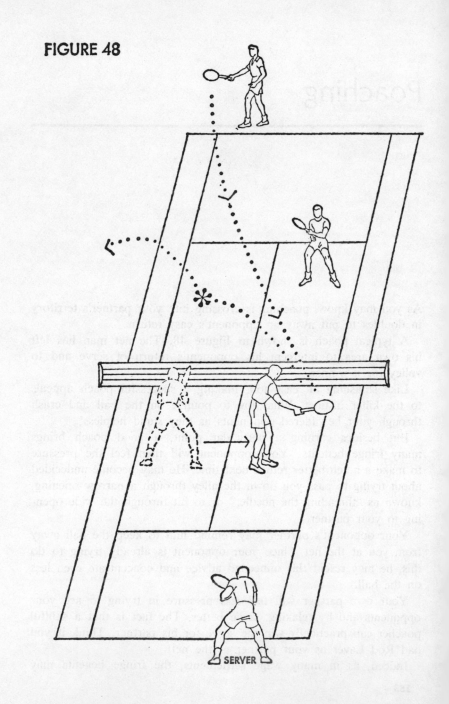

SERVER

outweigh the supposedly main issue: winning a particular point. For if you can make a couple of good poaches, you will undermine your opponents' concentration on returning the serve so that they will continually miss service returns. Even when you do not poach.

As mentioned earlier, about 30 percent of all shots in doubles are service returns. Thus, anything that you as a net man can do to make it even harder for your opponents to concentrate on returning service will help your partner win his serve.

A poacher can also kill soft balls much easier closer at the net than his partner can from backcourt or farther away from the net.

How to poach. Anticipation is the heart of poaching. You should lean forward, poised on the balls of your feet, your eyes intent on your opponent. Watch to see how he gets set to return the ball.

Is he digging in to slam it back hard? Is he moving in to take the ball sooner? If he is, you will have less time to decide whether to poach or to start moving for his shot.

Is he drifting back to take the ball on a lower bounce?

If he is, he gives you more time to diagnose where his return will go and to get moving for a poach.

Is he preparing to lob?

If so, get ready to drift back.

Watch the ball—not your opponent nor the area you are aiming for.

Once he hits the ball toward the middle, break to intercept it. Cut in toward the net, for the closer you are to the net, the easier to make a sharp angle or to punch the ball through the middle between your opponents.

Unless you can read minds, do not start until he hits the ball, or you may be caught flatfooted by a ball going down your alley.

Play as close to the net as you can get away with. If your opponents never lob because they think it is a sign of weakness, you can hang over the net and enjoy a poacher's holiday. If your opponents mix up lobs with drives, play back to cover your own lobs.

The odds favor a tall poacher, because he can reach farther, but if you are small and agile, you can poach almost as well. If you are heavy-footed and slow-moving, forget about poaching except in rare instances.

When you poach, you must go for a winner. If you merely return the ball while you yourself are out of position, you are giving your

FIGURE 49

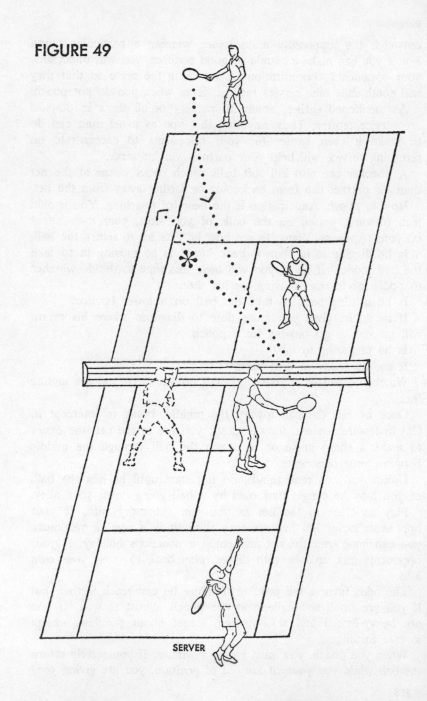

SERVER

opponents a setup. See Figure 49 for an example of a bad poach.

The net man has run way over into his partner's court and then merely returned the ball to the service line, where his opponent can pounce on it. See Figure 50, in which the opponent is firing a drive down the net man's alley before the server (the net man's partner) can reach it. Moreover, many times the net man tries futilely to return to his own territory to cover the passing shot down his alley. The result is that the net man's partner does not know which half of the court to cover.

Keep in mind:

1. In poaching, usually aim for the wide opening. Since you are moving out of position, make your play for the easiest putaway shot. Don't try for fancy angles if you can punch the ball through the center to win the point.

2. It is better to angle the ball away from your opponent as in Figure 48 than to blast the ball right at your opponent's partner at the net.

3. Do *not* remind your opponents of any errors of judgment they are making. If they have not lobbed against your poaching, do not remind them of their single-track approach. If they keep trying to return the ball high through the center, do not mention they haven't tried to pass you down the alley.

Sometimes successful poachers glory so much in making poaches that they chide their opponents, who then change their tactics.

4. If your opponents start lobbing, back up and stay back until they resume driving again. Most players prefer driving to lobbing their return of services, so pretty soon they'll forget about lobbing and start driving again—and give you a chance to resume poaching.

5. How often should you poach? As long as you can poach successfully.

Do not try to poach on each return. You will waste a lot of energy bouncing around, and your swinging futilely at balls going past you must distract your partner.

Also, a surprise poach deals a more effective blow against your opponents, who can't be sure when they should try to pass you down the alley.

Just as a little knowledge is supposed to be a dangerous thing, so a little success as a poacher can lead to trying harder and harder poaches with less and less success. It does little good to make one sensational poach and then miss three others.

FIGURE 50

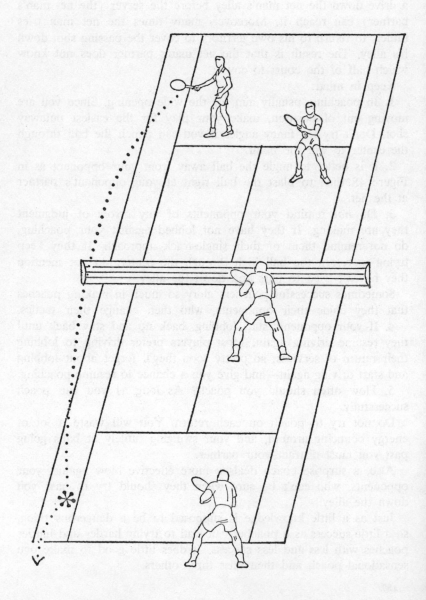

Keep track of which opponent you are doing best against in poaching, and try most of your poaches against him.

If you are playing with a much better partner, limit your poaches to only sure kills when your partner is way backcourt. Nothing distresses a better player more than to see a weak partner cross way over into the former's territory—and then make an error.

If you are playing with a much weaker partner, you will be tempted to poach constantly. You will figure that if the ball keeps going back to your partner, he will miss it sooner or later although you may be able to put it away.

This is fine reasoning, but there is a law of diminishing returns that works against overzealous poachers as surely as the law of gravity. You have undoubtedly seen matches in which one player recklessly invades his partner's court time and again—and then misses the shot. Or is pulled so far out of his own court as in Figure 50 that he can't handle the return shot.

In addition, the reckless poacher invariably bounces around the court so much that his partner can't tell which balls to take, so that sometimes the partner doesn't even try for balls he could reach and thus the point is lost.

There are thus some ifs connected with poaching when paired with a weaker partner. *If* you can poach to put the ball away; *if* you don't upset your partner so he can't tell which balls to take; *if* you can rest content at times and make surprise poaches; *if* your occasional poaches disconcert your opponents so that they watch you instead of the ball—then, my son, you are a worthy poacher.

This applies to poaching in club, team, or tournament matches where the weaker partner doesn't mind hitting fewer balls so that his team will win.

However, in fun matches with nothing at stake such as the usual weekend games, the weaker partner will resent the poacher who tries to hog the court—regardless of how successful he is. And justifiably so, for if the weaker partner hits only 15 percent instead of 50 percent of the balls, he will miss a great deal of practice, which he obviously needs. Not to mention the pleasure of *playing* tennis instead of standing around *watching* his partner play it.

If your partner poaches too much:

1. Stop praising him for his excellent shots. A little praise merely

elevates his concept of himself as a roving champion. You should, instead, regard him as a fractious horse whom you will have to keep under tight rein.

2. When he misses a couple of poaches, you should remark that an axiom of tennis states that a poacher must put the ball away. The more you sound like a professor lecturing dull pupils, the better.

3. You can start poaching yourself, and if he complains, comment that he has been giving you an example by his poaching so much. If he reminds you of the axiom you quoted to him, you say that then both of you should stop poaching so much.

4. You can run up and swing your racket at the seat of his pants—and apologize profusely. You say that the ball was so clearly in your part of the court that you couldn't help swinging at it. After you swat him a couple of times (always of course apologizing profusely) he will get the message.

The odds favor poaching

1. When your partner serves down the line to your opponent's backhand in the deuce court.

2. When your partner serves wide to your opponent's backhand in the ad court. Few players can return down the line to your alley and many times will return through the middle.

3. When your partner serves a high-bouncing ball to your opponent's backhand, and sometimes, depending on your opponent's skill, to the forehand.

The high bounce forces most players to take the ball farther back from the net in order to hit it around their waist lines; and the farther back a receiver stands to receive serve, the harder it is to surprise you, since you have more time to diagnose his shot. Also, it is harder to return a high-bouncing ball low over the net.

4. If your partner gets most of his first serves in. Then most of the time your opponents will feel more pressure in returning the ball.

5. If your opponents never lob. You can play closer to the net.

6. When your opponents stand back of the baseline to receive serve. The farther back they stand, the more time you have to decide whether to poach.

7. When your opponents return high, slow balls over the net.

8. If you have been exchanging shots in a close rally at the net while your partner has not been hitting any, the next ball that comes partly on his side should be yours. The player who has

been hitting a couple of balls usually is following the ball better than the bystander and can deal better with it.

9. When the ball comes high over the net on your forehand side.

The odds disfavor poaching

1. On your partner's weak second serve.

2. When your opponent in ad court returns serve low through the middle. You will have to volley low on your backhand and won't be able to make a sharp angle.

3. When your opponents drive balls with heavy topspin that drop quickly after crossing the net. You will be volleying *up* instead of *down* on the balls and thus not making a forceful shot.

4. When opponent stands inside the baseline and takes the ball on a rising bounce. This gives you less time to decide where he will hit the ball.

5. When your opponents mix lobs with drives. You will have to stand farther back from the net to cover lobs over your head, and this makes it harder for you to take the ball close to the net for a poach.

How to practice poaching

1. Rally with a player who stands on the baseline. Tell him to hit balls slightly on the other side of your half of the doubles court. Then practice racing in close to the net and trying to angle for a putaway.

2. Practice fast starts by leaning forward, poised on the balls of your feet, and breaking in diagonally to the net.

3. Look for the laziest, slowest-moving player for a partner. A lazy player really doesn't want to run if he can help it, for he prefers hitting only balls that bounce near him. This type of partner will appreciate your going after balls that he might have to exert himself for. It is no coincidence that a lazy player will always hunt as a partner for an energetic young sprout who doesn't mind running all over the court to retrieve balls.

4. Play in easy matches. You will feel more relaxed, and the weaker players will not place their returns as well nor hit as hard as your regular competition. Also, if you miss a few your partner won't mind as much.

Playing easy matches will sharpen your eye for judging how far you can go for a poach—and what you can do with the ball afterward.

5. Play in tougher matches and keep trying to judge how far

the tempting balls are going past you. Like a .350 hitter who learns not to bite on bad pitches, you can train yourself to judge which balls to poach on.

If you find that balls two feet past the middle elude you, limit yourself to balls one foot past the middle at first.

6. Usually it is more favorable to poach on your forehand side. If the ball is shoulder high or above your head, you can kill it even easier than a ball at a lower height. But if the ball is head high on your backhand, you may find it harder to deal with, since most players can't hit as hard off high backhand volleys as off high forehand volleys. Moreover, if you poach on your forehand side, you are usually taking a ball heading for your partner's backhand. But if you poach on your backhand side, you are taking a ball headed for your partner's forehand.

7. At times, fake a poach by making a start toward the center, and then draw back. Your opponent may decide to belt the ball down your alley—where you are waiting. But do not keep faking a poach, or you will waste energy and put your opponent on guard.

Rafe Osuna, one of the fastest men ever on a court, would stand

FIGURE 51

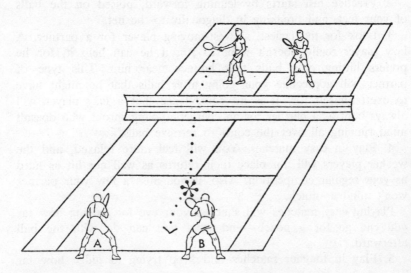

FIGURE 52

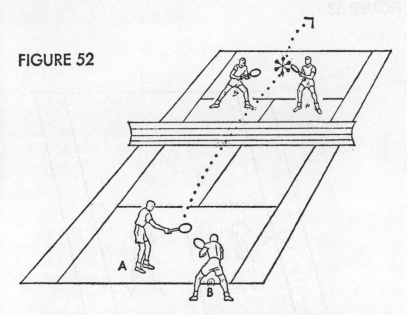

absolutely motionless at the net and then suddenly burst over like a rifle shot to poach. Your best bet, then, is to keep your opponents in suspense by not giving yourself away too soon.

Backcourt poaching. What about balls that land backcourt between two players, one of whom is decidedly stronger than the other? Should the stronger player *always* take the ball?

If a ball lands in the middle of the court, then in most instances the player who can take it on his forehand should take it. Usually, he can do more with it. The exception is when a player's backhand is much better than his partner's forehand.

See Figure 51 for an illustration of the positions of ad court player A and his partner, deuce court player B. Should player A, who has a powerful forehand, take a ball that lands within two feet of the center and up short? Or should player B take it because he is closer and it is on his side of the court?

Answer: If player A has a powerful forehand, he should take the ball. He can pounce on the ball and crack it past the opposing net men because the odds favor him. See Figure 52, which demonstrates this action.

What if a ball lands way back on the baseline and two feet

FIGURE 53

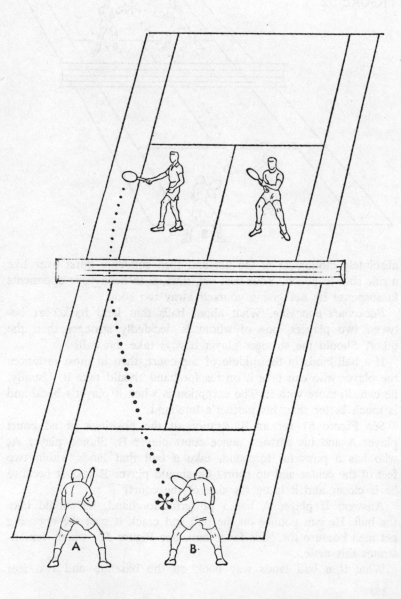

inside deuce player B's court? Should player A, with a powerful forehand, take it? See Figure 53 for an illustration of this situation:

Answer: This is a different situation than that shown in Figure 51, because now player A must hit for a winner. If he does not hit a winner, he is caught out of position. Also, it is much harder for him to make a winner from the baseline than from near the service line.

See Figure 54 for what happens if player A takes the ball by invading the territory of partner B.

Even though player B possesses no great backhand, he should take the ball—either by hitting a backhand through the middle or by lobbing over the head of player D. See Figure 55 for an illustration of his two choices.

Defense against poaching. A successful enemy poacher is a pickpocket who steals your rightful points, an angry gnat who buzzes in your bedroom at midnight, a thief in the night who makes off with your garden furniture, a trespasser who fishes in your private creek. He can cause more upset dispositions than a petulant tyrant of a bureaucrat, can create more ill feeling between partners than a practical joke, and can break down morale worse than a prison diet of bread and water.

To counteract his depredations, many tournament players will start off the first game in returning serve by banging a couple of drives down the alley of the opposing net man. They may lose the point, but they do serve notice to the net man that they may keep on trying more attempted passing shots. This tends to "keep him honest" and to stay on his own half of the court in fear of being passed. Many net men would prefer passing up a dozen chances to poach in fear of being passed just once down the alley and thus drawing the ire of a partner.

Similarly, if you lob over a net man's head once or twice at the start, you cause him to fear being lobbed over again and to stay away from the net. Unless, of course, he merely calls to his partner, "Yours," and moves over to the other side.

Here are some measures to use against the poacher:

1. Watch the ball! Many players get so upset at being poached upon that they start watching the poacher to try to outguess him. Keep your eye on the ball until it hits the strings of your racket. This will also make you concentrate more on making your shot.

2. Follow through! C-a-r-r-y the ball on your racket by following

FIGURE 54

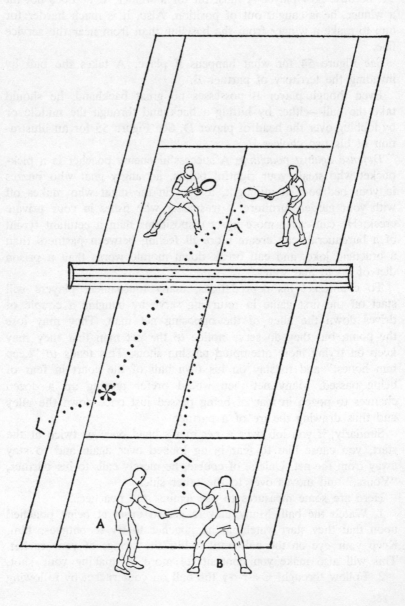

through on your stroke. Make up your mind ahead of time whether to try to lob, a passing shot, or a crosscourt return, and then make the shot regardless.

3. If possible, stand in closer to receive the serve. You can hit the ball back sooner and give the poacher less time to cross over. Also, if he starts too soon, you can cross him up with a drive down the alley or a lob over his head.

4. If your opponent serves too hard or too accurately for you to return consistently on his first serve, your partner should stand back on the baseline also. The poacher will then feel less incentive to poach, since it will be harder for him to put the ball away.

Ralston and McKinley frequently would vary their positions in returning first serves by one or the other standing back with the receiver on the first serve.

Of course, your partner should move up to volleying position when you receive the second serve.

5. Decide what kind of shot you will use, and when the serve comes, go ahead with it. If you decide to hit down the net man's alley and he doesn't move, go ahead anyway. Many players try in vain to outguess the poachers, and in so doing, don't place their shots at all.

6. If you have fast reflexes, you may hold off deciding what shot to use until the serve comes. Then, if the net man starts over before you hit the ball, you hit down his alley or lob. But this takes more skill, and you have to watch the poacher out of the corner of your eye while the serve is coming at you. Try this sometime against inferior players to practice before you attempt it in a hard-fought match.

7. Hit your crosscourt returns lower over the net (about a foot) and not too hard. If you crack the ball hard, the poacher need only stick out his racket, and the ball will bounce back on your side. Hitting an easier shot gives him no pace.

Rafe Osuna, who shared in the Wimbledon doubles championship, would return serves low over the net and with little pace so that the volleyer had to lift up on a dead ball.

8. Glance at the poacher before the serve to see if he bends his knees and is leaning forward on his toes. Lots of poachers rest at times since they can't poach on every return. If he looks as though he is relaxed, return crosscourt.

9. If the serve goes to your forehand in the deuce court, you

FIGURE 55

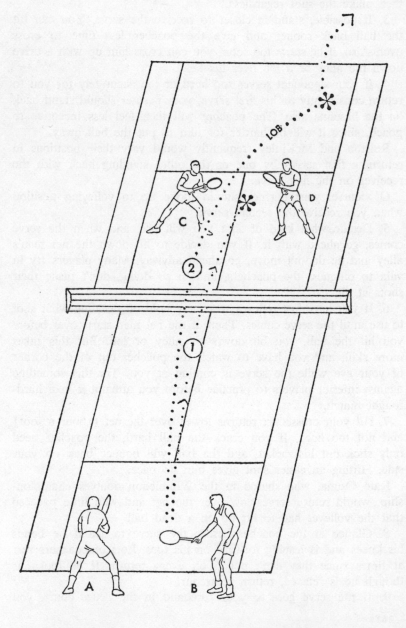

can easily hit down the line. But if the serve goes to your back-hand, forget about hitting down his alley.

If the serve goes to your forehand in the ad court, you may still try the down-the-line shot, although it is harder to make than in the deuce court. If the serve goes to your backhand, you will find it much harder to hit down the line. Here it is better to mix up lobs with sharp crosscourt returns.

Once in a while, try running around your backhand and hitting your forehand down the line.

10. Most players feel chagrined when a poacher wins a point. They grudgingly admit his skill, and their distress only serves to whet the poacher's appetite for another kill.

Instead, compliment the poacher on his putaways. You then appear the very soul of sportsmanship in commending an opponent's fine play. Keep praising the poacher, and what does he do?

He overpoaches. He becomes dizzy with success and fancies him-self as another Rafe Osuna dazzling his opponents with sharp angles. Instead, he begins stretching too far, waving his racket vainly at balls so that he confuses his partner. Inevitably, his partner complains that he should have let that last ball go by—especially if the poacher has swung at and misjudged the ball. But you keep on showering the poacher with praise and adding, "Too bad you missed that last one."

The poacher determines that he'll kill the next ball that comes over no matter where it goes. You return the serve, and he makes a mighty leap and smacks the ball into the net. His partner plain-tively cries, "I could have had that one!"

11. The best way to outwit the poacher is to make crosscourt shots way over and low. Nobody ever poached on Budge's back-hand return. But there is another method that is easier in the long run against the poacher. The lob.

Tournament players can run back and kill lobs all afternoon long. But weekend players do not smash lobs consistently and do not like running back. Thus a lob works much more devastat-ingly against average players.

Consider also the temperament of a poacher: By nature, he is restless, endowed with a killer instinct, determined to win points by power rather than by retrieving, quick rather than phlegmatic, a gambler at heart instead of a careful bookkeeper. He wants to keep hitting the ball continually and crowds the net for action.

FIGURE 56

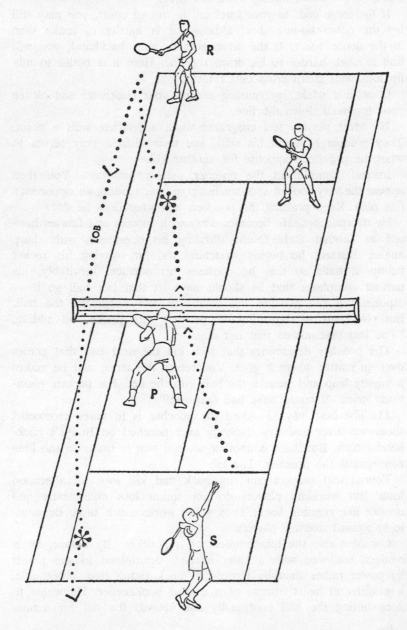

R

S

P

LOB

What is the one situation he hates most?

To stand around waiting for a ball to come to him.

So you lob over his head.

You want to break up his habit of crowding the net and thus making successful poaches. Tournament players can play back from the net and then rush in to cut off a shot, but nontournament players usually stand right on top of the net because that is the only way they can volley—by slamming down on the ball. They don't know or haven't bothered to learn how to volley from farther back.

So when you lob over his head, the poacher will either have to let those balls go, or if he is eager to hit some balls himself, he will pull back from the net. Great. Standing farther back from the net, 1. he can't volley half as well, and 2. he can't make the angles as he could up close.

So now you resume driving back your return of service. Soon the poacher will feel unhappy at staying back and will drift up to crowd the net again. So you resume lobbing. The advantage lies entirely with you, since he either has to hang back or crowd the net, and you can modify your shots accordingly.

If the poacher is the stronger of your opponents, you should lob back to the weaker opponent rather than over the poacher's head. This follows the accepted practice of directing as many shots to the weaker partner as possible, because he is more likely to miss. Also, the poacher becomes impatient to join in the rallies and will extend himself too far into his partner's territory.

If your two opponents are equal: When receiving service in the deuce court, lob over the poacher's head down his alley on his backhand side. This makes a hard shot for his partner to return offensively. See Figure 56.

This also affords you and your partner a great chance to storm the net yourselves, as shown in Figure 57 for the following shot. Naturally, the server won't always return the ball to the receiver who has stormed the net. But Figure 57 does show how two men up hold a great advantage over an opposing team of one man up and one back. The fact that the poacher plays close to the net (he has moved over when his partner went for the ball over the former's head) makes it easier for the opposing team to angle the ball between the server and the poacher.

When receiving service in the ad court, the same tactics won't work as well, for the poacher's partner will take the ball on his

FIGURE 57

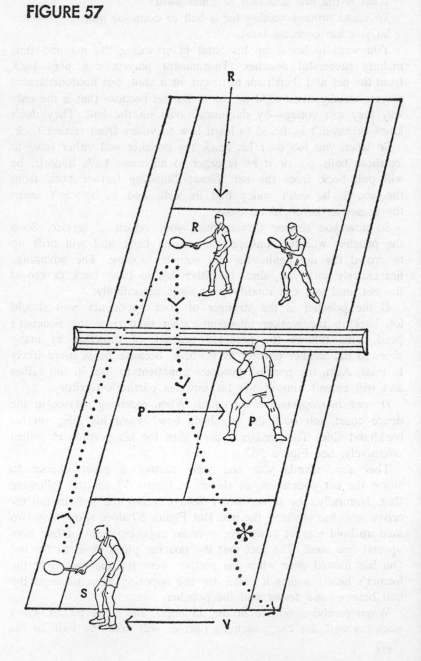

forehand side where he can drive or smash more easily. Therefore, you should lob back to the poacher's partner on his backhand side.

However, if the poacher's partner is slow-footed or heavy-set and does not like running, lob over the poacher's head on both sides. The partner will soon tire of chasing after balls and will suggest to the poacher to draw back and take his own lobs. Even if the poacher rejects this advice, it will create friction between the partners because the backcourt player will feel he is carrying an unfair share of the burden.

Unscrupulous players are known to capitalize on this situation by sympathizing with the backcourt player in whispered asides. "Too bad your partner at the net doesn't take his own lobs," says Machiavelli, Jr. "You shouldn't have to run so much on a hot day."

The backcourt player feels self-pity that his partner is taking advantage of his good nature and grumbles at the injustice. In turn, the poacher feels he should cover the net like a circus tent and his partner should take all lobs—regardless of how far his partner has to chase for them.

If the poacher is weaker than his partner: Many times the stronger partner will command his partner to stay close to the net and only take balls within his reach. That way, the poacher figures, the weaker partner can't miss too many balls. You should lob over the poacher's head because:

1. You will be playing to the weaker partner.
2. You will be forcing him back from the net.
3. You will be tempting him to take balls he shouldn't.
4. The backcourt player will have to run a great deal more.

What if the poacher never draws back from the net?

Keep lobbing, but mix up drives so the server can't start running over for a lob. Also, the poacher won't be sure when he should try to go back for a lob.

Keep relaxed. An important factor in outwitting a poacher is to keep relaxed. If an eight-year-old child were the net man, you would return service much better because you would hit without tension. But the moment an aggressive net man starts poaching, the normal reaction is to tense up and poke at the serve instead of making your usual returns with more follow through and c-a-r-r-y-i-n-g the ball on your racket.

Take a couple of deep breaths, and concentrate on the ball. Decide whether you will lob or drive. Then watch the ball.

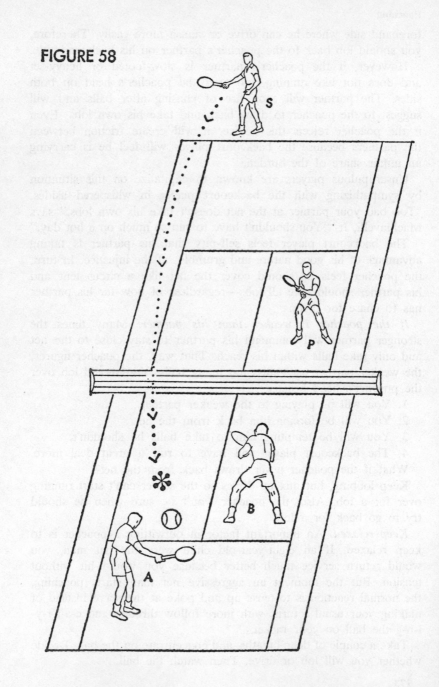

FIGURE 58

FIGURE 59

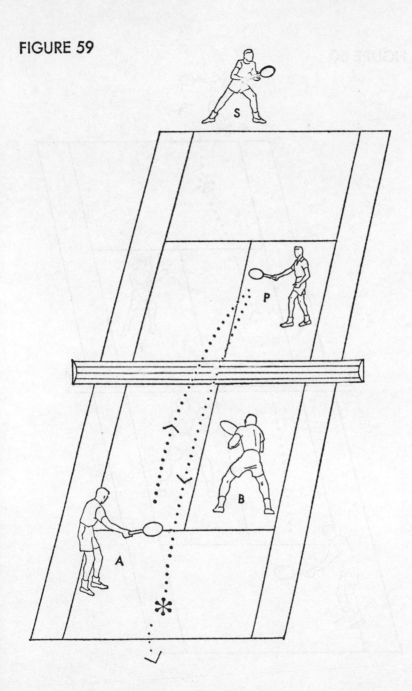

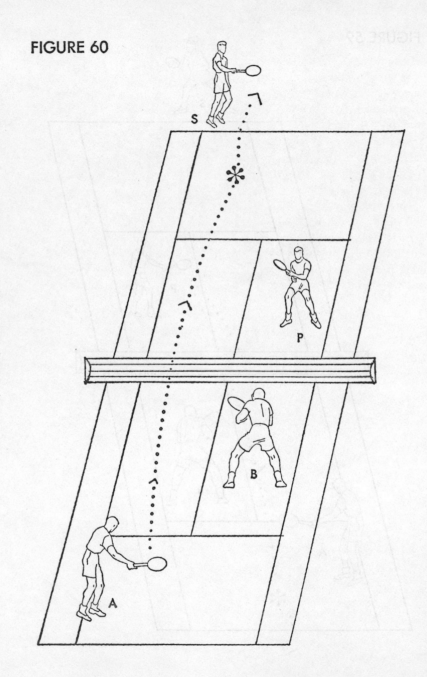

FIGURE 60

Practice your lobs or mixing up lobs and drives by taking on weaker players. Try lobbing close to the alley lines and to returning service way over into the server's court, far out of reach of a poacher.

When you practice, you thus make more automatic your responses when facing a poacher. By foiling the poacher, you break up the other team's morale, since all players dislike a poacher as a partner who fails to bring off poaches.

Should you try to outguess a poacher on an approach shot to the net? Figure 58 illustrates the situation when player A, with partner B already at the net, has a short ball on his forehand. Should he try to pass the poacher, P? Or should he drive to the poacher's partner, S?

Answer: If A tries to pass P at the net, P usually will move in and volley down the middle for the point, as shown in Figure 59.

Instead, A should drive deep to S and thus isolate P at the net, as shown in Figure 60. Then, with both A and B up at the net, the odds heavily favor their winning the point.

Tactics in Doubles

Position at net. When your partner is serving, you should stand three feet inside the singles alley line and about halfway between the net and the service line. You stand off to one side at first so that the serve won't hit you and to give the server plenty of your opponent's court to aim for.

Then if your opponent returns to your partner, you move to the center of your court, as shown in Figure 61. The symbol V stands for volleyer, and the dotted lines indicate where he moves after the receiver returns the serve. The shaded area indicates the territory he can cover.

Many servers will instruct their partners to "stand real close to the net and then you can't miss the ball." This is true because you'll never get a ball to miss—or to hit.

Look at Figure 62. The symbol V designates the volleyer who "stands real close to the net." See how little of the shaded area of the court he can cover—about 13 percent. This is an unlucky number for him, because it means that his principal exercise will be bending over to retrieve the balls for his partner. He might as well rent a rocking chair and relax watching the balls go by.

Actually, the server is saying, "Let me hog the court." He has no right to do this. Naturally, you want to win the match but you also want to contribute your efforts to that end, otherwise, it will be like pairing with Rod Laver against two 10-year-olds—a hollow victory.

FIGURE 61

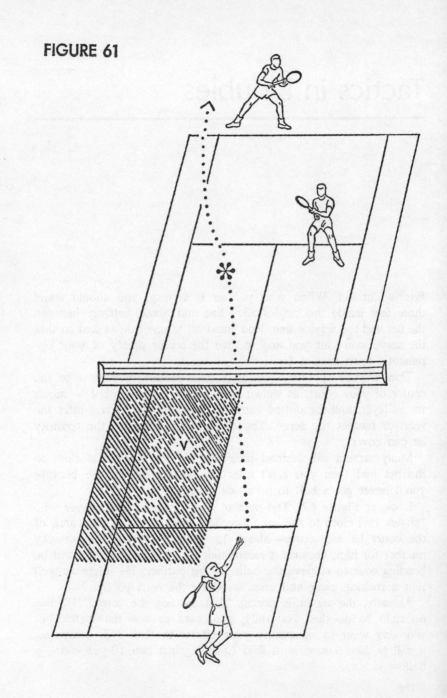

It is true that if you are playing in a tournament with a far better player, he should take a greater percentage of the shots, if possible. Note the phrase, "if possible."

There is a law of diminishing returns for partners trying to hog the court that works as inexorably as the law of gravity. Thousands of matches have been lost by overzealous partners chasing madly all over the court crying, "Mine—I'll take it!" They take that particular ball all right but leave the rest of the court wide open. Worst of all, they confuse the inferior player until he doesn't know which, if any, balls he should take.

If you play "real close" to the net constantly, you will find yourself lost if you have to play farther back. You will thus be unable to hold up your end in matches where you play with an equal or an inferior partner, or in singles when you have to rush the net.

Hence when your partner directs you to "play real close," tell him you are playing just for the fun of it—not to win, that you are just out for the exercise and want to hit some balls, too. "After all, it's just a game, isn't it?"

This statement of the traditional Anglo-Saxon attitude toward games usually undermines opposition, since it makes you appear a gentleman and the other a boorish clod. It helps also if you speak as though addressing a peasant unfamiliar with the traditions of the noble sport.

Rushing net on service. When you serve, you should rush up to join your partner at the net. Most points in doubles are won at the net, and the team that dominates the net usually wins.

However, there are exceptions. When you follow your serve to the net, you must get up inside the service line to volley. If you are slow-moving and can't run up quickly enough, your opponents will be hitting balls at your feet.

Then you might stay back, wait until your opponent returns the serve, and then on hitting his return, hustle to the net. That way you can concentrate more on getting a good first serve in and forcing a weaker return.

If you find yourself tiring from running up every time, stay back once in a while. Then you can catch your breath and perhaps throw your opponents off balance by not knowing whether to hit deep or short.

If you can't volley, stay back against strong opponents. But go

FIGURE 62

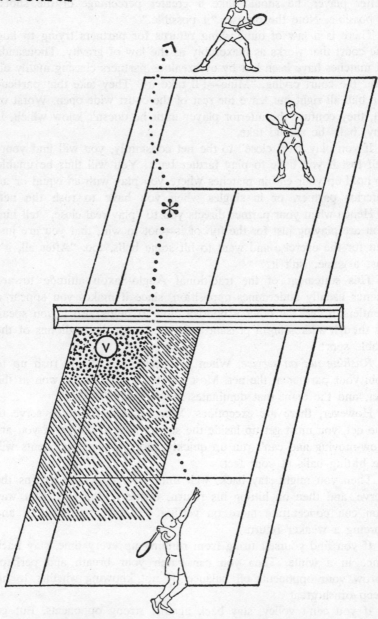

up to practice your volley against weaker teams, because to move up in class, you must be able to volley.

If your partner hangs right over the net and your opponents keep lobbing over his head, it does you no good to rush in on your serve. You should stay back until you can force a weak return. Suggest to your partner that if he stands back a bit more from the net he will be able to hit more balls instead of watching you all the time, and that it will make it tougher on your opponents to win points. Most of all, do not show any displeasure over having to cover lobs over your partner's head, or your sadistic opponents will then unleash a lobbing attack.

If your partner can't get most of the lobs over his head, you should advance only to the service line. From there you can run back for lobs over your partner's head or can move in closer to volley your opponents' drives.

Another exception to running in on your service is whether you can cover the lobs over your own head. If you cannot handle them satisfactorily, you should stay back on your serve. Go up only on weak or short returns. Naturally, to improve your game you should learn to improve your smashing. See the chapter on the smash.

First volley. The hardest volley to make is the first one. You are running up, not sure which way the ball is going, and you may have to break to either side or turn around and run back.

Thus you should give yourself as much margin of safety on your first volley as possible. That means hitting it deep, away from your opponent at the net (receiver's partner) and not trying for a sharp angle. If you serve to the deuce court, try to volley through the middle to your receiver's backhand. When you serve to the ad court, make your first volley deep to the receiver's backhand. That pushes him back to the corner, where it's hard for him to make an offensive shot.

Once you and your partner are entrenched at the net, the odds greatly favor your side.

Grand delusion. You serve, and you rush the net. The ball comes floating up to you and you try to bat it down the throat of the receiver's partner, who is standing a couple of feet inside the service line. You figure that once you blast the ball past him, you win the point outright.

Once in a great while (about one out of nine times) you do blast the ball past him. But once out of nine rates a mere 11 percent.

This shot is a grand delusion because it looks much easier than it really is. Consider the following objections:

1. You can make the shot eight out of nine times if you are within three feet of the net. But most of the time on your first volley you will be from fifteen to eighteen feet from the net. The result is that you will tend to hit downward on the ball far too much. Check the shots you miss, and you'll find that mostly you are hitting them into the net.

2. You will be tempted to look just once more at the receiver's partner before you hit the ball. That's just enough to take your eye off the ball and misjudge it a fatal fraction.

3. You will be discarding a highly favorable percentage in your favor for a highly risky shot. It's like passing up an ocean voyage aboard a majestic ocean liner to cross in a launch.

4. In self-defense, the receiver's partner may block back the ball for a winner between you and your partner.

5. The pros play the percentages by nearly always making that first volley away from the receiver's partner.

6. Don Budge, one of the all-time greats, would invariably hit his first volley deep to the receiver's court. He has told me that he sees little advantage in risking blasting the ball at the receiver's partner when he can make sure of the point by volleying deep to the receiver.

The exception in this instance is when the receiver's partner keeps moving toward the middle on your first volley. Then, "to keep him honest," you may volley where he left—in his alley. Or if the receiver's partner is decidedly inferior to the receiver, you may chance this shot more often.

Serving in doubles. The server holds a great advantage in doubles, as you can see by reading the scores of doubles matches. The scores of even the tournament winners triumphing over mediocre teams are 6–4, 7–5, or even 9–7, while the singles winner crushes his ordinary opponents by 6–2, 6–3, 6–1.

Let's face it: The receiver finds it much harder to hit the ball past the server's partner at the net in doubles. When the receiver misses, the next time he tries even harder to play the ball out of the server's partner's reach by hitting too far outside or too close to the net.

To capitalize on this advantage, you should make it harder for

FIGURE 63

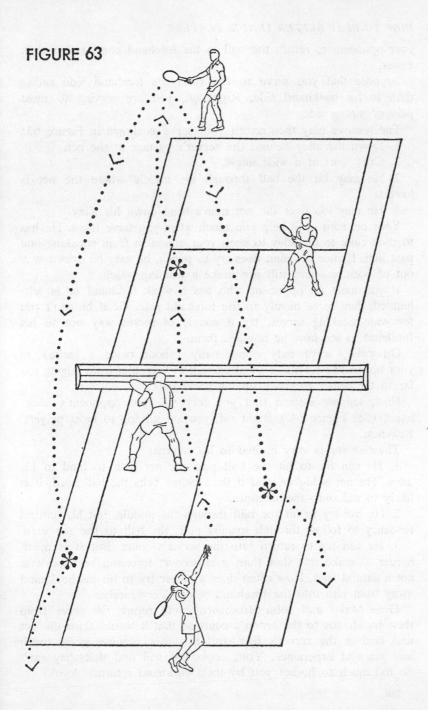

your opponent to return the ball in the forehand court rather than easier.

Suppose that you serve to the receiver's forehand side rather than to his backhand side. Right off, you are serving to most players' strong side.

The receiver may then return your serve as shown in Figure 63:

1. Down the alley behind the server's partner at the net.

2. Crosscourt at a wide angle.

3. He may hit the ball through the middle where the net is lowest.

4. He may lob over the net man's head down his alley.

Your net man can't help you much when you serve there. He has to stick close to his alley to keep your opponent from sneaking one past him. If your net man does try to poach, he may be drawn way out of position—and still not make a winning poach.

If you meet an opponent who has a weak forehand or is left-handed, then serve mostly to the forehand side. Or if he can't run for wide-breaking serves, try a couple of serves way out to his forehand to see how he handles them.

Otherwise, serve only occasionally (about twice a game) to your opponent's forehand—just enough to keep him from edging too far to the center to cover up his backhand.

Now, suppose instead that you serve to your opponent's backhand. (See Figure 64.) Right off, you are serving to most players' weakness.

The receiver is very limited in his returns:

1. He can try to hit the ball past the net man to land in his alley. The net is higher, and if the receiver belts the ball hard, it is likely to sail onto the sidelines.

2. He can try to hit the ball through the middle, but his natural tendency to follow through usually pulls the ball to the net man.

3. He can try to return into the server's court. But it is much harder to make this shot than a crosscourt forehand because it is not a natural shot. How often does a player try to hit his backhand away from him into the forehand court? Very rarely.

Gene Mako and John Bromwich could return the serve from their backhands to the server's court so that it would skim the net and land at the server's feet. But this shot requires great touch and years of experience. Your opponents will find that they can't do too much to bother you by their backhand returns.

FIGURE 64

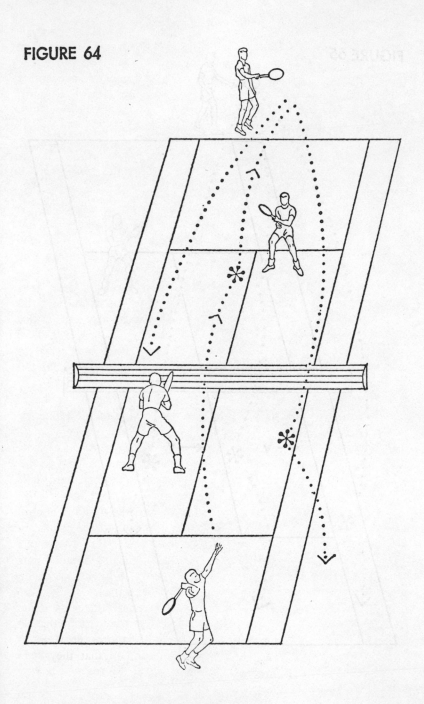

FIGURE 65

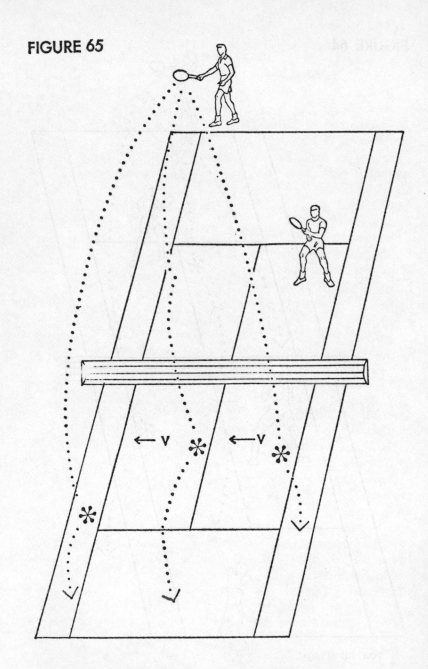

4. He can try to lob over the net man's head. This could be your opponent's best return if he can lob to your net man's backhand side, for if your net man can't get it, you have to run over to take it on your backhand.

However, if your opponent often lobs his backhand return, your net man should play back farther from the net. Then if your opponent hits a weak return through the middle, your net man should charge in on it.

Shifting the defense. In football, when the offense takes the ball around an end, the defense shifts over to that side to break it up. Likewise, in doubles, when you or your partner hit a ball into your opponent's alley, you two should shift over to cover the vulnerable area.

This vulnerable area extends from the alley on the same side in which the ball lands to half the opposite court. If a ball is hit into the other's forehand alley, you need not worry about the ball being hit way crosscourt into your own forehand alley. Any ball hit hard in that direction would sail out by miles, and any floater going that way would be easy for you to cut in on and put away.

Figure 65 illustrates that when the ball is hit to an opponent's forehand alley, you and your partner should shift to that side. The partner nearer the forehand alley should shift about two feet over from the middle of his side of the court to cover the down-the-line shot. The other partner should also shift in that direction to cover the middle, because he doesn't have to worry about covering his own alley.

This shifting puts the odds in your favor, since the team at net usually wins most points from a team backcourt.

If you find that when you are backcourt, the opposing team at the net does not shift, then hit for the opening. If your opponent doesn't shift to cover his alley, fire the ball there. If your other opponent stays right in the middle of his side of the court instead of shifting over, then drive through the wide opening between your opponents.

When your team hits a ball to the opponents' backhand alley, you shift in that direction, as shown in Figure 66.

This shifting back and forth keeps you on the balls of your feet, and your movements tend to take your opponent's eye off the ball he is trying to hit.

If you hit a ball to the center of your opponents' court, you

FIGURE 66

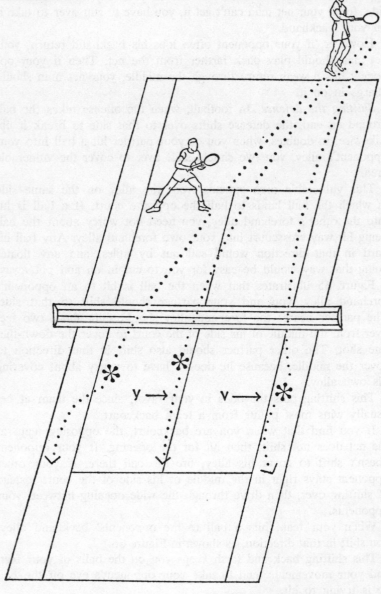

and your partner should draw a little closer to the middle, since their obvious shot is through the middle. If your opponent tries to hit down the alley, he will have to soften his shot to keep it in, and then you can move forward in plenty of time.

Hitting down the alley. You've probably faced lots of players in doubles who keep trying to pass the net man down his alley.

They think there's an opening down the alley and figure that once the ball passes the net man, it's gone. But if they hit through the middle and the net man misses it, the server can still get to it.

This sounds like a fine theory, like all the theories about beating the races or Las Vegas until you consider the odds.

First, the net is six inches higher at the end than in the middle. Second, there is very little margin for safety. The alley is 4½ feet wide, and the net man should be able to cover all but two feet by merely extending his racket. If he takes a step, he can cover all the alley.

There is a width of two feet to shoot for on the forehand court. If the receiver hits a little too soon, he pulls the ball right to the net man. If he hits a little too late, he hits outside.

Another factor is that if you start banging balls down the alley, the net man will start to hang over to cover his alley—and creep closer to the net besides. Then what do you have to shoot for?

You should return the serve down the alley only if:

1. The net man is always trying to poach on balls hit through the middle. One or two passing shots down his alley and he'll soon decide to stay in his own territory.

2. The serve goes wide to your forehand in the forehand court, and the net man does not shift over to cover his alley. Then you've got a wide opening to shoot for.

Remember that if you return the serve through the middle, it is hard for your opponent to make much of an angle. The net is lower there, and you can make your return much tougher to handle, because it will come lower to the volleyer. And it's always tougher to bend down and volley upward than it is to take a ball high and volley down on it.

Look at Figure 67 to see what happens when a service return goes to the net man. See how the net man can easily angle it between the receiver and his partner.

All that applies about returning serve in the forehand court down the alley goes double for returning in the backhand court. From there it is harder to hit a forehand drive slightly crosscourt down the alley, and it is even harder to hit a backhand down the line. This plus the fact that you are hitting to the net man's forehand volley, which is usually better than his backhand volley, which he uses in the other alley.

Let the uninformed player try all afternoon to return serve down the alley past the net man. Let him pile up a flock of errors. But you be smart and play the percentage returns through the middle and crosscourt.

Return of serve. While we're at it, let's consider how you can improve your own return of serve. Some experts believe that returning serve is the No. 1 shot in doubles—more than the serve itself. Undoubtedly top-flight doubles players like George Lott, John Bromwich, Gene Mako, and Don Budge returned serve far more consistently and accurately than usual.

Bill Crosby and Bobby Perez were ranked No. 2 in 1955, although they did not even play in the National Doubles tournament. Dozens of other teams that year served, volleyed, and drove better, but none could compare with their phenomenal return of serve. They could go a whole set and miss only two returns of serve apiece.

The most important feature about returning serve is to get the ball back over the net to give your opponent a chance to make an error. About 40 percent of winning returns of serve are due to the server's team erring. So forget about trying to make winners off your returns every time.

Where should you stand? You should stand as close as you can. The closer you are to the net, the less chance of being pulled way out of court by a wide-breaking serve. Also, it is easier for you to make an angle and harder for the net man to anticipate your return. And if the server rushes in, he has less time to reach the net.

Standing in closer takes practice, so try it first against weaker players. Then use it to discomfit your regular opponents.

Try standing on the baseline or a foot inside. Don Budge used to stand way in so that if a server hit a wide-angle American twist, Don would take it on the rising bounce before it could break and pull him way out of court.

Shorten your backswing. Unless the server stays back, there is no reason for taking a big backswing to blast the ball. The harder you

FIGURE 67

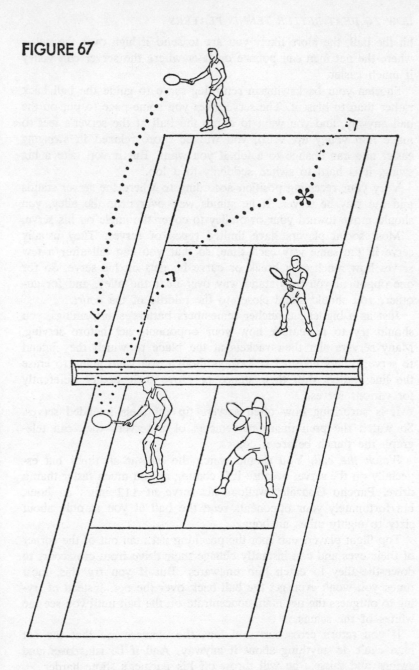

hit the ball, the more likely you are to send it high over the net—where the net man can pounce on it or where the server can volley it much easier.

Shorten your backswing in returning serve to guide the ball back rather than to blast it. The serve gives you some pace to put on the ball anyway, and you want to dump the ball at the server's feet to make him volley up. Also, you will be more relaxed in swinging easier and can change to a lob if you want. But if you take a big swing, it is hard to switch suddenly to a lob.

Vary your receiving position according to where the server stands and the way he serves. If he stands way over near the alley, you should move toward your own alley to cover the angle on his serve.

Most social players have limited types of serves. They usually serve in the same way each time, so that you can tell after a few serves how much of a break or curve he gets on his serve. So for one opponent you may stand way over near the alley, and for another, you should stand closer to the middle of the court.

Just as a big-league pitcher remembers batters' shortcomings, you should try to remember how your opponents act before serving. Many servers aim their rackets at the place to which they intend to serve; others take a last look as though you were going to erase the line; others shift their stance or move their bodies differently for various serves.

It is surprising how often servers tip off their intended serves. So watch the preliminary movements of a server—they can telegraph the punch before it comes.

Watch the ball. You should watch the ball at all times but especially on the serve, because it is coming at you much faster than a drive. Pancho Gonzales wallops his serve at 112 miles an hour, but fortunately your opponents send the ball at you at only about sixty to eighty miles an hour.

Top-flight players can spot the poaching net man out of the corner of their eyes and can instantly change their drive from crosscourt to down-the-alley to catch him unawares. But if you try this, most times you won't even get the ball back over the net. Instead of trying to outguess the net man, concentrate on the ball until you see the whites of the seams.

If you return crosscourt and low, the chances are that the net man can't do anything about it anyway. And if he runs over and swings and misses, he will throw off his partner's shot.

Height over the net. Tournament players can skim the ball a few inches over the net, but they practice so much more than you do that naturally they can play all their shots much closer to the net and the lines.

Aim your returns about a foot over the net. That gives you plenty of margin of safety, and your opponent still can't volley it too decisively. And if he volleys up and short, come in to drive for the opening.

You want to keep those returns going back steadily so that your opponent has to earn the points he wins. And if he's average, he'll even miss your easy shots once in a while.

The lob. Variety of attack is the spice in the cake of victory. If you keep pounding your opponent's backhand on every shot, he will eventually improve his returns. If you keep hitting your returns short at the server's feet every time he rushes in, he will start handling them better because of all the practice you're giving him. Also, because he knows exactly what type of shot you're going to give him, he will prepare better.

So you should mix up your returns. Bear in mind the experiment wherein a mouse is conditioned to push one button to earn some cheese; if he pushes another button, he gets a shock. When the buttons are changed, the poor mouse doesn't know when he pushes one whether he will get cheese or a shock. The uncertainty sends him into a mouse brand of nervous breakdown.

You should try to perform the same process with the server. Throw up a lob occasionally instead of driving all the time. See the chapter on the lob for the mechanics of lobbing.

It is true that top-flight players rarely lob in doubles because they all kill most lobs and can run faster than a child to the nearest candy store. But the weekend player can't smash as hard, nor as consistently, nor race as fast, nor keep chasing all afternoon for lobs.

His overhead is erratic, and the more he chases back and tires, the more erratic he becomes—until finally he merely tries to return your lob instead of killing it.

Does this mean you should spend a dull afternoon pushing up lobs instead of indulging yourself by swatting the ball? Not at all. In fact, when you force your opponents to hang back from the net in fear of being lobbed over, you can unleash even more drives at their feet.

The best place to lob when returning serve is from the forehand court. Lob down the line to the net man's backhand. See Figure 68.

If the net man crowds the net, he won't be able to run back in time to get the lob. Then the server will have to stop in coming up, turn, and chase back for the lob. The net man will probably cross to the other side of the court as indicated in Figure 68.

If you make a good lob, the server will have to take it on his backhand and won't be able to make a forcing shot. Once you see that you've made a good lob, run up to the net to volley the server's return.

Now the odds shift to your side, because a team with two men at the net dominates a team with one man up and one man back. If you can, volley between your two opponents. If not, volley deep to keep the pressure on your opponent backcourt.

Unless he is a young eager beaver, the server will get tired of running back for your lobs. He will probably complain to his net man to play back farther to cover his own lobs.

This is a hopeful sign for you, because it may be the first indication of friction that will drive a wedge between your opponents. If the net man pulls back, he will leave the center wide open, since nobody can poach as well from this new position. Also, because the net man is most likely not used to volleying from that far back, he won't volley as well. You should then drive through the middle where the net is lowest, and you can keep the ball lower with increased safety.

If the net man remains back, lob occasionally to the server. Then the server will become undecided whether to stay back and wait for your lob or to charge in. But even when he does run up, he will tend to advance slower and won't get as close to the net as he used to—and he will have to volley up more.

Keep an eye on the net man, because he won't feel comfortable playing way back. He'll start edging to crowd the net as before, and then you can lob over him.

In a while, the server will become as frustrated as the mouse not knowing which button to push to get food. He may even decide to stay back all the time on his serve—which is just what you want, because then you can drive deep but not too hard to give yourself time to follow your return to the net.

When you do lob, it is usually better to decide ahead of time whether the server stays back or not. The same with trying to pass

FIGURE 68

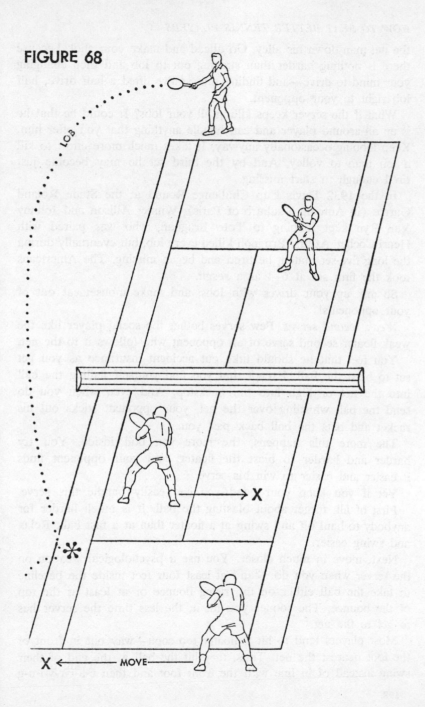

the net man down his alley. Go ahead and make your shot, because there is nothing harder than starting out to lob and then changing your mind to drive—and finding that you've lifted a half drive, half lob right to your opponent.

What if the server keeps killing all your lobs? It could be that he is an all-around player and can handle anything that you offer him. Keep lobbing occasionally anyway. It takes much more effort to kill a lob than to volley. And by the third set he may become just tired enough to start missing.

In the 1932 Davis Cup Challenge Round at the Stade Roland Garros (in Auteuil, a suburb of Paris), Wilmer Allison and Johnny Van Ryn kept lobbing to Toto Brugnon, who was paired with Henri Cochet. At first Brugnon killed every lob, but eventually during the long five-set match, he tired and began missing. The Americans took the fifth set at 6–4 as a result.

So mix up your drives with lobs, and make mousemeat out of your opponents!

Weak second serves. Few serves bother the social player like the weak floater second serve of an opponent who follows it to the net.

You feel that he should take out accident insurance as you get set to blast the ball. Except that you find yourself flailing the ball into the net or high into the backstop. And even when you do send the ball whistling over the net, your opponent sticks out his racket and bats the ball back past you.

The more this happens, the more you boil inside. You try harder and harder to blast the floater, and your opponent finds it easier and easier to win his serve.

Yet if you keep your head you can easily handle this serve.

First of all, forget about blasting the ball. It is much harder for anybody to haul off and swing at a floater than at a fast ball. Relax and swing easier.

Next, move in much closer. You use a psychological weapon on the server when you do. Stand at least four feet inside the baseline to take the ball either on the rising bounce or at least at the top of the bounce. The sooner you hit it, the less time the server has to get to the net.

Most players tend to hit a floater too soon—way out in front of the foot nearest the net. Thus, they hit the ball at the end of their swing instead of in line with the front foot and then c-a-r-r-y-i-n-g the ball on the racket. See the chapter on the backhand about making sure you c-a-r-r-y the ball on your racket.

Since the serve floats to you, you can get set easier for it and thus can play it closer to the net than returning a hard first serve. Try to hit the ball at the server's feet where he has to volley up defensively so that you or your partner can come in and pounce on his high return.

Lob the floater back once in a while. The server is so used to everybody trying to blast his serve that your mixing your returns can confuse him.

If the server stays back, drive deep to force him way back. This gives you more time to rush the net and makes it harder for him to deceive you about his type of return.

Singles

Singles differs so greatly from doubles that they often seem like two different kinds of sport. You are the captain of the ship in singles; often in doubles, when paired with a much better player, you are merely a deckhand. You must rush the net in doubles, while on clay you can often win in singles without going to the net once.

In singles, everything you do directly affects your opponent while in doubles, you or your partner may be affecting each other far more than your opponents. In doubles, you can get away with a weak backhand, but any weakness in singles immediately exposes you to a withering cannonade from your opponent.

But singles affords a challenge in singlehandedly planning and executing the destruction of your opponent. You can figure out ways and means to overcome your opponent with no second guessers hampering you, as in doubles.

There are all kinds of ways in which you can improve your singles without training rigorously or developing superstrokes. In science, knowing what to ask in a problem is half the answer. In tennis, knowing what and how to play is half the victory.

As said previously, before you even pick up a racket, you are geared to play a definite type of tennis. This depends on your physique, your conditioning, the type of court, and your temperament. However, whether you're a confirmed baseliner or an eager

FIGURE 69

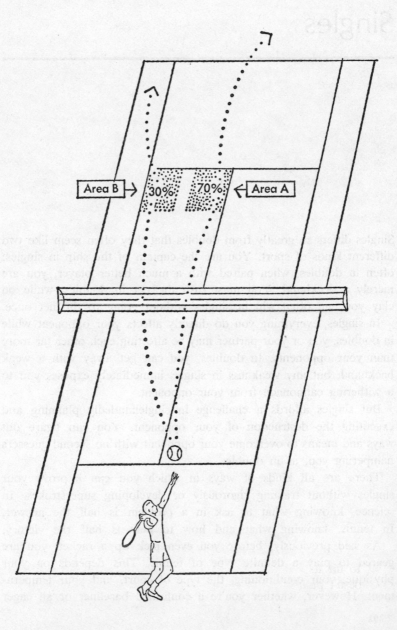

Area B → 30% 70% ← Area A

net rusher, you should still make use of certain principles that will enhance your game.

Let's consider the serve. You may have read the chapter on the serve, but let's repeat again: You should get 70 percent of your first serves in. Deep, too. You will then automatically improve your ability to wage tennis warfare.

You should work to place your serves. Assuming that you are not rushing the net, you should direct 70 percent of your first serves into the deuce court to your opponent's backhand, as shown in Figure 69, into area A. Thirty percent should go to area B. However, if your opponent displays a devastating forehand, cut down your serves to area B to only 10 percent.

You should direct most of your serves to your opponent's backhand, since it's usually weaker than his forehand. If it is stronger or if he can't or doesn't like to run, serve wide to his forehand more often.

You should direct your second serves most of the time to his backhand. You cut down on his angles and make it easier to defend against his return. Once in a great while, you should serve a second serve wide to his forehand as a surprise. The pros keep pounding at an opponent's weakness, and so should you.

In serving to the ad court while remaining on the baseline, you will frequently find that your opponent is standing way over to cover up his backhand. Many players feel tempted to move really close to the center service mark and blast most of their serves down the line to his forehand, area B as shown in Figure 70. They feel they can then sneak one past their opponents who are crowding way over on one side.

This is a great idea, but it brings up some questions:

1. Can you serve consistently into area B? If you merely serve to the middle of the court, your opponent can crack his forehand easily to your backhand. Or if you never get your first serve in, you are throwing it away.

2. How does your opponent return your serves? Does he step into them with the greatest of ease, or does he mis-hit or poke at them? Remember, your serve to his forehand in the ad court never breaks as wide as in the deuce court, so you can't force him to run as far to hit it.

3. Doesn't pulling your opponent toward the middle of the court make it easier for him to handle your return? When you serve wide

FIGURE 70

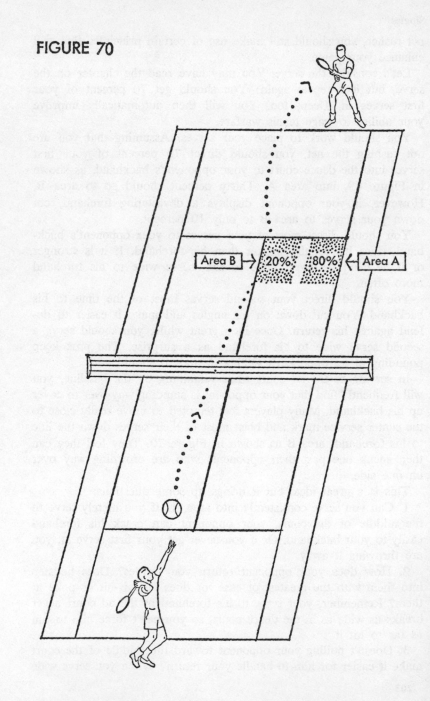

Area B → 20% | 80% ← Area A

to an opponent in the deuce court, you can force him so far out of court that he can't get back in time to handle your return.

Therefore, unless your opponent demonstrates a weakness in running to hit his forehand, you should quit serving to his stronger side. Serve mostly to the area shown as area A in Figure 70 to try to force him to run around his backhand, and thus push him way out of court.

See Figures 71 and 72 for the trap that receiver falls into when he runs way around his backhand. Notice how his return in Figure 72 leaves the whole court wide open.

You should serve nearly all your second serves to the backhand in the ad court. Serve them deep, and you'll keep your opponent back on the baseline, where it's harder to make winning returns.

Should you rush the net on your serve?

You can learn a lot by watching the pros and by trying to model your game after them except when seeing them serve and rush in. They are conditioned for this and can volley and smash decisively. But the weekend player usually finds that it takes too much effort to rush in all the time. Then, too, playing on a slow surface like clay dictates much less net rushing, since you can't volley as forcefully as on cement.

Actually, because the pro rallies are so short, you will see more stratagems useful for the weekend player by watching a top-flight women's match. The women will run each other around, mix up their shots, rush the net, fade back for lobs, pull off soft drop shots, and angle their smashes so that you will see a great variety of strokes. Compare that with a typical men's pro match of serve and volley, which has become so dull that all sorts of variations on limiting the serve are being suggested.

Meanwhile, back to your own game: Certainly, an occasional foray to the net may surprise and disturb your opponent and prevent him from grooving his returns.

But you should ask yourself:

1. Are you running in fast enough to volley in front of the service line? If you aren't, you'll be making weak volleys, and the percentages will mount against you.

2. How does your charging in affect your opponent? Some opponents become upset at seeing you storming in and try to blast you off the court. If you can duck fast enough, they'll be knocking the fences down with their swings. Other opponents put up

FIGURE 71

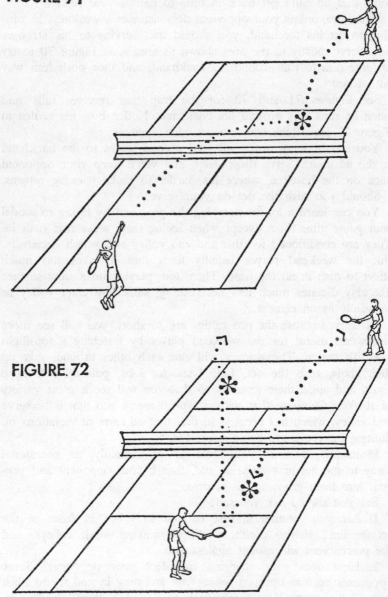

FIGURE. 72

weak lobs. Still others hit better because they have targets to aim for—the openings past you.

3. Is your opponent improving on his returns? If he is, forget the constant running in. If you stay back at times, you may disconcert him so he doesn't know whether to hit deep or short returns.

4. Is the added effort worth the extra points? If you are young and can run all day, keep going in. If you play only twice a week and are older, you may not have much left for the final set. Bill Tilden was a genius at deciding how much energy to save, and nowadays Pancho Gonzales measures out his energy as though with a computer. Pancho never takes one extra step he doesn't have to and kills lobs with just enough power to win the point. Similarly, you want to save some strength for the extra effort in the final set that will topple your opponent.

Return of serve:

1. Make every effort to hit back the serve. Over 25 percent of points are lost by the receiver simply not getting the ball back into play. No matter how badly you return the ball, you are still forcing your opponent to make a good shot to put it away. Since he's not a computer, he's likely to miss even a setup, and if he does, he may become so irritated that he will miss another setup, which gives you two free points.

2. If the server remains on the baseline, return high (a racket length) over the net and *deep*. The best defense is a deep return, and many times it is also the best offense. *Think deep.*

3. If the server rushes the net, hit the ball about a foot over it. Let the pros skim the ball over the net; you should allow yourself more margin of safety and give your opponent a chance to miss. If his serve puzzles you, aim to return it right at him. Since the ball won't be coming straight and true off your racket, your returns will vary and thus perplex your opponent.

4. As you improve your steadiness in returning serves, try to place them more accurately to the backhands of your opponents. When facing easy opponents, try to sharpen your accuracy.

5. Reread the chapter on the return of the serve to check on ways to improve your returns.

Tactics:

1. Work to become steadier. Eight out of ten points are lost because the player actually hit the ball with his racket but didn't get it back into court. Against erratic juniors and wild-slugging

adults, you need only keep the ball in play and your opponent will obligingly knock it out for you. Unfortunately, this alone will not suffice against most other opponents. But many matches are decided by one player simply outsteadying the other.

You should not pat the ball back, for this would chain you to the lower echelons of players. You should try to return the ball with a fair degree of speed and *deep*.

2. To move up in class, you must take the offensive. Keep your opponent so busy defending himself that he can't get set to unleash any thunderbolts or to figure out what would bother you.

A. The easiest way to put your opponent on the defensive is to make him run. Hit the ball from one corner to the other, and when he rushes the net, lob over his head to cause him to turn around and run back. You can usually spot the eventual winner of a match by noticing which player is doing less running.

B. Look for and pound his weakness. When warming up with him, notice what kinds of balls he likes and what kinds he dislikes. Does he crack low-bouncing balls and merely paw at high-bouncing ones? Does he favor the net or avoid it as you would a panhandler? How does he move? Easily and with no effort or awkwardly?

How does he move going toward the net? If he moves forward with reluctance, he probably hates to take the net. So feed him short shots to pull him up and then see how he handles lobs and passing shots. If he rushes in with delight, he enjoys playing net and does better there, so keep him back with deep shots.

How does he deal with soft floaters? Does he step right in to crack them with all his might to the corners? Or does he poke at them and swing hard only at fast drives? The answer will tell you whether to give him a change of pace by mixing floaters with fast balls.

Everybody has a favorite shot or two. Try to find out what his are: Crosscourt forehand, angled volley, backhand return of serve deep to your backhand. Some players never lob on their forehand, so edge in closer to the net when hitting to their forehand. Others lob off their backhands as though firing bull's-eyes from a rifle to the baseline.

Everybody, except the experts, hates to play some shots: High-bouncing balls on the backhand; low, short balls wide to the forehand; or high backhand volleys. Study your opponent, and notice his expression when he misses a shot: The more he scowls, the less he likes the shot.

C. Play according to your own temperament. To thine own self be true, and it follows that you will perform far better than accepting the advice of a player with an opposite temperament.

If you like to slug the ball, go ahead. A cautious player who beats you may suggest you play the same careful way he does because he has the soul of a computer. Disregard him, but you might try hitting medium-pace balls sometimes.

Similarly, if a net rusher type urges you to charge up all the time but you know your volley isn't half as sharp as your accurate backcourt drives, stay back. You could practice volleying against weaker opponents, but most likely you still will feel more at home roaming the baseline.

If you don't hit hard but can run a marathon runner into the ground, make like a rabbit. Chase after all the balls, but see if you can't return the ball at sharper angles so you won't just be pushing the ball back.

If you like to figure out your opponent's weaknesses and then feed him the ball he doesn't want, ignore the advice of a slugger to cut loose on every ball.

D. That shrewd oldster, Socrates, admonished, "Know thyself." Figure out your own strengths and weaknesses, which shots work for you and which don't, at least not yet. Many players possess delusions of grandeur about their strokes and keep trying a shot that comes off more rarely than a forty-to-one bet at the track.

For instance, some players keep trying to pass the net man down the alley regardless of their low percentage of successes. Granted that you can have an off day on any shot, you should keep track of your percentages, and when a shot doesn't work, try to determine why it doesn't. Is it because of poor execution or because it's a bad shot to try anyway?

E. In the heat of battle, you can't always tell why you are losing points. Many times a player comes in on a short ball, hits right to his opponent's forehand, and loses the point when the opponent belts the ball past him. The player will berate himself for volleying so poorly, when the truth was that his poor approach shot lost him the point.

Try to figure out why you lose points. Is it your own fault in the way you hit the ball, is it where you hit the ball, or is it your opponent's luck or skill?

You will improve your game if you thus try to correct your mistakes. Experts constantly check on what loses points for them, what brings them victories. They can tell you years later about certain shots that worked for them in a match because they are concentrating on what works and what doesn't.

Problem:

Your opponent forces you wide on your forehand, as shown in Figure 73. He then moves to the middle of his baseline to await your return. Where should you hit the ball—to his backhand or to his forehand?

Answer No. 1: Many players would return the ball to the opponent's backhand as shown in Figure 74. They think they should play to an opponent's weaker side at all times.

Answer No. 2: Figure 75 shows what a disaster this return brings, for now you will have to dash madly to your backhand side to cover the Deadly Diagonal. You are now running at the end of a pendulum, and even if you win the point, you will have used up a lot of energy. Moreover, if this sequence continues, you will wear yourself out in no time.

Consider how much better you will fare if you hit your forehand crosscourt, as shown in Figure 76.

Now you are forcing your opponent to run. If he hits to your backhand, you can start chasing him at the end of a pendulum.

Remember: *One good angle deserves another.* If you are forced wide on either side, your best return is to crosscourt right back in the hope of making a better angle.

Problem: Player A in Figure 77 runs a little around his backhand to take a ball on his stronger forehand. His opponent, B, is awaiting his return from the center of his baseline. Where should player A direct his shot?

1. To his opponent's forehand down the line?
2. At an angle to his opponent's backhand?

Answer: You would be amazed at the number of players who elect to hit down the line (shot No. 1) to opponent B's forehand. They seem to think that this shot will upset their opponents by thus playing to their strong point.

However, unless opponent B is sleeping standing up, see how he

FIGURE 73

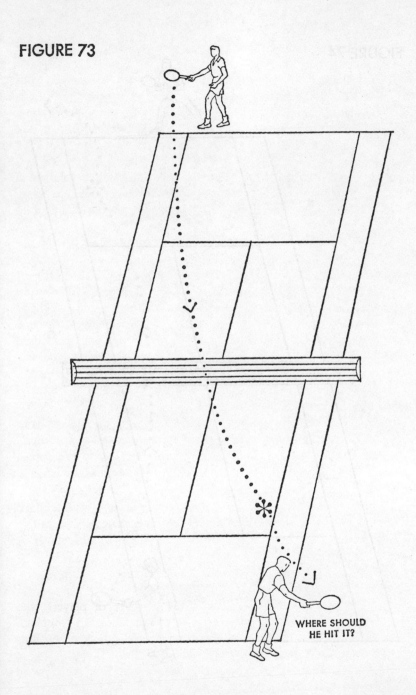

WHERE SHOULD
HE HIT IT?

FIGURE 74

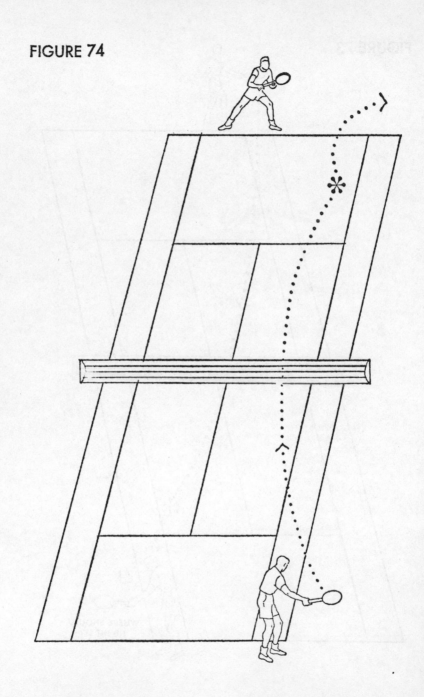

FIGURE 75

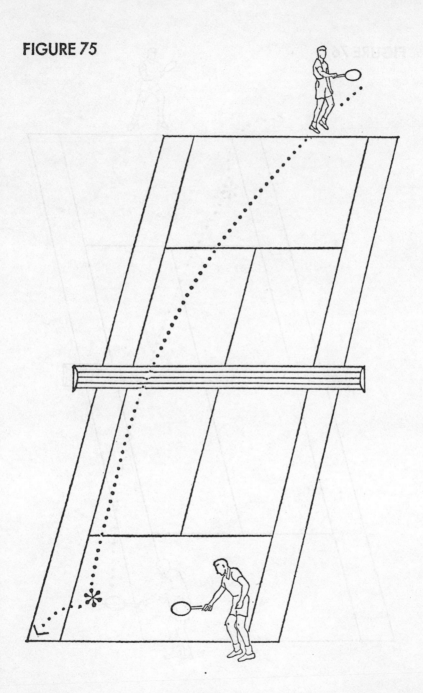

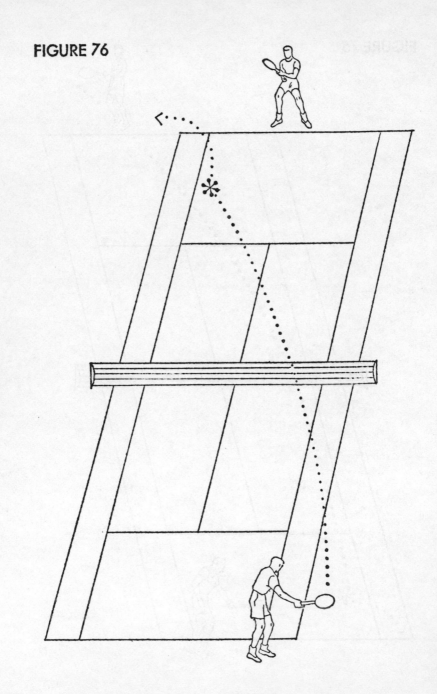

FIGURE 76

FIGURE 77

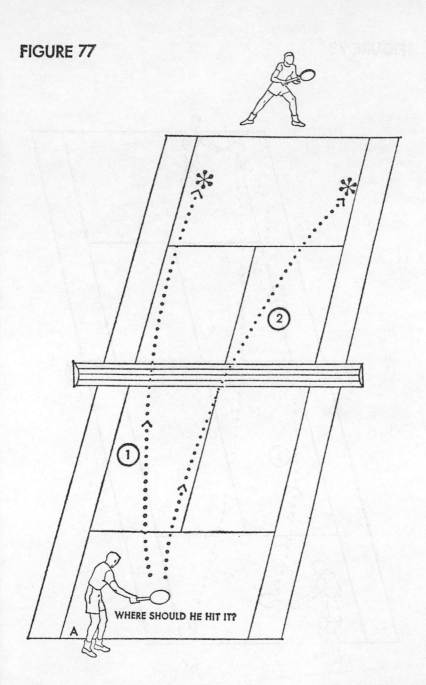

②

①

WHERE SHOULD HE HIT IT?

A

FIGURE 78

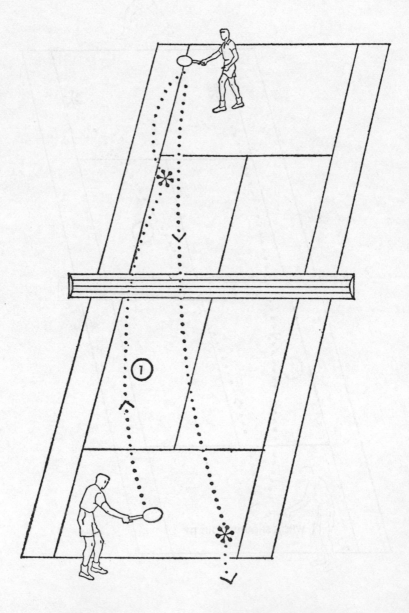

FIGURE 79

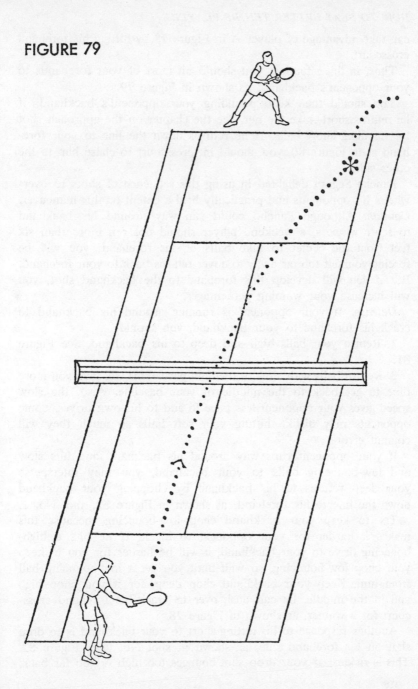

can take advantage of player A in Figure 78 by hitting his forehand crosscourt.

Thus, in this situation, you should hit most of your forehands to your opponent's backhand, as shown in Figure 79.

You should then keep pounding your opponent's backhand. If he returns short, take the net. See the chapter on the approach shot for handling short balls. If he returns down the line to your forehand as in Figure 80, you should hit crosscourt to chase him to the other side.

Pancho Segura delighted in using this sequence of shots to overwhelm his opponents and practically held a patent on this maneuver. *Caution:* Although Pancho could run way around his backhand to score winners, a weekend player should not run more than six feet from the center to take balls on his forehand; you will be forcing yourself too far away to cover returns back to your forehand. But if you will develop this forehand to the backhand shot, you will increase your winning percentages.

Defense. If your opponent is running around his backhand to crack his forehand to your backhand, you should:

1. Return your balls high and deep to his backhand. See Figure 81.

2. Return balls with slow or medium pace. This will give you more time to get back to the middle of your baseline. Also, the slow speed gives your opponent less pace to add to his own drives. Some opponents may dislike hitting your soft balls so much they will commit errors.

If your opponent runs way around his backhand and hits slow and low-bouncing balls to your backhand, you may intersperse your deep returns to his backhand by chopping your backhand down the line to his forehand, as shown in Figure 82, shot No. 1.

Try to keep your backhand chop low-bouncing, because this makes it harder for your opponent to hit it. If he hits a high-bouncing drive to your backhand, it will be harder for you to keep your chop low-bouncing, so wait until you get a low-bouncing ball from him. Keep your backhand chop deep, for if you chop high and in the middle, he can dash over to crack his forehand crosscourt for a winner, as shown in Figure 78.

Another response to his hitting short to your backhand is to drop shot on his forehand side, as shown in shot No. 2 in Figure 82. This is riskier: If your drop shot bounces too high or too far back,

FIGURE 80

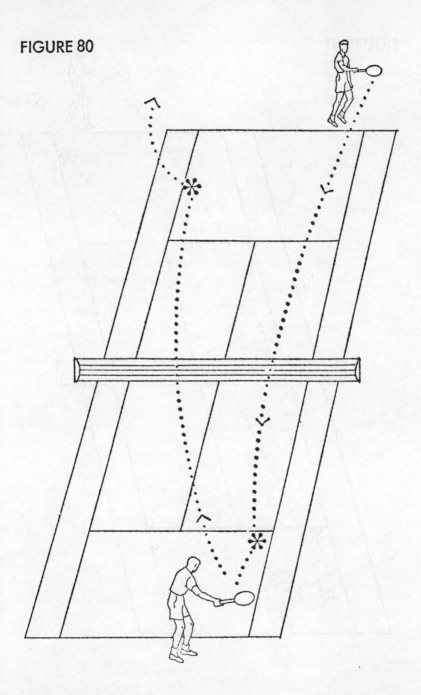

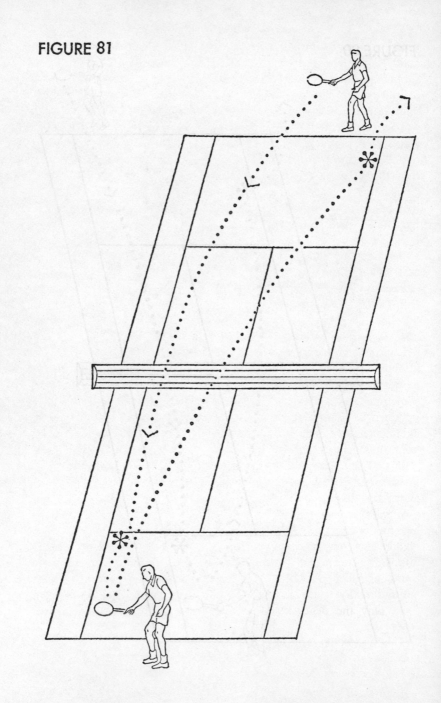

FIGURE 81

you're a goner. But if your opponent is slow-footed and if you have a good touch, you can rack up an occasional point. This drop shot should be generally used as sparingly as garlic in a salad dressing— a little goes a long way. You should use it to surprise and confuse your opponent but not as a steady point gainer.

The net effect of your chopping backhands down the line is to cause your opponent to think twice about running way around his backhand. It will also cause him to run much more than you do and thus tire him out that much sooner.

Usually, a player who runs around his backhand does so because it is admittedly weaker. When you chop down the line to his forehand, you pull him over so that now you can pound his weak backhand.

Practice this chop down the line against weaker opponents, and you will add another weapon to your arsenal.

Tactics. Never change a winning game, pronounced that old master, Bill Tilden. If you are beating an opponent in exchanges from the baseline, keep it up. Don't start rushing the net or lure him to the net.

Lots of times an opponent doesn't realize your weakness nor attempt to undermine it. He may be plodding along, half resigned to defeat and persisting in the type of game you enjoy. If you try something else and start missing, a light bulb will flash on in your opponent's brain. He'll think, so that's the kind of shot he doesn't like! Let's give him lots more of it. The next thing you know, your opponent is walking off the court in triumph.

If you are winning by rushing the net, keep going up. If he doesn't like high-bouncing balls on his backhand and openly frets at missing them, give him a dozen more.

While it is true that if you feed enough shots to a player, he will eventually improve in returning them, you needn't worry about giving him too many. For even though you may aim a high-bouncing serve to his backhand, you may find that it angles sometimes instead to his forehand. Thus you are mixing up your game without really trying.

So play the percentages by continuing to pound his weakness. *Never change a winning game.*

The opposite axiom is *Always change a losing game.* What do you have to lose by changing? Of course, it sounds simpler than it is. Suppose you are losing from the baseline. Now you should

FIGURE 82

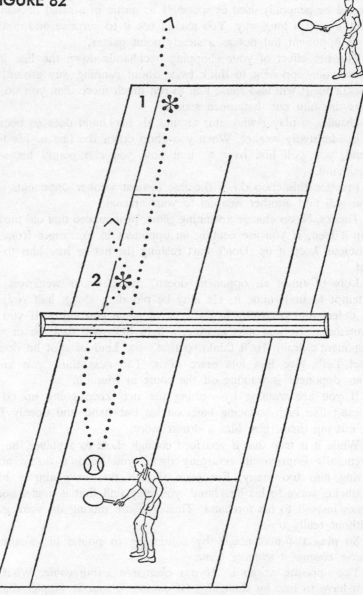

change by rushing the net? Fine, except that you are playing on clay and you not only don't possess a net game, you can't even beg, borrow, or lease one. So now what?

Consider then why your opponent is beating you: Are you trying to hit harder than he is? Are you hitting balls short instead of deep? Are you aiming your drives just barely over the net instead of to the baseline? When he forces you to one side, do you return to the middle instead of at a crosscourt angle?

Are you serving only one-fourth of your first serves inside? When you have to go to the net, do you make your approach shots deep to his backhand, or do you just push the ball right back to him?

You can see that there are lots of ways you can change a losing game. When he rushes the net, do you always try to pass him instead of tossing up a few lobs? If you like to rush in and he's passing you, wait until you get a better chance to put pressure on him before going up.

Thus, when you are losing, think of changing your style of play. Try hitting a different type of shot to your opponent than you have been to see how he handles it. When losing, think *change*.

Practice. A weatherbeaten myth is: To improve, you must always practice against better players. Rarely has one myth deceived so many players for so long a time with so little reason.

If you played the world pro champion every day, all you'd learn would be to duck faster. You would have no time to think about footwork, stroke production, or tactics.

You should play against all types of players with all kinds of games: the slugger, the slowpoke, the retriever, the wily professor. Of course, you don't want to waste your time on a player who can't even return a ball—unless you are trying to sell him something or persuade her that you are an athlete with charm.

To improve you must correct your weaknesses, and the best way to practice is against a weaker player—at first. Against a weak player, you can tell yourself, "Move your feet sooner . . . start the racket back faster . . . get your weight going into the backhand . . ." because the balls are coming at you more slowly or closer to you. Practice your backhand or your volley against a weak player, and you will feel more relaxed and can give more time to the actual mechanics.

Then take on a player of your own strength. Now the balls come faster to you, and you have to run more. Good. Now you can sharpen your stroke against the grindstone of your opponent. You have to react quicker, but this challenge should speed you up. The harder balls give you more pace to hit off of, and you naturally get a greater feeling of satisfaction making these shots.

After your stroke has obviously improved, play against a better player. First, a note of caution.

A Class A player can always get a game with a B player, so it is up to the latter to make the game interesting and enjoyable for A if he wants a return match. Interesting by making A work for his points and enjoyable by B's manners.

When you are facing a better player and he starts winning, the normal reaction is to bemoan your luck, complain about bad bounces or the wind or that your racket has sold out to the enemy. But nobody likes to play a grumbler, because you are robbing him of his feeling of triumph in making shots.

Hence, even though it requires great efforts, force yourself to be the very model of a model opponent. Applaud his good shots, be honest in your calls, and if he wins, say, "You played well today." Not a word of your own shortcomings.

Human nature being what it is, the other fellow will feel compelled to reciprocate with a compliment on your shots. He will add, "Too bad the wind was blowing your lobs out . . ."

Many players strive to be good sports against better opponents, but since they display good manners so seldom, the effort diverts attention from their strokes, and their games suffer. It is well to practice good manners against usual opponents so that it becomes a habit and you can then concentrate entirely on your shots against tougher opponents.

Concentration. One word that can lift your game without buying expensive equipment is: *Concentrate.*

When on the court, think only about your own match. Forget the other matches around you or your plans for the next day. Concentrate on where and how you should hit the ball, what your opponent likes and dislikes, and the score.

Some players should rent out their ears as radar equipment, for they can pick up sounds inaudible to dogs. The instant a faint clicking, clacking, booming, honking, or whispering sounds from a mile away, they stop playing. They also stop thinking about the match to express their displeasure at the noise of butterfly wings fluttering.

Jack Kramer labels such players as having "rabbit ears." The least sound disturbs them and throws off their delicately attuned mechanisms so that they lose easy matches.

During the 1966 Pacific Southwest tournament, Roy Emerson was playing a quarter-final match while workmen were hammering in putting up the temporary north grandstand of the Los Angeles Tennis Club center court. Many players would have gone berserk at the irregular noises. Then a helicopter came over. Most of the spectators looked up, but not Emmo. He banged his serve, rushed the net, and punched the ball away. He played as though in a noiseless vacuum intent only on winning.

This is the stuff that champions are made of. Bill Tilden was playing Billy Johnston in a Forest Hills final when a plane crashed nearby. After a pause, the players resumed the match. Tilden knew that he himself couldn't do anything about the plane or its occupants, so he did the next best thing: He channeled his thoughts entirely on winning the match. Which he did.

Concentration is a habit of mind. All players want peace and quiet when playing, but you can train yourself to ignore disturbances, whether they be workmen pounding away at the street pavement, a baby crying, or the whirring of a movie camera. Moreover, if you really concentrate, you will possess an edge over the opponent who is easily distracted.

Players who learn their games on the public courts possess one advantage over the country club players: They become accustomed to interruptions, strange sounds, movements behind and around them of people passing through. Many times, promising juniors who are "gymnasium fighters" unused to public appearances find it hard to beat mediocre opponents at public courts. The solution is for them to work out there occasionally to develop greater powers of concentration.

Make a game out of developing your own concentration. When you find yourself woolgathering or gazing into the distance, transfer a coin from one pocket to another. You may find yourself loaded way down on one side when you first try this. If you find a dozen coins one time, try the next to cut it down to nine. And then down to zero in succeeding times. You will play better and enjoy the game more as you concentrate better!

Play to the score. While every point in tennis counts, there are some that mean much more. The first point of a game does not mean as much as an ad. Ellsworth Vines once said that there were from five to seven points really important, really decisive, that turned the tide of the set.

Certainly, the long-drawn-out games are the most important, for they mark the turning points. Ever notice how a player will battle hard for the first set to lose it at 7–5 and then drop the next set 6–1?

In a game, the 30–15 point is a key point. If you lead 30–15 and win the next point, you have him 40–15 and are an odds-on favorite to win the game. So try real hard at 30–15.

If you are down 15–30, don't try for a big shot close to the lines. Keep the pressure on him, but let him try for the sensational shot, for if you lose this point, you are down 15–40.

If you are down 0–40, you might as well go for broke. No sense chasing all over the court wearing yourself out. Try to make him run so he has to use a little more energy to win the point. Try a drop shot on clay or lob him if he rushes the net.

If you win that point and lag 15–40, play cautiously. Return deep so he will have to make a better-than-average shot. Keep the pressure on him without hitting all-out. Win that point and it's 30–40. Still avoid trying any fancy shot or really sharp angles. Once you get it to deuce, you rate a psychological advantage because he knows he has lost a real lead, and it irks him. If you get ad, you can take a chance, for even if you miss, the score is still even.

Similarly, when you lead 40–0 or 40–15, you can try big shots because your opponent has to defend, for if he misses once, he's lost the game.

If the third and fifth points of a game are important, so are the fourth and seventh games of a set. By the fourth game, it is usually 2–1 and only rarely 3–0. Hence if you lead 2–1, strive to win the next game to lead 3–1. This could upset a front-runner type of opponent who loses heart when falling behind; if you win the next game, you lead 4–1, practically the set.

The climax of many sets comes in the seventh game. It is usually 4–2 or 3–all. If you lead 4–2, you should make extra efforts to win the game to lead 5–2. If you are down 2–4, you have to win the game to stay in contention, for if you are only at 3–4, you could break service to tie the score at 4–all.

Moreover, if you can bring the score from 2–4 to 4–all, you

have gained the psychological advantage of coming from behind. You should then keep the pressure on to lead 5–4. It would be his service and actually almost even, but the fact that you now lead after lagging cannot help but disturb your opponent.

At 3–all, it is a question of which one cracks first. The set is usually half over, and whoever can gain an advantage first is most likely to keep it. If it's his service, go after him, for if you break it, he doesn't have too many chances left to break back.

"Victory is an inclined plane," said Marshal Foch. If you win your serve and lead 4–3, and then break his, your opponent will suddenly realize he is down 3–5 and has only one chance left, your service, to retrieve himself from defeat.

Should you make an effort to win a set when you are down 0–4 or 1–5? In a three-out-of-five match, you might content yourself with making your opponent run as much as possible. But in a two-out-of-three-set match, go all out.

The winner of the first set in two out of three usually wins the match, so try despite your opponent's lead. Besides, if you start hitting better, you may still lose the set, but by the time you start the second set, you are rolling in high speed.

In three out of five sets, the all-important set is the third. The laggard who by now is feeling the strain of the three hard sets thinks that he will have to work even harder to win two more. This dread cuts down his resistance and makes him hit too hard too often to end points quickly.

The extra effort you exert to win the third set will end the match much sooner for you in the long run.

For Ladies Only

More females are playing tennis than ever before and for a variety of reasons: Some play because they find it a pleasant way to keep a trim figure without monotonous exercises and to remain supple like a teenager. Some play because they find it a social asset in meeting new friends. Some girls take up the sport because they like the percentage odds in their favor—one girl to no less than five male players. Not just ordinary men either, but healthy, success-oriented, and above average in means and intelligence—prime marriage prospects. Some girls play for the fun of cracking the ball and winning matches and thus unleashing their competitive urges.

But whatever your reason, when you first take up the game, you think first of—clothes, naturally. You may already own blouses, Bermudas, slacks, Capris, or shorts of various colors. If you're a blonde, the chances are that the colors are definite and strong enough to contrast with your own coloring.

If you go to a public park, you may see other girls wearing outfits of red and blue and yellow—anything they happened to have. But nothing marks a player as being a novice more than bright colors. Save your money and don't buy clothes of that type.

White is the enduring fashion for tennis, and although designers are always threatening to change the color scheme with vivid shades, they sell mostly to the newcomers. One girl tennis player who backed such a designer lost her shirt and panties on the deal.

229

So stick to white for shorts and blouses and dresses. Wear a colored sweater or red belt or perhaps colored tassels on your socks for color and you'll look like an expert.

Tennis dresses are favored over shorts, especially by tournament committees who still haven't entirely become reconciled to women not wearing long white stockings and dresses down to their ankles. Would you believe that the first woman to play without stockings was considered only one notch higher than Jezebel? Your main problem is, how do you look in shorts as compared with a tennis dress?

Some tennis dresses would make Helen of Troy look like a rag-picker, while others would make a wallflower look like Cleopatra. You may have to try on twenty to find one that looks and feels right when you go through the motions of swinging a racket. The prices may astound you, but you have to remember that there is a very limited market for this type of dress. If you can, wait until the end of the season (even in Southern California) when the stores have to unload, and you may buy one for half the price.

You can tell much more about tennis dresses by going to a tennis club and seeing what the other girls are wearing than by listening to a dozen salespeople assuring you that *this* is what *they* are wearing this season.

When it comes to shoes, remember you will be running and jumping, so get a pair of real honest-to-goodness tennis shoes. Not a pair of thin sneakers with thin soles that burn your feet, nor play shoes nor leisure shoes. Close your ears to salespeople telling you they look chic on a tennis court. Buy real tennis shoes.

Put on a pair of wool socks and then try on tennis shoes that give your toes room to wiggle in. If you cramp your feet, you can't run as well, and how can you smile at people when your feet are killing you? The shoes may feel like weighted deep sea diver's shoes compared to your featherweight street shoes at first, but real tennis shoes will enable you to play much better tennis.

Women have a phobia about their feet looking too big, as though men judge women first of all by the size of their feet. I played with Gussie Moran of lace panties fame and noticed she was wearing oddly painted shoes left over from her tour. Afterward in commenting with the two men who played with us, I said, "Did you ever see such odd shoes?"

"What shoes?" asked the two men.

230

Who looks at a girl's feet when she's wearing shorts? So buy your shoes for comfort.

Racket. See the chapter on equipment, which deals with rackets.

Playing your own way. Women do not look like men. Thank Heaven! They do not think like men, and they do not walk or run like men. So why should you try to play tennis like a man? Very few women can rush the net, drive, and smash hard like men. It takes tremendous effort to serve the American twist, rush up two feet within the service line to volley decisively, or fade back to kill a lob. This type of game demands quick reactions, accurate strokes, abundant vitality, and intense concentration. Only a few women players develop this, after years of hard practice.

Yet the men you play with will constantly exhort you to "play more like a man." In trying to do so, you will wear yourself out while making a lot more errors than necessary. This doesn't mean that you should play patball but that you should make use of your own capabilities and not those of a man who possesses one-third stronger grasp, exceeds you from six to twelve inches in height, and can run much faster. Compare track records of men and women. Evidently Mother Nature decided the men should run faster so they could catch the women.

So you should learn the shots that work best for you in playing a woman's game, and then you will improve faster.

What should you learn first of all?

1. Try to walk, hike, or run as much as you can. Since high heels are apparently here to stay, it won't do much good to beseech you to wear low heels as being more healthful. But since tennis is two-thirds running, you can improve your moving to the ball by using your feet more.

Walk an extra block, park an extra block from a store, walk downstairs, walk around the block when window-shopping. Get a skipping rope and skip rope two minutes a day, *every* day. You will be surprised how much practice like this will improve your running in tennis.

Then when the others suggest an extra set, you won't have to tell your male partner that you'd rather sit this one out.

2. The serve is the most important single stroke. Practice throwing a ball overhand to develop the same motion as the serve. Try to reach up when you serve, since the higher you hit the ball, the more chance it has of going in.

When you get a chance, take a dozen old balls out on a court and practice your serve. The chapter on the serve emphasizes the wisdom of getting seven out of ten first serves inside.

3. *Practicing with men.* When you first start out, you may play with girl friends who hit the ball easier than you do and so give you lots of time to think about how to swing, etc. However, aside from the social angle, practicing with men can provide better means of improving.

For one thing, men get more balls back because they can cover court better, and so you get more balls to hit in a shorter time.

Incidentally, if a much better male player asks you to play, you should tell him you are a beginner or haven't played too much. Then if he still wants to rally with you, he has been warned and knows what to expect. In fact, he might even be pleased at your playing better than he expected. This is much better than for a girl to tell a man she's played for years in tournaments and then go out and not return ball one.

Men usually hit the ball harder than your girl friends, so the ball may seem to hurtle at you too fast for you to get set. If he cracks the ball way to the other side and you can't reach it, it's not your fault. But if you actually hit the ball with your racket and don't return it, you are probably starting your swing way too late. You are probably waiting until the ball bounces before you start to take your racket back. The instant the ball crosses the net you will know whether it's going to your forehand or backhand. So start your racket back right away, and move toward the ball.

If the ball comes right at you, take it on your forehand by stepping sideways a couple of short steps.

Practicing with men will make you move faster provided the man doesn't blast every single ball. If he does, all you're practicing is your ability to duck. You can then suggest you will have better rallies if he would hit the ball easier. Otherwise, try to hit the balls so he has to run way over to retrieve them, and after a while he'll get tired and ease up on his hitting.

4. *Advice from men.* Every man I've ever seen go out on a court with a girl will start telling her how to play—no matter whether he can hardly hit the ball or has just won Wimbledon.

Some of this advice may be good, some bad. How do you tell which advice to heed?

If your male opponent makes a simple suggestion like bending your knees or starting your racket back sooner, fine. But if he overwhelms you with a torrent of advice that would take a computer to assimilate, he's exposing his ignorance of skillful coaching. He's expecting the impossible, so don't try to act on it. Suggest that if he limited himself to just one suggestion every five minutes that you would have more opportunity to practice it.

Or you can pretend (as females do when not wanting to accept other advice from males) not to hear him.

Don't be surprised if the next man you play with seems to offer advice that contradicts the first one. Untrained coaches try to make their pupils play the way they do themselves, which would be fine if you were a carbon copy. Since you aren't, you might remind your friend that men are supposed to run twice as fast and hit twice as hard as women, so he shouldn't expect too much of you.

If he seems upset at your missing balls, think how he would feel if you cracked the ball back twice as hard as he did. This happened to Alice Marble, one of the all-time greats, when she trounced her high school hero—and never saw him again.

Remember that your friend is trying to be helpful and that rallying with him will improve your game. If his torrent of advice bothers you, tell him sweetly that you could concentrate much better if he didn't talk while you're hitting the ball.

5. Hit deep! Regardless of your grip or swing, try to hit long, deep balls that land close to the other's baseline. Aim your balls (by lifting up more) at least one racket's length, if not two, over the net. Even if you hit the ball easily to the other's baseline, you will make it harder for him to win the point than if your ball skims the net and bounces on the service line.

The best defense against a harder hitter is to start your swing sooner, aim higher over the net, and c-a-r-r-y the ball on your racket. You will then be using the other's speed to send your own ball back harder.

6. Learn a backhand chop. If you can manage to return balls on your backhand, even with reduced speed, you will lift your game over that of a girl who merely pokes her backhands. See the chapter on the backhand.

Learning a backhand chop will also aid you in learning the lob. This is the most underrated shot in mixed doubles but can become your deadliest.

7. Learn to lob. Read the chapter on the lob to discover how to

233

equalize your game against an opponent who hits harder and runs much faster. Lobbing over a man at the net requires far less skill and effort than trying to drive the ball past him.

Against women, the lob is the greatest weapon since the hatpin. If men dislike consistent lobbers, women hate and detest them. For no other stroke in tennis can wear them down faster, destroy their offensive power, and weaken their will to force the issue as the lob.

Running back for a lob takes much more out of a woman than a man. The thought that you will lob if they rush the net will deter them from storming up far more than your hard drives.

Gene Mako, the noted doubles champion, claims that all a woman needs is a lob and a drop shot (a soft shot just over the net). When the late Maureen Connolly returned from winning Wimbledon, he counseled her against changing her winning backcourt game to a net-rushing game.

"They'll kill you with lobs," he warned.

She followed his advice and kept on crushing her opponents with backcourt thunderbolts until an untimely accident put her out of competition.

As mentioned in the chapter on lobbing, your opponents won't like it because you're not giving them the shots they prefer. They may comment bitterly or subtly about your lobbing, as though it were illegal, unsportsmanlike, and deceitful. You may remind them that Pancho Gonzales, who blasts opponents with serves, can also cut them down with skillful lobs.

8. Learn to volley. You may ask, "Why bother learning to volley if it's so easy to lob over your head?"

Most players won't lob when they see you up there. They'll try to slam the ball past you. It's more fun, so although many players realize it's easier to win points by lobbing, they'll still keep trying to hammer the ball past the net man.

Besides, you'll play net much more in doubles than in singles, and you do want to improve your mixed doubles game, don't you?

Oddly enough, the most important feature of volleying well is not how you make the stroke so much as how quickly you move. The stroke itself is simple: Read the chapter on volleying.

I mentioned this before, but it's worth repeating: Practice facing the net, leaning forward on the balls of your feet, your knees bent, your racket pointed toward your opponent. Then dart forward to intercept the ball. If you stand flatfooted, the ball will seem to come at you like a rifle shot.

Practice at first against easy floaters, which help you develop the habit of moving into the ball. As you improve, have your friends hit harder balls that make you move faster.

Many partners in doubles will want you to play right on top of the net—especially your male partners. They figure that since they play much better, they should play all the balls they possibly can. This may be all right if you are in the finals of a tournament and want to win a trophy.

But if you let your partners stick you on top of the net regularly, you will never learn to volley. You will get very few balls, since naturally you can't miss. You may also develop the habit of pushing your racket in front of you as a shield and thus returning the ball right back to your opponents instead of angling the balls by volleying correctly. You will also become so bored watching your partner doing all the playing that you won't concentrate.

As said before, the volleyer in doubles should stand halfway between the net and the service line. Your opponents will then direct more balls at you in the hope of winning points. You may then miss some. Fine. This is what you are playing tennis for: a chance to return balls, and if you miss, try harder next time.

Your partner may implore or command you to play really close to the net. You may then tell him: A. You have come to play tennis and not to be a bystander. B. Ask if he would rather play singles. C. Point out that feminine tournament players play back to cover more shots. D. Pretend to agree, but back away when he serves. E. That you are just playing for fun, aren't you?

Remember, as long as you play on top of the net, you are playing low-echelon doubles and you'll never be able to play better matches because you aren't carrying your share of the load.

Keep reminding yourself to volley *deep*. Most players miss volleys by hitting downward too much into the net. No matter how soft a volley you make, if you hit it deep, you give your opponents a chance to miss. So think *deep* when you volley.

9. *Learn return of serve.* A girl who can manage to get the ball back over the net in returning serves is a jewel beyond price. Once you return the ball to the server, the odds shift greatly from the server to almost even.

As said before in the chapter on return of serve: Await the serve by leaning forward on the balls of your feet, your knees bent, your racket pointing at the server. You will then start faster.

Once the serve clears the net, you should know whether it's going to your forehand or your backhand. Start your backswing right away. Most girls swing late at men's serves because they start way too late.

Watch the ball until you see it hit the strings of your racket. Think of c-a-r-r-y-i-n-g the ball on your racket as you follow through.

When the man serves, try to return the ball through the middle to the girl's half of the court. The man will usually try to take the shot if it's at all within reach. If he keeps doing this, the girl won't know which shots to take.

A great return of serve in doubles is to lob over the girl's head at the net. The man has to run over to cover it, so that when he does take the net, he's afraid of getting in too close or he can't get the lob over the girl's head. Naturally, then he can't volley as well.

When the man hangs back from the net, then drive the ball to land it at his feet. You don't want to lob all the time, for it's not much fun, and your opponents will get used to them.

10. Learn to smash. Read the chapter on smashing to learn about moving your feet into position. This is the hardest part of smashing, because if you face the net, you can't smash well.

You don't have to develop a powerful smash, but if you learn to smash consistently and to the other girl, you will keep the ball in play until your stronger partner can crack it. As you improve, you will find that smashing consistently will win you a lot of points against pushers.

Practice smashing a little every time you rally. You will sharpen your eye in depth perception and in judging how far to move for lobs. If you stand halfway between the net and service line and then back up ten feet, you will cover most of the usual lobs. Try to take some lobs every time you play instead of automatically letting them go for your partner.

Practice throwing balls overhand to develop the smashing motion. Practice turning sideways and backing up until you can do it without thinking. This will then become automatic.

Try to smash to the girl. It is up to her to get out of the way, and if you should happen to hit her, it will teach her a lesson so that when a man hauls off and smashes, she will have retreated to safety.

11. Learn to drop shot. Read the chapter on the drop shot, and you may lift your game faster than a jet plane takeoff. On clay, a skillful drop shot can upset the rhythm of a better player with classic backcourt strokes by bringing her to the net with a drop shot and then lobbing over her head.

A drop shot should be used sparingly on cement or asphalt and works much better against women than men. The more slow-footed your opponent is, the more you should use it. If your opponent runs like a cheetah and loves to play net, forget about drop shots.

You can tire your opponent much more by making her run up for drop shots and back for lobs than by chasing her twice as much from side to side. It is that much harder to run up and back. A fringe benefit is that after having to rush up for a couple of drop shots, your opponent is likely to slam the ball in desperation to end the point right there because she fears your lob.

A drop shot works well even against experienced tournament players except for confirmed card-carrying net rushers like Billie Jean King. Diminutive Anita Lizana of Chile won Forest Hills by mowing down her opposition with deceptive drop shots mixed with lobs and deep drives. In the 1937 finals, she nullified the slugging of Panna (Yahyah) Jedrezejowska, who had been blasting her foes off the court, in a straight-set victory, 6–4, 6–2.

What if you are a born slugger? The kind who cracks the ball much harder than her competitors? Many sluggers have no "touch" and operate at only one speed: full power ahead.

Admittedly, it is harder for a player with a powerful forehand to change to the opposite extreme and softly lift a ball just over the net. Most of the time you would be better off to go ahead and slug the ball. Helen Wills Roark, who blasted her forehands, rarely used drop shots, nor did Maureen Connolly.

However, if you chop your backhand, you will find it much easier to adapt your stroke to make drop shots and to disguise them more easily. But be sure to vary your drop shots with deep drives to increase the difference between the two strokes. If you hit your drives on the service line, your drop shots won't seem too different.

12. *Playing against other women.* You may feel at first that playing other women calls for far less effort than playing against men. Certainly women usually hit easier and can't cover court

like men. But this means longer rallies on both sides and more sustained effort to win points.

You might also think that women care less than men about winning, because they are much more polite to each other. Your opponent will call sweetly, "I'm sorry, but your serve looked out. Would you mind playing two?" You know darned well you just aced her.

Another comments, "*Too* bad. You *just* missed. You're having such *dreadful* luck with your backhand today."

Or: "My, what a *beautiful* forehand! I've never seen you hit *so* many in a row." She sounds as though it was pure luck.

The compliments and condolences fly back and forth like so many feathers in a pillow fight. But it's no pillow fight when women face each other. It's a battle to the death with no holds barred. Male tournament players can battle each other to exhaustion week in and week out and go out on the town together. But in some famous feuds between women players they haven't spoken to each other for years except to say, "Rough or smooth?"

Men pretend they are playing merely for exercise, but women try to perpetrate the illusion that tennis is merely a social function like five o'clock tea. Don't be deceived by this aura of excessive politeness.

Women battle harder against each other than against men. Most women don't try as hard against some men because they don't want to beat them and upset their egos or because they think the men are superior anyway.

But taking on another woman is a different story. The tricks and stratagems employed by women against each other in tennis would make Machiavelli seem a Simple Simon. Women invented psychological warfare long before there was a name for it.

Does this mean that a tennis court is a miniature chamber of horrors and that a kind, sensitive creature like you will be devoured alive? Not at all. You'll relish defeating another woman by using your head while she is wearing herself out by using only her feet.

You simply have to remember to use a different set of virtues when opposing other women, as against men.

A. Patience. It takes longer to win a point, so you should develop patience. Don't be in a hurry to win slapdash. It takes longer to pick up the balls, to change courts, to end a rally. The pace of a usual women's doubles match is so much slower and hence less

pleasing to watch than men's that it has been said that in case of
fire in wooden stands, the quickest way to clear the crowds would
be to put on a women's doubles.

Fortunately, women possess an abundance of patience from having
had to deal with children, especially the males over twenty-one.
You too can learn to wait patiently while your opponent shuffles
over to pick up a ball. She's probably tired from your chasing
her all over the court and wants to catch her breath.

If you recognize situations like this, you remain patient because
you know that your game is triumphing over hers. So while you
wait, review your tactics and plan your next attack.

B. Try to make your opponent run. Males like to run just for
the fun of it and to keep in training. But world champion Suzanne
Lenglen based her whole game on chasing her opponent all over
the court. Hit the ball where your opponent isn't, and keep her so
busy defending she won't be able to get set to crack one. When
faced with where to hit the ball, choose the opening that forces
her to run the most.

C. Insist that your opponents make decisions. An aura of excessive politeness lays a heavy hand on women's matches. A weekend women's doubles match takes twice as long as men's because
of the constant discussions about whether a ball was good or not.

You serve a fast ball to the outside corner and your opponent
swings and misses. Does she congratulate you on serving an ace?
No. Does she remind herself to start faster the next time? No. Does
she decide next time not to stand over too far to cover up her
backhand? No.

She will call politely, "I'm sorry, but I really couldn't tell just
where the ball landed." She turns to her partner. "Could you?"

Her partner isn't about to end a lifelong friendship by saying
it was a clean ace. She says she couldn't tell either.

Your opponent then trots back, picks up the ball, and returning
it to you, calls with the air of a princess dispensing largesse to a
peasant, "Take two."

She has robbed you of an ace and managed to appear generous.
Why doesn't she call it out? Because if she calls too many good
balls out, she will feel guilty and suspect that others consider her
a cheat. Or perhaps she couldn't really tell.

As said before, the code of tennis sportsmanship demands that
if a ball lands close to the line and you do not see it hit outside

the line, you must give the point to your opponent. Not tell them to play it over or take two.

To cure your opponents of this take-two business, you must:

I. Not pull the same trick yourself. You will have to make decisions one way or the other. You can be polite while saying, "I'm sorry but it's out," or "I'm *so* sorry, it's *just* out."

II. Suggest to your opponents that it will speed up the game if everybody calls the ball one way or the other. "It *does* take up a lot of time replaying points," you can say. You may also add that people are waiting for the court, that you have to catch a train or meet a boy friend or husband. Or go to the hairdresser.

You might also point out that in tournaments they do not replay close balls. Or that the time you save will allow for another set.

D. Women like to talk and exchange ideas anytime, anyplace. And during a tennis match, they feel a compulsion to comment on every single point: "Beautiful shot. . . . Oh, too bad, you almost reached it. . . . My, we were lucky to win that rally."

Sometimes all four women comment at the same time, and it is debatable if they ever bother to listen to each other.

A male player who slugs everything can talk all the time because he doesn't have to think about tactics. All he has to do is keep slugging. But women's tennis demands much more concentration because women rarely can haul off and slug a winner.

The more anybody talks, the less she concentrates. So you will be smart to let the others chatter while you keep thinking only about the match.

To show how distraction can ruin one's game: In a recent tournament, losing player A commented to winning player B that the latter's skirt would fly up when she served and sometimes catch in the back. That otherwise the dress did look very chic.

Winning player B began to think more about smoothing her skirt down after serving than she did about winning points. Her concentration vanished and with it her chances to win.

When you stop talking and start concentrating, you will notice which of your opponents volleys better, lobs better, or scrambles better for the ball. You will keep track of which shots of yours work best against them and which fail. You will notice how your opponents tell you ahead of time by little preparatory movements what they intend to do with the ball: drive, lob, or chop. Thus warned, you will handle their shots far better.

You may say that your group plays tennis only to be sociable and have a good time and that conversation oils the wheels of good will. Uh-huh.

Try this experiment: Emphasize your sparkling conversation, your gracious and witty replies, your good-natured remarks at the expense of your tennis. Allow your opponents to win easily. After all, it's just *pour le sport* that you're playing, isn't it?

Repeat this experiment several times. You will then discern a certain coolness toward you when making up teams—as though you were Typhoid Mary. Nobody will seem to want you for a partner. The better players will avoid you as a carrier of contagious disease.

You may ask if you have to become a malevolent Lady MacBeth intent only on the destruction of your opponents' games to become popular. Not necessarily, but it would help.

Just concentrate solely on your tennis, and you can't help doing better than the others with the wandering attention. Win most of the time and you will suddenly become popular again. Everybody will want you for a partner.

E. The dinker (a player who pushes back every ball with no speed at all) poses more of a problem to women than to men. Men find it easier to rush the net and cut off the dinker's soft returns. But except for competent women tournament players who also can take the net or blast weak returns, the rest of the women players dread opposing dinkers.

What can you do against a dinker?

I. Hit deep to the corners. Most weekend players tend to hit hard but short drives at the service line that the dinker can handle. Hit the ball way back to force the dinker back of her baseline. If the dinker then returns short, use a drop shot.

Dinkers hate playing net. Once you have brought her in close, lob over her head or drive past her.

II. If the dinker does not return short even when you hit deep but floats the ball back high in the air to your baseline, you can't use a drop shot on her.

Instead, move in from the baseline and take her floaters on the fly to volley them to the opposite corner. No sensational winning volley, but it will force the dinker to run faster to the other corner. The way to beat her is to give her less time to get back into position.

Since her floaters come slowly over the net, you have more

time to make your volley. Keep it deep, since you have less margin of safety of volleying that far back from the net. Remember: You don't have to end the rally in a hurry, because she has to run faster than you do and cover more ground.

After you take a few volleys like that, she will try to keep her returns lower over the net. This means that with her lack of speed she won't be able to hit as deep as before. Fine. When she hits short, use your drop shots.

Don't let her rest between games by allowing her to stop to talk when changing courts. Helen Wills Roark avoided such time-delaying tactics by purposely changing sides at the opposite net post from her opponents.

Above all, remain patient when you miss setups against a dinker. Most players regard dinkers as the lowest form of human life because their strokes are usually awkward. They feel they should overwhelm them love and love because dinkers don't hit the ball hard. However, as said before, the main object of tennis is to get the ball back over the net, not to see which player can hit harder.

F. Call the score after every point. The server should call the score, but if she doesn't, you should. The points last longer in women's tennis, and it is thus easier to get mixed up about the score than in men's play, with shorter rallies.

When you change courts, tell your opponent, *"You* lead 3–2" or *"I* lead 3–2" instead of "Two–three in games."

And no matter how far ahead you are, don't feel so sorry for your opponent that you fear to call the score out loud. A lead of even 5–1 can dissolve like fog before a hot sun, and your opponent may insist later after winning two games that it was really 4–2 at that point.

Besides, calling the score helps you concentrate on the match at all times.

G. Learn how to lose tennis matches. Sometimes you don't want to win one against a sales prospect, business superior, or boy friend.

Anybody can throw a match by knocking the ball into the fence, but this is so obvious it defeats its own purpose. The methods that enable you to practice your own game at the same time are:

I. Play to your opponent's strong side.

II. Practice your own weak shots.

III. Aim closer to the corners and your percentage of errors will rise.

IV. When your opponent tires, stall to give him a chance to catch his breath.

V. Tell him you don't want to bother changing sides and then you take the worse side: the sunny side, or against the wind.

Curiously enough, you will find that when you relax and hit the ball with no tense effort that you will play better than ever. Keep playing to your opponent's strong points and practice your own weak shots. Then even if you win, at least you have kept the score closer.

Mixed Doubles

Masculine viewpoint. On the surface, mixed doubles seems to present the most gracious aspect of competitive tennis. In the beginning, each man is courteous and pleasant to his partner and opponents and the compliments fall like petals from a rose bush. But as the match goes on, each man plays harder to prove his superiority not only to the other man but to the girls.

What is the best way to win at mixed doubles?

Gene Mako says, "Choose the better girl player."

What if your partner is not only weaker than the other girl but your male opponent is better than you?

You can still win if you use your head—and without trying to hog the court. Here's how:

1. As skipper of your team, you may feel like offering advice to your partner based on your greater experience and skill. Tons and tons of advice.

Let's consider how great players act when burdened with weak partners. When Bobby Riggs pairs with a novice to take on another expert and partner for a hundred dollars a set, you might think that Bobby would shower his partner with tons of advice. Especially since Bobby's partner is lucky to reach most balls with an eleven-foot pole, let alone make good returns.

But instead, as mentioned earlier, Bobby speaks briefly before the match, comments once every four games, and speaks otherwise only to encourage his partner. Meanwhile, the stronger of the opponents is overloading his camel of a partner with a burden of advice a trailer truck couldn't carry. Result: Bobby scores another "upset" victory.

Bobby knows that you can't teach a girl to volley like Billie Jean King or run like Rosemary Casals in one year, let alone in one session. He knows that if you inundate your partner with advice, you will only confuse and baffle her.

You may suggest that she lob over the other girl's head, get her first serve in, try to c-a-r-r-y the ball on her racket and thus follow through more, and hit the ball through the middle. You space out these suggestions, of course. But you do not tell her to run faster, jump higher, hit as hard as you do, make pinpoint volleys, or return smashes off your short lobs. Don't expect miracles unless she can walk on water.

Women tend to regard advice as criticism, and this makes them play worse. Besides, if you keep telling her what to do all the time, your own game will suffer.

Before the match, impress on your partner that you don't care how fast she serves her first serve if she'll just get it in. Your opponents will always stay back to receive her first serve, and that makes it easier for you to poach on their returns.

Getting her first serve in will save her a lot of energy that will enable her to move faster and longer. She will run less risk of serving doubles and also of giving opponents a weak second serve to pounce on.

You and your partner should hit as many balls as possible to your girl opponent. The odds will favor you, and her partner will then try to take even more balls that are hers.

Never slug a ball right at her. This is considered very bad manners. Her partner would be justified in slugging you with the ball.

Your best shots directed at a girl are those just barely within her reach. Hit through the middle on her side or lob just over her outstretched racket. If her partner is typical, he will start telling her to let the balls go, and she'll become so confused she won't swing at balls right to her.

Who should serve first in mixed doubles? Most men usually start serving for their team, and this is usually on the shady side. This makes it easier for them to win their serves.

But it is the women's serves that usually determine the match. Yet they will then have to serve on the sunny side and thus find

246

it even more difficult to hold their serves. Lots of times the wind is also against them.

I feel that the girl should start serving on the shady side, and with everything possible in her favor. The man won't mind serving in the sun, and it won't lower his power much. Meanwhile, the other team's girl player will be struggling to hold her serve on the bad side.

If the girl thus serves first, she will rate you a true gentleman and will be inclined to fight harder to win the match.

If your match is really important, such as the finals of a tournament, you may win it by going all out to take every single ball you can reach. That is, you place the girl right on top of the net. Of course, you won't feel like playing another game for a week, but perhaps the trophy will console you.

However, if your opponents are smart, they will lob just over her head and chase you all over the court and eventually wear you down and you will lose the match.

So in the long run, if you expect to play with a partner more capable of holding up her side, you should place her back from the net. Halfway between the net and the service line is fine, but if she doesn't know how to volley too well, then she should play back six feet. She will then be able to cover a lot of lobs, and it will be harder to put the ball in back of her from an angle at the net.

More balls will be hit to her, but this will make the game more interesting to her and will improve her volleying with the added practice.

If your male opponent is hogging the court, hit to where he should be. Tell yourself ahead of time that you will hit down his alley regardless, and then you won't be trying to make up your mind in the middle of a point. This will tend "to keep him honest" and stay more on his own side of the court.

Don't try to overpoach. Some men try to poach on every ball that crosses the net. You will waste a lot of energy making futile rushes, you will confuse your partner as to which balls she should take, and you will end up being passed on your own side time and again. If you can't put the ball away on the poach, you are leaving yourself open to their return—on the side you just left.

You should always act as though the match is as trivial as chasing butterflies. This leaves you an out if you lose since it really wasn't important. More important, you may mislead your opponents into taking the match too lightly while you and your partner are going all out.

When your girl partner makes a good shot, praise her, especially if against your male opponent. He may not mind your scoring against him but that a mere girl should outwit him may upset him.

If your partner misses a few, hold back on your criticisms. If our mixed doubles partners never missed any balls, they wouldn't be playing with us, they'd be on the pro tour.

If the other team generously accords your team extra serves when they return an "out" serve, then you should do the same for them. If you want to deny a hard serving opponent an extra serve when you belt the ball back on an out serve, then you will have to refuse to accept extra serves yourself. If he serves much harder than you do, then exchanging the extra serves would work a hardship on you so you should refuse them.

When you coach your partner, you should sugarcoat your advice with, "You're hitting your forehand well but how about trying a lob when you're forced way back of the baseline?"

If you are losing by trying to outhit your opponents, try another type of attack. When the man charges up to the net, chop the ball easily at his feet. Or float a few lobs over his partner's head.

In mixed doubles, most men tend to overhit to win the point in a hurry. They feel that if they don't put the ball away right then that the next ball will go to their partners, who will undoubtedly lose the point. This isn't always true but you yourself shouldn't fall prey to this delusion.

Keep the ball going back and tell your partner that you don't expect any spectacular shots from her. If you both keep the ball in play, your male opponent may blast it out through overeagerness.

In returning serve, if your partner can't keep it away from the net man who kills it, you should stay back on the baseline. Similarly, if you can't make a good return on the serve, your partner should stay back on the baseline. From there, you can both defend better against weak returns.

Feminine viewpoint. Many ladies prefer mixed doubles because male partners are usually more polite than feminine partners, the tennis presents a greater challenge with the men running faster and hitting harder than in a ladies' doubles and also because the matches can broaden your social outlook. In fact, if you improve enough, you may be invited to play with three men and what's wrong with being the only female on a tennis court?

However, although mixed doubles matches may begin on a light-hearted note, don't be lulled into thinking that it doesn't matter who wins. Men remain competitive creatures in all tennis matches and would prefer an expert Lady MacBeth as a partner to a dub Helen of Troy.

During a match, concentrate, concentrate, concentrate. Let your feminine opponent idly watch other matches going on while her own game suffers. You concentrate and play your best and next time both males will want you for a partner.

Read the chapters on doubles and tactics in doubles. You will see that some suggestions that apply in men's doubles do not apply to a girl who doesn't run as fast. For example, when you are up at the net and the ball goes way over your head, your male partner should try for it.

Try to hit as many balls as possible to your feminine opponent especially, because she is more likely to miss than her male partner. In case of doubt, hit through the middle and on the side of your feminine opponent. Make a real effort to get your first serves in for even if you don't serve hard, your opponents will stay back to receive it. If you do miss a first serve, get your second serve in, regardless of how easy it is. Serving doubles in a mixed doubles match is a crime since you are giving away a point instead of making your opponents work for it.

Naturally, you will miss some shots but try not to apologize or you will be calling attention to your mistakes. The less you say, the more others forget since they are thinking mostly of their own shots.

Because of their intense desire to win, men players want to take as many balls as possible. This is all right if you are playing for some grand trophy but in a social match, the only way you'll improve is to hit a lot of balls. If you don't improve, you will limit the number of male partners who will play with you.

Your male partner should take the balls through the middle and those over your head. He should poach at the net (see the chapter on poaching) only if he can kill the ball. If he merely stabs at it, he will leave himself open at the side he left.

If your partner runs way into your court time and again and takes your ball, keep swinging. Aim for the seat of his pants, because if you hit him on the head, it might splinter or warp your racket. Then say sweetly, "I'm *so* sorry. But you did run right in front of me. And this is *my* half of the court, isn't it?"

Keep repeating, *"My* half of the court" to remind him that unto each of you is granted one half.

Never applaud your partner when he has stolen a ball way on your side. You will only encourage him to keep robbing you of shots.

As I mentioned before, all male partners mean well, but some may keep showering you with advice. If he gives you a little at a time and it is helpful, fine. Otherwise, tell him sweetly that you're not a computer and just can't remember to do everything at once.

As a very last resort, advise him, "If you'd started sooner, you'd reach those balls. . . . Bend your knees . . . Watch the ball."

You can endear yourself to your male partner by resolutely refusing to indulge in chatty comments with your feminine opponents about nontennis items, such as dresses, parties or other people. Think only of tennis and you'll make a much better player.

Go over these features from time to time and later, you will apply them unconsciously to win more matches.

Last of all but certainly not least, is the fact that romances flourish on the tennis court like flowers in a greenhouse.

I was once teaching a beautiful model, a beginner, when a world famous player stopped by to watch. It took me all of two minutes to realize he was not there to study my teaching methods. When the lesson ended, he offered to buy me a cup of coffee and asked my pupil if she would care to join us. We accepted.

During our coffee break, the player displayed a great deal of interest in furthering her tennis career and rallied with her after her next lesson. He not only began giving her free lessons but took her to dinner as well. In fact, he ended up marrying her. The player? Pancho Gonzales.

Madeline and Pancho now have three delightful little girls who combine Madeline's beauty with Pancho's warm personality. As for me, I lost a pupil but gained a rating as Cupid's helper, second class.

For Seniors Only

Will playing tennis make you young again? Will it restore your madcap, tempestuous youth when you considered dance bands more important than your bank balance? Will you start frequenting teenage movies and collect pictures of popular singers? Will you read *Downbeat* instead of *The Wall Street Journal?*

Not very likely. And just as well.

Will tennis slim down your waistline and reduce your figure to that of a collegian again? Tennis could but not unless you also (gulp) cut down on your eating too.

But playing tennis should keep you more alert, more positive in your reaction to life, and add years to your life. Dr. Paul Dudley White and other heart specialists have declared that regular exercise promotes health and longevity in older people.

You could get regular exercise by going through calisthenics, trotting around a track every morning before breakfast, and doing pushups in the evening. But who would follow such a dull routine? Only a professional athlete whose livelihood depends on keeping in top condition.

To see the beneficial effect of tennis on older people, you should watch a senior veterans (over forty-five years) tournament in California. (There are also divisions for over fifty-five, over sixty-five, and even over seventy!) Nonplaying spectators are usually amazed to learn they have underestimated the ages of the players by ten or fifteen years. One reason for this younger appearance is that the seniors generally lead a healthful regimen to maintain their tennis skill. But another reason is that playing tennis sustains flexibility and suppleness of muscle so that the seniors do move around like younger men.

Some spectators are amazed not that the seniors play so well but that they can play at all at their advanced ages. Yet there are literally hundreds of players in this country over sixty and some even nudging seventy who play a respectable game. The late King Gustav V of Sweden, who played until his mid-eighties, is a notable example.

However, regardless of its effect in promoting radiant health, tennis affords recreation that demands so much attention that you can't think of outside problems.

Senior beginners. This group also includes former players who are taking the game up after a lapse of some years.

The chances are you feel toward tennis like a child does toward getting a bicycle. Tennis presents something new and different and adds a new dimension to your way of life.

This enthusiasm can greatly aid you in improving your game and thus getting more fun out of it. In fact, this desire to play tennis is considered the most valuable asset by veteran tournament players. We'll discuss this desire later in the section for them.

Meanwhile, what should you do to improve rapidly?

1. Work yourself into better shape, but make haste slowly. Begin walking more and riding less. Park your car a block or two farther away, and avoid shortcuts. Stroll around the block a couple of times on your lunch hour or before going to bed.

Walk downstairs instead of taking the elevator. Walking is the easiest form of exercise, but don't try any five-mile hikes right off, or you'll wake up the next morning a mass of sore muscles.

Gradually increase your walking, and you'll be walking easier and with more of a stride. Then you'll be exercising your feet, your legs, and your heart.

See the chapter on conditioning for more exercises. Get a leather skipping rope and skip rope a little every day. Learn to lift up your feet and bounce, and you'll reach a lot more balls in tennis.

2. As you exercise more, you'll find that you sleep better. Many brain workers deliberately exercise with dull physical routines with none of the fun of tennis in order to sleep. So you should not

only spend more time on tennis but also allot more time for sleeping.

For sleep not only "knits the raveled sleeve of care" but builds up and reinforces your stamina. Athletes sleep from nine to ten hours to build their vitality, and you should now sleep more than before.

Taking a short nap does wonders also. Some doctors claim that a short nap during the day is worth twice the same length of night sleep. Many athletes take catnaps before crucial tests of their mettle.

3. Work on your strokes. Aim to secure a rounded game instead of relying on one powerhouse stroke.

A young player can run all over to cover up a weak backhand or storm the net constantly to avoid backcourt duels, but a senior player doesn't have an unlimited line of energy credit in his own bank. Your model should be the skillful Ulysses rather than the bold Achilles—the master of many strokes who relies on guile to succeed instead of furiously attacking with just one.

If you lack a volley, study the chapter on volleying, and practice. You'll find your improvement pays off in winning more points and putting more pressure on your opponents.

By thus adding to your arsenal of weapons, you become a better player and a tougher competitor.

4. Analyze the other fellow's game. Sometimes a doubles match turns into a cozy coffee break in which all four make frequent comments on every point and try to say something funnier than the last remark. In fact, some such matches are more interesting to listen to than to play in.

However, the essence of tennis is to triumph against obstacles, and you will be losing more than you win if you chatter so much that you lose your concentration. If you join in such friendly, talkative encounters, you should be the Great Stone Face, the non-talker.

Then concentrate on the failings of your opponents. Do they prefer low-bouncing balls on the backhand? Give them high-bouncing balls in the corner.

Do they prefer a series of hard drives? Mix up your drives with slow floaters to break up their timing.

Do they run around their backhands in receiving service? Serve wide to the forehand once in a while to keep them honest.

Are they slow in running up for short balls? Drop a couple of easy balls just over the net. Then lob their return over their heads. Do they play right on top of the net? Lob to the backhand side. Most players form habits or patterns of shots. They will prefer hitting crosscourt forehands when you take the net against them instead of down the line. They will try a dozen times in a set to hit the return of serve down the net man's alley—whether he stays or moves over to poach.

Study your opponents' habits and thus prepare yourself to reply to their shots.

5. Don't try to cover every single ball that comes over. If your opponent makes a perfect drop shot, save your breath to compliment him. Then the next time he tries it, start sooner. If he keeps making drop shots, keep complimenting him to conceal your annoyance, for if he thinks that you're annoyed and disgusted, he'll relax and use the drop shot more effectively. However, if you don't seem discomfited, he may try to make the drop shot even more perfect—and end up using it too often or lose his touch.

At any rate, do not waste energy chasing balls that are hopelessly gone. The chances are that even if you reach them, you won't be able to do much with them.

Incidentally, if your opponent chases madly after a ball, you may encourage him to keep chasing these hopeless shots by murmuring, "Good try. You almost got it. You can certainly run." Thus encouraged, he'll try to run as though he owned the Fountain of Youth—until he runs out of gas in the second set.

A youngster can and should play all day long. He is trying to learn shots, to size up situations, to meet different types of competitors for tournament experience. But a senior should learn to pace himself.

If you haven't played much and you are starting in again, you will be able to play more as you go along. But there comes a point when you just can't play eight sets in a row—or perhaps four sets. Whatever your limit is, you should stay within it. If you are feeling tired after three hot sets and they want to play a fourth, stop right then and there.

The reason is that you'll play sloppily, not get into position, or slap any old way at the ball. You'll be setting your game back a notch by slipping into bad habits.

Besides, if you quit while you still feel like a little more, you'll play your next match the next day or weekend with more zest.

6. You are facing a youngster who brims over with vitality. How can you counteract his overwhelming advantage in energy, since he can run all day?

The best answer is change of pace. Give a young sprout a couple of hard drives to the same place, and by the time he gets a third one, he is hitting in a groove and cracking the ball for winners. Hit a hard drive, then a soft floater, then a really deep one, and keep varying the pace.

Try to push him off court with short-angle shots. Most youngsters when forced off court try to blast for winners.

If he rushes the net on you, mix up short balls at his feet with lobs. Whatever you do, lob deep. If you lob short a few times, you sharpen his overhead until he can really kill a fairly good lob.

If he stays backcourt mostly, feed him a short ball. Lots of youngsters can hit for winners from the baseline, but learning to hit approach shots takes patience and practice. More of them miss so-called easy approach shots than hard-hit drives backcourt.

Don't try to outslug him unless you happen to possess a better forehand. Kids like speed, and usually the more you give them fast balls, the better they hit them.

Invariably, when playing a junior, he becomes disgusted at missing shots and he'll scowl, mutter, scold himself, hit the ball against the fence, and perhaps even fire his racket into the fence. If you're human, you can't help feeling sorry for him. Poor kid, he just can't cope with your game because he's having an "off" day.

So you let down a little and quit pressuring him into chasing all over the court. Junior starts to get a few more balls in and you happen to miss a couple. Suddenly, the dark clouds disappear from Junior's face and a sunny smile flits over it. Now he's got you on the run, and you feel dismayed at the sudden change in fortunes.

The next you know, he's grinning in victory and saying you did put up a good fight—while his face tells you he thinks he can beat you any time.

Juniors are like revolving doors in changes of mood. Watch a couple of juniors playing, and you'll see more histrionics than in an all-star movie. They take everything big—their successes and their failures. But just because you've made a couple of good shots that depress him doesn't mean that he's giving up. All he needs is to pull off a couple of winners himself, and his confidence returns like the tide coming in.

So once you've got Junior on the ropes, keep him there. Force him on the defensive, and keep him off balance with your change of pace. Don't pause to show Junior how to improve his backhand or to offer him advice. Wait until after the match ends before telling him to serve easier to get more aces. He may listen to your advice and begin to follow it—and send you down the chutes to defeat. Do not give him the same shot all the time, or he'll learn how to cope with it.

Always try to end a match against Junior as quickly as possible. The longer the match goes on, the more it favors the younger player. Mother Nature has loaded him with energy, so that he can afford to waste bushel baskets of it, while you can't afford to waste handfuls.

Even when it comes to taking a rest, he'll recuperate faster than you do. Bill Tilden told me that he never took rest periods when he got older between the third and fourth sets against young opponents. He reasoned that while the rest would aid him somewhat, it would rejuvenate the younger player much more.

Many seniors do not like opposing juniors because of the latter's actions on the court: the frowning, the groaning, the muttered epithets, the ups and downs in moods. These actions may annoy you, but the junior is giving you practice against faster shots and quicker reactions, and these tend to speed up your game. Junior also tends to rush the net more, and this gives you a chance to practice your passing shots and your lobs.

Opposing senior players. When you take on another senior, you will face an entirely different opponent from a hard-slugging, erratic, speedy junior.

Where Junior tends to rush over, retrieve balls, and fire a serve before you are quite ready, Senior tends to dawdle between points to husband his strength.

Junior may become upset over your peculiar shots, but Senior has played against so many different kinds of games and strokes that your particular brand does not surprise him.

Everything else is reversed. You should try to make Senior run, run, run. And the longer the match goes, if you make him do the running, the more likely you are to win.

For Seniors Only

Junior usually plays his own game and ignores yours. A cagey senior will try to size up your game and ferret out your failings— so he can pounce on them.

Where Junior goes around muttering to himself over missing shots, Senior will be talking directly to you, purposely or not; lavishly praising your game to cause you to let down; offering sympathy for your errors so you'll feel self-pity and quit trying; or stalling by stopping to converse with you as you change courts. Senior will be gauging the effect of his remarks on you, while Junior is so wrapped up in his troubles that he doesn't care how you react.

Juniors are more gullible and more easily taken in, while seniors are suspicious of your motives. Juniors usually possess orthodox stokes executed more smoothly, while a group of seniors will display awkward but effective strokes dating from a museum. The answer is that the juniors nowadays start off much better with smoother strokes than did the seniors, whose best models were awkward and ungainly strokers.

Seniors are in no hurry to win a point, because they play more cautiously from having learned the hard way that eight out of ten points are won by errors and only two by clean placements. Don't try to blast a senior off court, since he'll return so many that you'll lose confidence and revert to dinking.

Look for the weaknesses in a senior's game. He has probably developed patterns and habits of where he hits the ball and how hard on certain shots. He may stand way off to one side to serve to you. Try returning crosscourt and then down the line to see which shots he handles least effectively.

Many times a senior has illusions of grandeur about bringing off a shot because he has happened to make a lucky one early in the match. For instance, you are standing right on top of the net and he tries to pass you down the line with hardly a foot to spare on the outside alley line. If he does pass you, you should congratulate him, and every time he keeps missing it, you should shake your head and say, "Tough luck. I thought you had me." If you're lucky, he'll keep trying to make the perfect shot all through the match.

Try to keep your patience when you play a dawdler who takes forever to pick up a ball, go back, and serve to you. He may not be trying to stall but simply does not move quickly any time.

Since seniors usually prefer the backcourt, use more shots to draw them up than against juniors. And lobs work better against seniors, for they don't smash as hard to kill them outright and don't retreat as quickly. However, seniors are more likely to stay as far back as the service line from the net, so that you have to watch to see where they station themselves after coming up on a short ball. If a senior parks himself at the service line, your best answer is to hit a drive (not too hard) about a foot over the net to catch him at his feet.

To embellish Francis Bacon in his essay, "Of Youth and Age," *"Men of age object too much* to innovations in tennis or business; *consult too long* for two seniors in doubles will hold more conferences between points than an advertising agency with a million-dollar client; *adventure too little* in suddenly rushing the net from back-court or trying a brand new shot; *and seldom drive business home to the full period, but content themselves with a mediocrity of success."* Or, seniors who once establish a lead in a match are inclined to coast the rest of the way.

So once you get an opponent on the run, don't let up. Keep the pressure on him and he won't be able to call forth a sudden burst of energy to counteract your tactics as a junior could.

For Parents Only

Breathes there a parent who never to himself has said, "If I guide my child the right way, he may become a champion."

Certainly many parents have guided their children to the top-flight ranks. The parents of René Lacoste, Suzanne Lenglen, Sarah Palfrey Danzig, Anita Lizana, Earl Buchholz, Dennis Ralston, Frank Froehling, Jr., and Cliff and Nancy Richey all started and aided them.

There is besides an endless list of parents who have guided their children into enjoying the game as a pastime and into becoming tournament players.

So how soon should you start your child at tennis?

Ken Rosewall started when he was eight years old and never quit. Alex Olmedo played briefly at nine and didn't start again until the ripe old age of fifteen.

Patricia Henry Yeomans, former national girl champion, handed sawed-off rackets to her twin sons, Bill and John, when they were two years old. That's right, *two* years old. She did it only to keep them busy batting balls while she was playing a match on the next court. If starting very young would produce champions, they would now be dividing the world trophies. For they learned under ideal conditions: playing the year round in Southern California with the best equipment and competition available and counseled by parents who know every angle of the game. (Father Ed twice won the

National Hard Court Seniors' Singles.) The fact is that if the Yeomans family kept all the trophies they won, they wouldn't have room in the house for dishes, books, or clothes. Let alone furniture.

However, although the boys have done far better than most college players, other boys who started later have overtaken them. One reason might be that the parents didn't stand over them with paddles to make them practice endlessly. Or because they lacked the mysterious quality that marks the champion that Billy Talbert labels X. Or as Pancho Gonzales puts it, a player must also be hungry—like himself, Alex Olmedo, and Pancho Segura—filled with an intense yearning to become a champion.

Thus starting at a very early age does not guarantee the Wimbledon trophy.

Perry T. Jones, who has guided the destinies of thousands of tournament players, stated that a child should start at about nine years of age. He asserted that the years from ten to fifteen are the most important to learn the muscular habits of stroking the ball, moving about the court, and adjusting to the speed and direction of the ball.

Most pros think the child can start batting balls for fun at any age provided the child is strong enough to swing a racket. And keeps asking to hit tennis balls.

Let's consider the racket he uses. If you hand him your old racket, he may find it a warclub he can hardly lift. Pancho Segura started using two hands on his forehand because the racket was too heavy for him to swing any other way. Since he developed the most devastating forehand in tennis, you may ask, "So what's wrong with my child using a two-fisted forehand?"

Nothing, if he possesses Pancho's lightning reflexes, great stamina, and intense desire to win. Otherwise, your child may wind up with an awkward forehand.

If your child has asked to hit balls, buy him his own racket. It could be a junior-size racket if he's eight or nine, but not too cheap, please. I saw my first tennis match when Bill Tilden played against J. O. Anderson. I got inspired, saved my pennies, bought a fifty-nine-cent racket. It lasted two whole weeks of battering balls and made me temporarily quit tennis in the belief that only rich people with yachts could afford it.

But when I bought a better racket ($2.59), I could feel

the difference, so I decided it was worth saving up for and thus continued my unspectacular career. So get a racket with strings tight enough so your child can feel a ping when he hits the ball. That's all he wants at this stage—the deep satisfaction of cracking a ball in the center of his racket.

Start out by having him hit balls against a wall. Turn him sideways, hold his hand, and guide the racket back so that it will drop below his waist line and lift under the ball. Lifting under the ball at his age is very important, since the net is relatively much higher for him than for you.

After both hitting a couple of balls, drop a ball for him to hit. Drop some more balls until he connects, and then have him toss a ball for himself and swing at it.

Remind him, *"Lift* into the ball." Then after a while, ask him to repeat your instructions. In fact, when you give instructions, always ask your child to repeat them.

What do you think is the most important factor in the child's learning tennis?

To learn to watch the ball? No.

To learn the right swing? No.

To learn the right grip? No.

The most important factor is: Have fun.

At his age, he doesn't realize that some future day his tennis skill will enable him to make friends easily in a strange city. He doesn't realize he may earn his school letter and become a college notable. He doesn't realize he might even become champion. All he wants is to have fun.

If you shriek and yell at him for missing shots, he will become conditioned into thinking that tennis is a middle-class torture chamber. What would you think of a teacher who yelled, "Don't spell it CATT! And not RAT nor KATT nor CCATT. How can you be so stupid as to spell it CAAT? Wake up and don't write it KAAT."

Yet parents will frequently scold a child by pointing out his mistakes. *Be positive.* Tell him only what he should do.

If tennis pros coached like some parents, they'd end up in sanitariums or starve to death. Unlike the car rental firm that tries harder, parents try *too* hard.

Make your practice with him easy for both of you. Choose a day that isn't too hot, because then exertion becomes exhaustion.

If you plan to play a match that day, *first* go out on a court with him. There is nothing more wearing after playing some hard, fast tennis than to find yourself reduced to tapping a ball gently. Also, you would be tired and less patient.

After the child has practiced against the wall on his own, take him out on the court. The younger he is, the less you should tell him and the shorter the session. Praise and encourage him for the few times he hits a ball. Make him feel he is accomplishing something by just connecting with the ball—which he is.

The younger he is, the closer he should stand to the net with you on the other side. When you hit balls to him, remember that the ball that bounces around your waist line is bouncing around his shoulders. As he improves, move him farther from the net.

The cry most often expressed by parents in France is, *"Regardez la balle!"* In Spain, the parents who reign over their children exclaim, *"¡Miranda la pelota!,"* while in Germany, they exhort, *"Auf den ball achten!"* In Yugoslavia, they call, *"Gled' aj Loptu!,"* and in Hungary, *"Nézzd a labdát!"* In English-speaking countries, the parents bark, "Watch the ball!"

If you feel compelled to say something, you might as well call out, *"Remember Pearl Harbor!"* or sing out, *"Erin Go Bragh!"* Because if there is one thing the child is doing, it is watching the ball. That's his problem—that's all he's doing and all he's concentrating on.

Instead, tell him to start taking his racket back sooner. Veteran players will run for a ball, and then on reaching it, will suddenly think about starting their swing—which is too late. A child is no different. He's intent only on running to the ball.

After the child starts his racket back sooner, tell him to *"Lift into the ball."* When he does that, he will transfer his weight toward the net and hit harder with less effort.

A tennis axiom is: Better to hit the ball too far than in the net. Start your child off right by telling him: Take a good swing at the ball. Not with all his might necessarily, but so he will learn to place his feet farther apart and to move his weight into the ball.

If his attention wanders, stop the session. You should try to quit while he still wants more and then he'll be eager for the next time. Tell him after he practices for a while that you'll hit some more with him. This will give him an incentive to practice.

Make a game out of how many he gets over the net. Count

how many he gets in a row. "You made six in a row for your world record last time. Let's see if you can make it nine in a row this time."

Work on the forehand until he can return some balls before starting on the backhand. The younger he is, the harder it may be for him to swing on the backhand. Tell him to use two hands at first, and as he grows stronger, to release the left hand as he takes the racket back. Then give him lots of low-bouncing balls on the backhand to bring it up to his forehand ability.

Teach him the serve by starting with the very last part of the swing. He should hold his racket back on his shoulder and swing forward and overhand at the ball. Tell him it's as though he were throwing his racket. At first he may use the forehand grip, because this makes it easier to get the serve in. If small, he may start serving between the service line and the baseline, and then as he improves, he may move back to the baseline to serve.

Play games so he will appreciate the idea of hitting the ball within certain lines. Let him win a point once in a while to increase his confidence. Keep encouraging him when he makes a good shot.

After he plays games, bring him to the net so he can practice volleying. He should learn to block or punch his volleys instead of taking a big backswing, and he should become accustomed to playing at net. He will then tend to play more there as he grows taller and can reach more balls.

Your child will get more real concentrated practice from you than from a youngster his own age. But he will enjoy the latter more, so try to line up another child or children for him to bat balls with. If they become friends, they won't mind spending a couple of hours hitting balls intermixed with pauses for drinks of water and conversation. Lots of parents think children are wasting their time when they are not hitting a tennis ball, but this companionship is part of the joy of tennis. Youngsters can spend a whole day on tennis courts by interspersing the tennis with talk about schools, studies, boys, girls, and athletics and parties, meanwhile swallowing incredible amounts of food. It's good for them because they associate tennis with pleasant companionship and not just grim determination to hit so many balls over the net.

Teaching girls. Take two groups, one of four boys and another of four girls. Tell each group just to rally and practice their strokes. Leave the boys alone and they will choose up sides and start playing a match to see which pair can beat the other. Leave the girls alone and they will meet at the net and start finding out which other girls they all know and start discussing them.

Or: Boys are more competitive than girls, who are more social minded. As you knew in the first place.

So the first thing to do after your daughter starts playing is to find another girl she likes or will come to like to play tennis with. Two girls will play together if they are friends even if one is far better than the other. If they don't get along, they can both play equally well, but they will make all kinds of excuses to avoid playing together. So check with other parents in the neighborhood to find a likely opponent about her own age and school grade.

Boys of vastly different social classes will play each other all the time, but girls usually mix only with those of the same background.

As mentioned before, males run faster than girls, and enjoy running. To give a girl a distinct advantage over other girls, train her to run, run, run. Most girls don't like to run, and if you develop your daughter into running easily, she will cover the court far better and reach twice as many balls as the slow ones.

Induce your daughter into playing games like basketball with boys' rules and baseball. Skipping rope does wonders. Play catch with her, and throw the ball to one side so she has to run to catch it. Also have her throw the ball overhand. This will help her serve later.

The worst possible fate to befall a girl player is to go in for ballet dancing. Dancer Cyd Charisse has said, "Tennis is bad for my dancing."

This goes double for ballet dancing harming tennis players.

If Dante had included a separate portion of his Inferno for immoral tennis pros, he would have plagued them with near-sighted pupils who refuse to wear glasses, musclebound weight lifters, and dedicated ballet dancers.

You would think that dancers schooled in using their feet and legs would move more easily than nondancers, but it works the opposite way. The rigid locking of the knees and the tense, unnatural positions seem to combine to make it harder for a girl to bend her knees and let her body flow into the stroke. Any ordinary six-year-old boy will chase down a tennis ball better than a dozen dancers.

264

For Parents Only

When a tennis pro wants revenge on another tennis pro, he doesn't call up the local Mafia. He simply directs all longtime dancers to take lessons from his rival. The only worse pupil is a weight lifter who is so musclebound that he can hardly lift a racket over his head.

This is not to say that a once-a-week ballet class for a winter will ruin a girl's tennis. But if she continues year after year, she will never have to worry about beating her boy friends, even if they started the game the previous week.

Ballroom dancing is something else again. Usually any activity that uses your legs helps you in tennis, and tennis makes you use your legs. Basketball is wonderful for tennis. Tony Trabert played on the University of Cincinnati basketball team and found that it promoted great conditioning and agility. Lots of tennis players at colleges win the intramural long-distance events because they excel at running so much.

However, intensive swimming hinders the tennis player, for it develops the long muscles and slows down quick reactions. You needn't worry about your daughter spending a lot of time at a pool or beach and swimming too much since girls hardly get their suits wet when there are boys to talk with on the shore.

In fact, you can stimulate her tennis interest by practicing with her and pointing out that she has to develop enough to return balls before she can play with boys, and that the better she plays, the more likely it is that she will play with boys.

Should your child take lessons? Asking a tennis pro whether your child should take lessons is like asking an auto salesman whether you should trade in your old car for a new one. What else would he answer but, "Of course."

However—and I may be hanged in effigy by the coaches' association—lots of times he should not, especially at the start.

Every child has to learn to run for a ball, to judge the bounce, to develop his muscles, to take a healthy swing, to start his swing sooner. If he starts the very first time with a coach, he will have to spend time developing those faculties.

Isn't that what a coach is for?

Sure.

But any parent could just as well follow the directions about hitting the forehand to show his child. Any parent can hit balls to make the child run a little farther and improve his timing. The

265

child has to swing at thousands of balls before he learns the art of returning balls steadily. Somebody has to be on the other side of the net some of the time to correct and direct him.

This is why coaches insist that the pupil practice as much as possible. Some coaches make a pupil practice five hours at least between lessons. They know that lessons alone are not enough, and that lots of practice develops the child faster. Sometimes this insistence on practice can backfire.

I started the then six-year-old daughter of George MacCall, the illustrious Davis Cup team captain and promoter, by telling Polly that she must practice every single day against a wall.

Two weeks later George called unhappily and asked about her instructions to practice.

"She promised to practice faithfully every day," I said.

"But at five in the morning under my bedroom window?"

Polly had to be told there was a time and place for practicing.

Ah, the enthusiasm of youth! I recall getting up really early, hiking over to the Jackson Park tennis courts with a friend, climbing the locked gates, and playing for an hour before breakfast.

We would run like mad at the sight of the caretaker, but one morning he cornered us. He shouted that we were ruining the courts by playing when they were wet, and he threatened to call a cop. Nowadays a youngster would retort that his parents would sue him and the cop for false arrest, and that the caretaker would be thrown into prison if he so much as laid a finger on a minor.

But in those quaint days, there were no soft-hearted reformers excusing crimes as being due to bad environment or to the need for releasing tensions. We knew that if a cop caught a law-breaker, the judge would hand down the appropriate punishment. We threw ourselves on the mercy of the court, as it were, and promised to behave ourselves according to the regulations.

"After this, I don't want to find you kids trying to climb the high fence and breaking your idiot necks," said the caretaker. "There's a much easier place to get in—by the storage yard wall."

As we got better, we found that a bumpy clay court hampered our fun, so we became the guardians to keep off intruders when the courts were still wet. From our group, Scott Rexinger became the Big Ten Champion and James M. Farrin now Admiral (Ret.) played for the Naval Academy and later with his son, reached the finals of the National Father and Son Championship twice.

If anybody had tried to force us to play on boiling hot days, to play until the street lights came on at dark, to compete during gales that made the dusty courts like the Sahara during a sandstorm, and to sweep snow off asphalt courts, we would have rebelled. But to us, this was just part of the joy of playing tennis under handicaps.

So when you practice with your child, be cheerful even if it kills you. He will then regard tennis sessions as fun.

If you are uncertain about the wisdom of your coaching him, ask yourself:

1. Are you patient enough to stand on a court and hit dozens of balls to one special spot for him to practice?

2. Can you place the balls well enough to give him this practice?

3. Are your own strokes good enough for him to copy?

Make it easier for yourself by keeping the sessions short at first. Give them while you are fresh. Expect no sudden miracles for the child to learn in a few months what it took you years. When you find yourself growing irritated, quit.

If you have played for years, you should be able to place the ball where you want. This will sharpen your own accuracy by hitting with less speed but more control.

Amateur coaches tend to mold their pupils into the image of their own strokes. If they serve awkwardly but effectively, they tend to teach the same serve. If your own strokes are fairly orthodox, teach him, but don't force him to deliver exact imitations of yours.

Children develop in varying stages. One will improve greatly at first and then stay on a plateau for a while. Another will seem hopeless but gradually catch up. I once had a pupil who was the worst in the group and could hardly walk across the court without tripping on his own feet. He also had the loftiest ambition of all: He wanted to make his high school team.

I could have said that if there were five youngsters with rackets in the school he would be lucky to be sixth. But I told him to practice daily, keep the ball deep, and work to become a steady rather than brilliant player. He gradually improved so he could return a few balls, and this encouraged him to practice even more. He never did learn to volley with much skill, but he managed to develop a steady backhand and a punishing forehand. To everybody's surprise except his own, he ended up in his senior year as captain of the team.

Naturally, every struggling player won't do that well, but if he keeps at it, he may well surpass the athlete who doesn't practice. Most of all, if nobody tells him how awkward he is, he will keep trying and eventually develop a fair game.

Literally thousands of parents have guided their children into becoming better players than they themselves ever were and have instilled in them a lifetime love of the great game. You can do the same if you use your head in guiding them.

You should take him sometime to a tournament, especially a junior tournament. Explain that all players started the same way as he has. He can see youngsters of his own age hitting the ball and understand that it doesn't take twenty years to learn the game.

Guard against taking him to a day-long tournament or he may become bored by the matches; if possible, take along another young friend.

You should also take him to a tennis clinic. These demonstrations will not only explain the mechanics of the game but should stimulate his desire by his watching first-rate players.

You might start him out with a coach who gives group lessons. These don't cost nearly as much as private lessons and will bring him into contact with other players of his own age for practice.

Before signing for a series, check:

1. That he will hit balls most of the period.

2. That the group isn't too large for some individual instruction. If nobody ever checks his swing or grip, he won't learn too much.

I have given group lessons limited to eight, using two courts for an hour so that four players rally on each court during the whole time. Then I would go from one to the other to check their swings and recommend changes during the period.

Tennis camps also provide concentrated instruction and practice. Be sure to check with former pupils to determine the quality of the instruction and if they considered it worthwhile. Tennis camps are expensive, so you want to make sure you are getting your money's worth. However, since the practice is so concentrated, a real beginner wouldn't benefit as much as a more experienced player, since a beginner would get tired much sooner.

How do you pick a coach for individual instruction? Usually you are better off to choose one in your own area, since it would make it easier for your child to become acquainted with and practice with children in his own area.

People vary in their opinions of coaches as they do of doctors. Ask tournament players or officials to name the five leading coaches in your area. Then you may choose from the names that appear most frequently. Or have your child take one lesson and see how it works out.

You should impress on your child when he starts his lessons that he has to practice according to instructions, or you will stop the lessons. Work out a schedule with him as to how much time he can give to tennis; when he knows what is expected of him, he will follow the schedule much better than if it is left vague.

If you take your child to the coach, note what points he is stressing. Write them down if possible. Don't interpose your own opinions, because this distracts the child, divides his attention, and antagonizes the coach. Afterward, you may ask questions if something isn't clear in your mind or the child's.

You should ask the coach for names of other youngsters of the same age and ability for practice sessions with yours. Some of them may be better, some worse than your child. The one way to ruin a coach's day is to insist that you want your child to practice *only* with better players. If a child loses every time he plays, he won't develop enough confidence to beat a four-year-old. As I said before, a player should play with all kinds of players.

If your child takes a liking to another child who may not be as good, so what? If they get started practicing, they will learn much faster than sitting around waiting to play much better players.

Parents like to see their child as a magnified edition of themselves, with all their strengths and none of their weaknesses. Especially in tennis. They tend to expect too much too soon. If you feel that the coach isn't bringing out your child's ability or that his methods lack direction, you should change coaches. Some parents, however, shop around from one coach to another in a game of musical chairs to find one who will suddenly uplift their child to instant championships. Most often, the fault, dear Brutus, lies within our own progeny who lack the desire and talent to rise more quickly up the tennis stairway.

You should go easy on the child when he's starting out. Wait until he's really motivated to play matches before outlining a program to improve his game. When he loses, console him rather than berate him.

Youngsters take defeats much more to heart than veterans. Would you believe that I once became so upset over losing a match that I wouldn't wait for my ride, hiked nine miles back home, and then wouldn't eat dinner? Not even the apple pie à la mode with two scoops of ice cream? Nowadays if I lose a match, I know it wasn't my fault—my partner had an off day, or it was windier on our side than on theirs.

As for choosing an older or a younger coach: The young ones generate more enthusiasm, the older ones bank on experience. But I feel that you should mistrust a coach who makes all his pupils swing exactly the same way and play exactly the same types of games. There are as many ways to play tennis as there are players. The wise coach seeks to develop the inherent abilities of varying types.

If you have more than one child playing tennis, develop the older ones first, and keep them ahead of the others. If the younger ones become better, the older ones are likely to quit the game, since they would hate losing to younger children.

How can you tell if your child has talent? Oddly enough, if he is better than average at the piano or the violin, he will play better-than-average tennis. I have found a high degree of correlation between music and tennis, and some of my best pupils who improved the most rapidly were musicians.

Years ago, Perry T. Jones asked me if I would mind rallying with a boy from out of town who was playing in a junior tournament at the Los Angeles Tennis Club. I hit some balls, no instruction, with the lad, who seemed hardly taller than a net post. Later, Mr. Jones asked about the boy.

"He's amazing," I said. "He hits every single ball right in the middle of his racket, clean, crisp. What did you say his name was?"

"Ralston," said Mr. Jones. "Dennis Ralston."

It takes no skill to spot talent in a youngster like Dennis. It's as obvious as a beautiful girl in a group of fat matrons. It took no skill to spot talent in Jon Douglas, later a Davis Cup player nor in Ed Atkinson, who won the National Intercollegiate Doubles with Alex Olmedo.

Youngsters with talent move faster, more easily, hit with less effort, and anticipate like mind readers. They are perfectionists and sometimes vent their displeasure at losing like an Academy Award winning actor in a dramatic scene. They try much harder and practice longer.

Working on strokes is the mark of talented youngsters. If a child goofs off time and again, he may simply lack interest at that stage. But in the long run, he must discipline himself in striving to improve his strokes. The juniors today are like jet planes in stroke equipment compared with Sopwith Camels of the juniors of forty years ago. Parents can sometimes force or coerce their youngsters into becoming fair players, but the really talented ones feel the motivation within themselves. When they lose, it is like Napoleon at Waterloo; when they win, it is like Julius Caesar overwhelming the Gauls.

As a parent, you can do much to aid your child's progress. Play with him, encourage his progress, and remember that while you yourself may play the sharpshooting game of Rosewall, your child may pattern himself after hard-hitting, net-rushing Rod Laver.

Even if your child never becomes a tournament player, it is far better for him to chase balls on a tennis court than trying to elude police officers in a riot.

For Juniors Only

You are a junior who wants to improve. You may want to improve enough to make your high school team or your college team. Or you may want to go farther in tournaments, to win a local event, a state championship, or even to make the Davis Cup team. What should you do to become a much better player?

You will go much farther if you play according to the type of person you are than if you try to copy the methods of some expert completely different in temperament. But if you are starting out or haven't played much, you needn't decide right now whether you are a net rusher or a baseliner at heart.

1. *C-a-r-r-y the ball.* First of all, learn to hit the ball instead of merely poking at it. Learn to c-a-r-r-y the ball on your racket, and take a full swing. You need not slug the ball, but it's better to hit too far rather than in the net.

Study the chapters on various strokes to see how you should c-a-r-r-y the ball on your racket. This will enable you to get your weight into the ball, for after all, you must hit with some speed or you won't go too far in tournaments.

2. *Think deep.* Unless you are playing a net rusher who goes up all the time on anything, you can win a lot of matches by simply playing the ball deep. It's much harder for your opponent to earn a point from back on the baseline, and many times he

will become overanxious and give you a free point by making an error.

The pros skim the net with their shots because their opponents are rushing the net all the time, but you will be playing against slower opponents who can't rush in that quickly—unless you give them a short ball around the service line.

Hit your shots at least one or two racket lengths over the net to make the ball bounce near the baseline.

Later, when you want to rush the net yourself, you will find it easier to get in because your deep shots will usually bring short returns.

So think deep!

3. *Play steady.* Maybe you delight in slugging the ball now to mow down your opponents. Of course, you miss a lot of shots, but you may figure that with practice you'll get all those thunderbolts in. You might, but then again, you'll be losing a lot of matches you shouldn't lose at all.

Juniors are notorious for giving away free points in every game by slugging too hard on easy balls. You get your opponent way out of court, and all you need do is hit with fair pace to the other side. But instead you slug away, and the ball hits the net. The result is that your opponent gets more than one point: He feels encouraged to retrieve even harder because you may miss again, and you feel discouraged at missing, and this may upset you for a couple more points.

You need not *push* the ball back, but you can learn to hit with medium pace. Then sometime you'll face a wild slugger and you will discover that if you return the ball deep a few times, he will haul off and knock the ball out by a mile. You won't earn the match—he'll give it to you.

So learn to return the ball deep to the corners five, eight, twelve times in a row. In fact, if you hit the ball back seven times, you can then slug the ball any way you want on the eighth—because your opponent will rarely return seven balls. Unless you are playing in the higher echelons of junior tennis.

Sometime for the fun of it, see how many times you can rally with another player to hit the ball on the first bounce just to keep it going. See if you can actually return the ball one hundred times in a row.

Play steady, and you'll beat players with much better strokes and who hit a lot harder.

4. *Try to dominate opponents.* The essence of winning tennis is to force the other player on the defensive. Then he can't get set for his favorite shots, because you're putting too much pressure on him.

Try to place the ball from corner to corner, to lob over your opponent's head when he comes charging in. Make him run.

By learning to place the ball, you will be improving your game and, most of all, learning to dominate your opponent. You want to make him play your kind of game rather than have him force you to play his. If he prefers playing net while you do better backcourt, the more you force him to play backcourt, the less chance he has of making his favorite shots.

When you play a match, keep thinking about what your opponent does not like, and give it to him. The more he grumbles or moans, the more certain you know you are on the right track.

Naturally, you can't always feed him shots he dislikes, but by working on your own game, you can diversify your attack.

Maintain your dominance when you get a lead. Don't let your opponent "off the hook" by letting up once you've won the first set. Jack Kramer, former world champion, went out to beat his opponents 6–0, 6–0, 6–0.

Helen Wills Roark scored more one-sided victories than any other woman in tennis. To show how this established a habit in her, one time years later I was playing with her against Louise Brough and another male in a friendly match. We won the first set and were leading 5–2 in the second.

As we changed sides, I commented to Louise about how she'd been winning her serve and thus indicated that I felt she'd win it again and that this would leave it up to my following serve to close out the match at 6–3. But Queen Helen thought otherwise.

"Let's take her serve at love," she said.

Know something? We did because Helen played every ball as though it were match point against her.

Not a day passes at the Los Angeles Tennis Club but that players come in, saying, "I had him 5–2 in the third. . . . We had them 4–1 and my serve in the second after winning the first. . . . I had him forty–love on my serve at 6–5. . . ."

When they start off like that, you can write your own ending: The other team came back and trounced them.

The mark of all champions is domination of opponents and never giving them a chance to make a comeback. When you get a lead, pile up more points. Park your sympathy in the dressing room. You'll end up beating a lot of opponents with better strokes and greater knowledge but with only one failing: They let up.

5. *Never underestimate your opponent.* You may have easily beaten an opponent five times before, he may be using an old snowshoe of a racket, he may swing with awkward strokes and he may plod around the court like a broken-down mule. But never take an opponent too lightly.

Or you may join the crowd at the Wailing Wall of tennis as in the locker rooms at Forest Hills and Wimbledon. "How could I possibly lose to him? He has no strokes, no power, no talent . . . I beat him two, one and two a month ago . . ."

Juniors are the most unpredictable of all players. They can slam a ball into the corner as well as a pro and then miss an incredibly easy setup on the next shot. Their playing ability varies greatly from one day to the next. So even though you have climbed to a higher plateau from last year, it is still possible for you to slump to the depths while your supposedly inferior opponent plays over his head.

If you go into a match completely relaxed, you are psychologically unprepared to meet an equal opponent. You know if you expect to meet a tough opponent, you feel on edge, tense, nervous and can hardly wait to start playing. Mother Nature has poured adrenalin into your system to enable you to fight harder and longer, to race across court for shots you'd never dream of reaching in practice, to keep trying when dead tired and to force yourself to extraordinary efforts for victory.

But when you walk onto a court against a supposedly inferior opponent, you feel like joking, waving to friends and slapping any old way at the ball. Even when you lose a couple of games you still feel confident and loose—too loose. You figure you can turn on the pressure any old time.

You fall farther behind and start trying hard—too hard. You miss shots you should make. So then you hit easier—too easily. Your opponent moves in on your soft shots and knocks them off.

You lose the first set and get worried. You dig in and go all out. But your opponent has smelled the blood of a possible victory and he's playing over his head with the confidence of a winner. You try all kinds of shots but he's got an answer. You're struggling uphill while he's coasting all the way to win the match.

One trouble with underestimating an opponent is that you don't feel it is necessary to warm up before the match so you hit a couple of balls and then start cold. Meanwhile, your opponent may have warmed up beforehand and is ready to go top speed right off.

You should always practice all your strokes before a match if it is at all possible, either on a court or against a practice board. This will loosen your muscles, get you moving with the ball and groove your strokes.

You can't expect to practice for half an hour on the court with your opponent since in a tournament, you are allotted only three to five minutes warmup. You can try some serves, smash a couple of lobs, volley and drive backcourt. But you should do your real practicing an hour beforehand.

Back in 1938, Frank Kovacs provided the classic case of underestimating your opponent. Fun loving Frank was known as the carefree clown of tennis in those days. (My, has he changed! Now he is a hard working, conscientious teaching pro who has developed many fine players.) Frank was seeded No. 6 at Forest Hills and rated in singles much higher than unseeded Gene Mako, the doubles genius.

Frank didn't bother to practice before the match but Gene went out on the field courts with Don Budge and hit all his shots for more than thirty minutes.

Gene was sharp and ready to go when he rallied with Frank who slapped carelessly at a few balls and then the match began.

Frank never knew what hit him for the first nine minutes as he lost eight games in a row 6–0, 2–0 before he could manage to win a game. Gene scored repeatedly with his forehand against Frank's booming drives and breezed through the second set 6–2. Frank began bearing down and forced the third set to deuce before succumbing at 8–6.

Certainly, Frank would have done much better, perhaps won, if he had realized his danger.

You can guard against this upset if you go after your opponent right from the start. Develop the killer instinct of champions like Rod Laver. Even after he won the Grand Slam—the English, French, American and Australian championships—he tried just as hard, against all types of opponents. You can train yourself to do the same and avoid losing to inferior players.

6. *Develop a fighting spirit.* The popular definition of fighting spirit is something called forth like a genie out of a jug by a football coach. At halftime, when his team trails by three touchdowns, he arouses them with a pep talk, and they go charging out onto the field to mow down the opposition.

If only it were that simple in tennis. But fighting spirit in a tennis match is more like hacking your way through a jungle infested with poisonous snakes, plagued by swarms of gnats, lashed by thick underbrush, and harassed by unfriendly natives.

You will often find the heat enervates you, sudden bursts of wind betray your accuracy, and your faithful serve deserts you, while your opponent plays over his head and acts as though he could beat you with a snowshoe. You feel tempted to quit running so much to gain so little, to slug the ball to end points in a hurry, and to voice complaints such as "I just can't get going today." You spend your time thinking up alibis instead of how to turn the tide.

Fighting spirit means persevering on every single point and concentrating every single moment on how to win. You ignore the "unlucky breaks" of the net cords that drop dead on your side, the close ones you miss, and the "lucky" shots your opponent makes. Instead, you strive continually and forget the past points, which you cannot change, to concentrate on the next point, which you can determine.

Fighting spirit means controlling your temper. You don't become disturbed at missing shots and ape Santa Claus by giving the following points free to your opponents. You control yourself and let your opponent become tense and angry so that he misses ordinary shots.

Every year some junior comes along with lightning-fast reactions, a superb build, and great natural talent. He hits hard, covers court like a tiger prowling for prey, and displays a greater variety of shots than a dime store has items. The tennis officials are about to sing, "Happy days are here again, We'll get the Davis Cup back soon again" when they discover a slight flaw.

The promising junior loses his temper when he misses shots. He flails the air with his racket, cracks balls over the fence, and bemoans his incredible bad luck while his game goes into a tailspin. After he cools off, he manages to regain his form and seems about to overtake his opponent. Then he gets mad again. This time he gets into a deeper hole, but he can't get out in time to avert defeat by an opponent inferior in strokes, physique, and natural talent. But decidedly not inferior in controlling his temper.

It takes fighting spirit to control your temper when you miss so-called easy shots. But controlling your temper stems from habit. If you miss a question on a school exam, you don't jump up and down and throw your pen against the wall. You go on to the next question because of habit.

In the same way, you can train yourself when you miss a shot or gave your opponent the wrong shot, to disregard that point and think about the next one. All champions have developed this habit, which enables them to win even when playing badly or against an inspired opponent.

Maureen Connolly was once down 0–40 for three match points in a row to Shirley Fry in a Pacific Southwest finals. Maureen then returned the serve deep and kept pounding the ball to the corners for at least thirty balls in a row on each point. Imagine returning ninety balls in a row deep and to the corners while knowing that one single error would lose you the match! She finally won the match in a display of magnificent hitting.

Another advantage in controlling your temper is the disturbing effect on your opponent. He cracks a ball past you and expects you to show dismay. Instead you calmly pick up the ball and serve. His reaction often is to try to hit the ball even harder to prove that he can destroy your defenses. Let him. He'll hit too hard for his skill.

Bill Tilden said of poker faced René Lacoste that he felt he was playing an invincible practice wall, for no matter how great a shot he made, Lacoste showed no emotion.

Similarly, if you make a fine shot and the other player shows he dislikes it, you should really pour it on. Give him many more of them.

Fighting spirit means refusal to admit defeat, no matter how far behind. Pancho Gonzales lost the first two sets to Ted Schroeder at Forest Hills in 1949. The odds against Pancho winning the next three sets were about 15–1, since only four players out of sixty champions had ever won after losing the first two sets. But Pancho played as though the odds were in his favor and rammed home a victory in three hard-fought sets.

7. *Become an all-around player.* Learn a lot of shots: How to angle your backhand at a sharp angle when drawn in halfway; how to lob off the forehand as well as to slug the ball; learn a backhand chop on high-bouncing balls to chop them down at a net rusher's feet. If you play on clay, learn a drop shot.

As said before, Pancho Gonzales, who serves a ball going more than one hundred miles an hour, can also hit shots that drift like feathers just over the net. Hard hitting Arthur Ashe also lobs with great skill. The more shots you learn, the tougher you will become as a competitor and the more weapons you will have in your arsenal to use against one-stroke players.

8. *Watch better players.* Watch how a better player hits the ball. Forget about the ball going back and forth and look only at one player in action. See how he c-a-r-r-i-e-s the ball on his racket and follows through. Watch his footwork. Does he move into the ball, or is he falling backward? Does his weight flow into the ball, or does he hit mostly with his arm?

Check to see how far he gets when he rushes the net. Does he get past the service line when following his serve in? Does he get back easily for lobs over his head?

Sit with other competitors to listen to them discuss other players. It is impossible for a player who goes around the circuit of eastern tournaments before Forest Hills to conceal a weakness, for the players in the stands watching him soon learn it.

When you watch a match, notice which player is forcing the other, which one seems to be running out of gas. Sit in back of the court if possible to see how a wide-breaking serve can push a player out of position. When a player comes up on a short ball, check on how well he returns it, whether deep to a corner or only halfway, where the other can crack it for a winner.

You can't notice all these things at once, of course, but the more matches you watch, the better. Unconsciously, you pick up clues on how to get your weight into the ball because you will tend to copy the better players.

9. *Add a stroke a week.* To move up the tennis ladder, you should keep learning new strokes and shots. When starting out, learn these:

A. Forehand drive to opponent's backhand.
B. Forehand drive crosscourt to opponent's forehand.

C. Backhand chop crosscourt to opponent's backhand.
D. Serve to opponent's backhand.

Now, add one of these during your next weeks:
E. Serve breaking wide to opponent's forehand.
F. Backhand lob to opponent's forehand and backhand.
G. Backhand drive to opponent's backhand.
H. Volley: Forehand to opponent's forehand and backhand.
I. Volley: Backhand to opponent's backhand.
J. Smash: Letting the ball bounce and smashing to opponent's backhand.
K. Smash: Taking the ball on the fly and smashing to opponent's backhand.

Now you are ready to tackle the following advanced shots:
L. Approach shots: Forehand down the line to opponent's backhand—deep to the corner.
M. Approach shots: Backhand crosscourt to opponent's backhand corner.
N. Volley: Backhand to opponent's forehand.
O. Half volley.
P. Backhand: Chop down the line to opponent's forehand corner.
Q. Serve: Serve to backhand in the ad court and rush the net.
R. Serve: Serve to forehand in the ad court.
S. Smash: On short lob to the forehand side, smash at angle crosscourt wide to opponent's forehand.
T. Smash: On short lob to your backhand side, run around it to smash at angle crosscourt wide to opponent's backhand.
U. Return of serve: Chop your backhand return short to catch server coming in behind his serve.

After learning to use the advanced shots, you will find you are beating a lot of players who know only a few shots. Now you are ready to move up in quality by practicing these expert shots:
V. Approach shot: 1. Forehand: Sharply angled short crosscourt to opponent's forehand.
2. Forehand: Deep crosscourt to opponent's forehand.
W. Drop shot: 1. Backhand to opponent's backhand.
2. Backhand down the line to opponent's forehand.

X.   Drop shot: 1. Forehand to opponent's backhand.
    2. Forehand crosscourt to opponent's forehand at angle.
Y.   Lob volley.
Z.   Stop volley.

The most important feature of all is knowing when to use these tools, against which opponents, and how often. This knowledge you will gain from playing tournament or school matches. The more tournaments you play in, the sooner you will gain this experience, and the better you will become.

You will find to your delight that often, when losing to an opponent who is hammering down your defenses, you will change the score in your favor by changing your game to mixing up your shots and adding depth. This is the challenge of tennis; it is so complex and offers such a wide variety of shots and strokes that you may beat opponents who run faster and hit harder than you do if you use your head.

Thus, the more you learn, the more you will enjoy dueling with an opponent and seeing how you can outwit, outthink, or overpower him. When you are young, you will find more time to practice than later. Make the most of it, and you will reap many benefits that are unknown to you now.

Equipment, Training, and Conditioning

Equipment was discussed somewhat in the chapter, "For Ladies Only," but this chapter will go into more detail.

First of all, wear white. Colored clothes mark you as a beginner or as a person with abominable taste. Some pros wear colored clothes to stimulate crowd appeal, they claim, when what they really need is to play better tennis. One exception is heavy clothing worn in cold weather. The Australian stretch pants come in white as well as blue, but tournament players prefer the blue, probably because white stretch pants look too much like underwear.

Get shoes that feel comfortable, with heavy soles. Put on wool socks when you try on the shoes to learn how your feet will feel when playing. Some players wear two pairs of socks: A pair of cotton and a pair of wool and/or nylon.

Some players can play with no hat or cap to shade their eyes or take up perspiration. But the rest of us will find that a cap with a long bill makes it easier to play.

Rackets. Metal rackets have become popular in the past couple of years. Players afflicted with that dread disease, tennis elbow, have found them easier to swing than wooden rackets and many times have resumed playing with lessened pain and fatigue.

Other players have bought them because their games had stag-

283

nated at a plateau, and they felt that a metal racket would add power to their serves, accuracy to their drives, and perhaps wings to their feet.

Still other players bought them simply as status symbols. Wives have given them to husbands for Christmas and unwittingly set back their husband's games three years. Actually, a metal racket is like a sports car—it has its defects as well as its virtues.

Some metal rackets are very flexible; others are like wooden rackets except that they cost a lot more and won't warp. You can serve faster and swing more easily with a metal racket, so you can volley better, but since the ball pops off much faster, you will find that it is harder to control the ball on ground strokes. You do not hold the ball as long on your racket and do not c-a-r-r-y it as long, so you sacrifice accuracy. If you want to make sure of beating a hard-hitting but erratic opponent, give him a metal racket.

Another minus factor is that if you mis-hit a ball with a wooden racket or "on the wood," you may win the point because the ball spins erratically on the other side or even drops dead. If you mis-hit a ball with a metal racket, it simply won't go over the net or might even become stuck in the throat.

You should borrow a metal racket and try it out for seven different times to see how you play with it. If you are just starting or are a novice, avoid it as you would poison ivy. If you intend to buy one, search out a disgruntled hard hitter, and you may get it at a bargain price.

A metal racket should be one-half ounce lighter in weight than a comparable wooden racket. A man should use a wooden racket ranging from 13½ to 14¼ ounces, depending on how strong he is. Jack Kramer wielded a war club of 15½ ounces (these weights are all for strung rackets); Roy Emerson's racket is 13¾ ounces, light in the head, and with a 4⅝-inch handle.

If you like to slug the ball, you will prefer a heavier racket and an even or heavy-in-the-head balance. If you play consistently and prefer outmaneuvering your opponent, you will do better with a lighter racket and light in the head. The balance makes a lot of difference, since a light-in-the-head racket of 14 ounces will seem lighter in swinging than a 13½-ounce racket that is heavy in the head.

If possible, choose a racket that is unstrung in a shop that provides a string weight to put on the various frames, so you can tell how they feel when you swing them. If you pick out a racket that is already strung, check the condition of the stringing. Some rackets are strung months ahead, not too tightly, and with nylon. This is why some so-called bargains aren't really bargains. You get a good frame, but you'll have to replace the stringing.

Bernard Baruch, the financial genius, said he bought his straw hats in the winter, and you can save a lot if you buy a racket in September or the dead of winter.

You can also save money by buying a good used racket at a shop that has been in business for years and wants to keep your trade for many more years. Everybody loves a brand-new article, and so used rackets sell for a lot less as a result.

Training and Conditioning. Since tennis is two-thirds running, you should emphasize footwork in your training program. The easiest way to build up your legs is to walk. Walk an extra block whenever you get a chance. Get off the bus or park a block or two from your destination, and walk the rest of the way. Walk around the block on your lunch hour. Take the long route instead of shortcuts in walking between buildings or places. Walk downstairs when in stores and buildings. If you feel ambitious, walk upstairs one flight, and it will save a match for you someday because of your superior condition.

Start with an easy walking goal, and increase the distance. The Army starts recruits by marching them up and down the parade grounds. Next comes a three-mile jaunt around the camp. Each week the recruits march farther and farther, carrying a loaded field pack and a rifle and occasionally breaking into a sprint.

During the last week of training, the recruits march twenty-five —that's right—twenty-five miles in a continuous march with occasional breaks. Some do not make the full distance, but it is literally amazing that clerks who never ventured two blocks in a city could build themselves up in a couple of months to hike twenty-five miles at one time.

You can also build up your legs, wind, and condition by performing the following exercises:

1. After walking at least two miles a day for a while, start in your running program.

A. Run at an easy pace for five minutes to warm up your muscles.

B. Break into a sprint for thirty yards, giving it all you've got.

C. Walk for five minutes, interspersed with moving backward and sideways.

D. Run faster for five minutes.

E. Break into another sprint.

F. Do not sit down or take a shower right after a sprint, but continue to walk for a while to help recover your strength.

The sprinting is to make your leg muscles work harder, because if you run at the same pace all the time you are making no demand on your legs.

Another variation of this program is Pancho Gonzales' practice of running a quarter-mile and walking a quarter-mile for two miles within twelve minutes.

Also, run backward (great for speeding you up in fading back to smash lobs) and sideways to break the monotony.

If you cannot run outdoors or on an indoor track, run in a standing position. Or better yet, skip rope.

2. Skipping rope provides instant exercise. Few other single exercises call for so much exertion in so little time. Better yet, skipping rope does wonders for improving your agility and moving into position faster.

If you have never skipped rope before, you will probably hop twelve to eighteen inches off the ground at first. But as you skip more, you will find that you can lift your feet just a couple of inches off the ground and skip much faster.

Start by jumping with both feet at the same time. Whip the rope slowly, and then as you get used to the rhythm, hop on one foot and then on the other. To skip faster, use a leather rope, and hop just enough to clear the rope.

For variety, whip the rope twice as you hop once. Also try advancing and then retreating a few yards as you skip. Or cross your hands to whip the rope around.

At first, skipping a hundred times may seem a chore, but if you will skip every day, you will find that three hundred times presents no problem. To skip longer, break up the sessions by pausing every fifty times to walk around to catch your breath and swing your arms. Then skip another fifty times, or until you miss if longer before walking around some more.

Skipping rope brings more benefits if you skip a little each day rather than skipping ten times as much once a week.

3. To strengthen hand, wrist, and arm muscles: Squeeze a sponge

rubber ball daily to improve your grip on the racket. Keep the ball handy, where you can squeeze it occasionally—in your pocket, on your desk, or in your locker.

Do pushups by lying on the floor and then hoisting yourself up by pushing with your hands against the floor. This exercise develops your wrists and arms so that you can keep making your power shots even when tired.

Do a couple of pushups a day, and you'll find yourself able to increase the number as you go along.

If you can work out in a gym, use the light pulley weights to go through the same motions as hitting a backhand or a forehand.

4. To get more bounce out of your ounces of weight, you can do the same routine that Alex Olmedo did for years while practicing with the University of Southern California team. He would bend his knees and then fling himself up like a rocket while smashing with his racket at an imaginary high lob. When he started leaping, he looked like a man bouncing on a trampoline.

Many lobs that elude you now could be smashed for points if you could leap higher, as the pros do. Practice leaping as high as you can and swing your racket.

Another exercise is Don Candy's trick of jumping with knees tucked up to attempt to touch his chin.

Sometime while rallying before a match, limber up by jumping high for practice.

5. Bending exercises: Many times during a match you have to bend backward or twist to reach a ball. To keep your midriff muscles supple, do these exercises:

A. Stand with feet apart, holding arms out at shoulder height. Turn around as far as possible in one direction. Then repeat in the opposite direction.

B. Stand with feet apart and knees straight. Touch the tip of your left foot with your right hand. Then touch the tip of your right foot with your left hand.

C. Lie flat on a mat, and lift your feet to point to the ceiling. Now gradually lower them with a countdown of ten.

D. Sit on the floor with your feet anchored to a chair and your hands behind your neck, and lower your head to the floor. Then rise to a sitting position.

How many times should you do these exercises? You can start out with just a couple of times for each and work up to ten. But it is far better to do them a couple of times *every* day than to try to do ten each once a week.

6. Muscle tone exercises:

Dr. Arthur H. Steinhaus has come up with simple exercises that take little time and can be done anywhere.

A. Put a towel behind your neck. Pull your chin in, pull forward on both ends of the towel, and resist the towel with your neck with all your might for just six seconds.

B. Put the towel behind the small of your back. Pull forward on the towel while resisting by contracting the muscles of the buttocks and belly. Push back hard against the towel for six seconds.

C. Loop the towel under the toes of one foot. Pull up with both hands while pushing down with your toes. Hold for six seconds. Then do the same with the other foot.

D. Here's one you can do while waiting in line, window-shopping, or waiting for a traffic signal change. Stand up and draw in the abdominal muscles while contracting the muscles of the buttocks. Hold for six seconds. Do this six times during the day for a total of thirty-six seconds.

If you will do the other exercises, it will take only seventy-two seconds a day to increase your muscle tone.

7. Weight lifting: If you want some bulging muscles to impress others at the beach, go in for weight lifting. The hard hitters in tennis do not possess impressive muscles, but instead an especially keen sense of timing. Thus, Billy Johnston was and Pancho Segura is smaller than average size, and yet both rank as tremendous hitters.

If you do all the other exercises faithfully and have nothing else to do on a rainy afternoon, you might try lifting small weights. Otherwise, you'd be better off practicing your serve.

8. How hard should you work on exercises? If you are in senior high or college or engaged in making a tournament journey, you should push yourself to find out your limits. Work really hard in the morning, take a long rest, and work really hard again in the afternoon. Then finish with a mile run.

You'll not only find out your limits, but you'll expand your physical capacity to withstand tough matches.

However, the weekend players should avoid this strenuous workout. They'll wake up the next morning strained, pained, and sore all over. They won't be able to lift a cup of coffee, let alone a racket, and they'll shamble downstairs like a refugee from Alcoholics Anonymous.

A weekend player shouldn't expect to play five hard sets of singles and four sets of doubles in one afternoon, as a seasoned tournament campaigner can. A weekend player should content himself with getting into reasonable shape to play three sets of singles and two sets of doubles—perhaps just the singles. If he follows the exercises, he will undoubtedly increase his stamina, but with his lack of practice during the week, he can't expect to develop the same physical capacity of a tournament competitor.

Another reason for a weekend player not working so hard is that he naturally doesn't feel the surging urge of a player determined to win a higher ranking. If tennis becomes hard work, he'll give it up altogether. He wants to enjoy himself, and so if he does some exercises besides, he'll improve. But it usually isn't worth toiling like an Olympic champion to win a match.

So to the weekend player, do as many exercises as you can, but when you get tired, stop.

8. Smoking and drinking: No matter how many alluring television commercials or four-color magazine ads showing a brawny athlete lighting a cigarette you see, don't you believe them. No real athlete smokes to any degree. He can't if he expects to have any wind. Golfers, armchair fishermen, bowlers, and other practitioners of sedentary sports may smoke, but the other athletes who testify for pay are exaggerating the quantity they smoke.

If you are already addicted to smoking, you are enchained in a habit that demands tremendous will power to overcome. However, you might try to cut down, since every cigarette you don't smoke gives you added wind. Certainly if you intend to aim for big-league tennis, you will have to choose between smoking and tennis success.

A tournament competitor may console himself with a beer in the evening but should forgo the couple of hard drinks "to help him unwind." Alcohol stimulates the appetite but dulls the performance, Shakespeare observed concerning another activity, but it applies just as well to tennis competition.

The few ranking players in the past who went in for drinking learned the hard way that alcohol bars the way to the top rungs. If you're disheartened or disgruntled over losing a match, you won't find the remedy at the bottom of a liquor bottle. The remedy lies in your practicing the weak shots that led to your downfall.

If you're a weekend player, you need every advantage you can get. You don't have the long hours to practice or to condition yourself to top performance, but you can improve your ranking in a minute. Just substitute beer for hard liquor, and make it last longer. If you've been guzzling beer as though you owned the brewery, limit yourself to a couple of glasses instead.

You'll receive payment the next day on the court by weighing less, reacting faster, and gaining extra points.

9. Sleep, diet, and tournament hints:

No two players require the same amount of sleep, but once you determine your own needs, see that you get your regular sleep almost every night. If you are of college age, you can stay out really late one night and get away with it the next day once in a while. But if you are older or playing in a tournament, you can't afford to lower your stamina by staying up too late the night before.

If you have played a tough match and expect another one the next day, you better hop into bed early. This is also true in hot weather, which saps your strength, or when you expect to be in an especially grueling match the next day.

Some players have developed the knack of taking a nap between matches and of relaxing completely, even if for only fifteen minutes. Try to snatch a nap, and even if you do not fall asleep, you will be resting.

If you play a great deal, you should eat a lot of protein like meat, eggs, and cheese. Avoid fried foods and pastry that are harder to digest and add weight in the wrong places. A common fault among players is to nibble on candy bars and gulp down soft drinks all day and thus destroy their appetites for the evening meal. Some even make a lunch of sweets instead of eating a sensible and varied meal.

Another failing is to eat too big a meal too soon before playing. Many a player then finds to his sorrow that trying to digest a full meal while chasing all over the court demands too much of his body.

Actually, the meal you eat that day provides almost no energy. You get that from the food you ate the day before. So eat your steak the night before. If you play in the early afternoon, eat your regular breakfast, and then only a salad or fruit and toast at noon. You'll play much better when your stomach is practically empty.

During a match, you may lift your energy level by eating a candy bar or drinking tea with honey or sugar. But during a long, exhausting match, no food can destroy the fatigue wastes that accumulate in your body and slow you down. Ability to resist fatigue stems from your conditioning before the match.

On a hot day, you may feel tempted to drink a lot of cold ice water. The cold water takes energy from your system because the stomach has to warm it up and besides, you will become waterlogged. It's far better to take a mouthful of cool water and hold it there for a while before you swallow it. That way, the water will cool off your mouth and you won't drink as much.

You might also take a couple of salt tablets on hot days, but check first on a nonplaying day to see if you can take them without discomfort without food. Some players become nauseated if they take only the salt tablets with water.

10. Losing weight: Will tennis enable you to take off unnecessary poundage?

Yes, provided you cut down on eating. Some people exercise at tennis and lose weight temporarily but put it right back by eating starchy foods and drinking beverages high in calories.

Most people would lose weight if they just cut out the fried foods, pastries, and starches along with the extra snacks.

Index